Date: 6/11/14

BIO PARR
Parr, Jerry.
In the secret service : the
true story of the man who

PRAISE FOR
IN THE SECRET SERVICE

Jerry put himself in harm's way to protect Ronnie, and I am forever grateful.

NANCY REAGAN, former first lady of the United States of America

Jerry Parr saved President Reagan's life following the assassination attempt. . . . [Parr] directed the limousine to George Washington University Hospital. The president had a serious injury that caused blood loss significant enough that he initially collapsed with no obtainable blood pressure. Immediate treatment was essential. Stopping at the White House would have delayed treatment, perhaps causing a fatal outcome. This story and others are part of an excellent read in the book *In The Secret Service.* . . . I strongly recommend it.

JOSEPH GIORDANO, MD, professor emeritus of surgery, former chairman of surgery at George Washington University Medical Center

On the day Ronald Reagan was shot, March 30, 1981, Secret Service agent Jerry Parr made a split-second decision that literally saved the president's life, and that gripping story is told here in vivid detail. But the gift to the reader of *In the Secret Service* is much greater; it is an uplifting and exemplary American story of a man and wife dedicated to serving God by serving others.

RICHARD V. ALLEN, former National Security adviser to President Reagan and senior fellow, The Hoover Institution, Stanford University

Jerry Parr is an American hero. . . . He is known for his prompt, intelligent, decisive actions on March 30, 1981, when President Reagan was shot as he left the Hilton Hotel in Washington, DC. Jerry Parr's action that day saved the life of the president. He is highly respected by Secret Service personnel, active and retired. He continues to serve the people of this great country as a spiritual guide to the sick and bereaved. I was privileged to work with him throughout my own Secret Service career. This book . . . will give you an insight into the life of a Secret Service agent. It is not a life of glamour or recognition. It is a life of dedication and determination, loyalty and perseverance. Jerry Parr has set an example for future agents to follow.

CLINTON J. HILL, retired assistant director of the United States Secret Service

The Secret Service is the emblem of America at its best. Standing high above politics, it protects the lives of the leaders we elect and thereby guards our democracy itself. Jerry Parr is the Secret Service agent who personifies that trust. In March 1981, . . . Parr was the top Secret Service agent who made the real-time decision to get President Reagan to the hospital within that narrow window of time that separated life from death. . . . Only after he'd saved him did he tell Reagan his secret. It was the president himself, in his early Hollywood career, who had played the dashing Secret Service agent who inspired young Jerry Parr to join up so he could be there on the sidewalk next to him when the bullets flew.

CHRIS MATTHEWS, host of *Hardball with Chris Matthews* on MSNBC

JERRY PARR
WITH CAROLYN PARR

IN THE

THE TRUE STORY OF THE MAN WHO

SECRET

SAVED PRESIDENT REAGAN'S LIFE

SERVICE

TYNDALE HOUSE PUBLISHERS, INC.
CAROL STREAM, ILLINOIS

Visit Tyndale online at www.tyndale.com.

TYNDALE and Tyndale's quill logo are registered trademarks of Tyndale House Publishers, Inc.

In the Secret Service: The True Story of the Man Who Saved President Reagan's Life

Designed by Dean H. Renninger

Edited by Jonathan Schindler

Published in association with the literary agency of WordServe Literary Group, Highlands Ranch, CO, www.wordserveliterary.com.

ISBN 978-1-4143-7871-8   Softcover
ISBN 978-1-4143-8748-2   Hardcover

Printed in the United States of America

19   18   17   16   15   14   13
7   6   5   4   3   2   1

Tout est grâce.

GEORGES BERNANOS,
The Diary of a Country Priest

CONTENTS

Prologue   *1*

PART 1: MY RENDEZVOUS WITH DEATH 5

1. Just Another Day at the Office   *7*

2. Inauspicious Beginnings   *19*

3. From New York to Dallas:
   "The President Is Dead"   *47*

4. Vietnam: Going from Bad to Worse   *79*

5. 1968: The Year from Hell   *113*

6. Two Deaths   *133*

7. Sinners and Statesmen:
   Watergate and the World   *151*

8. Up and Down the Ladder   *177*

9. Shots Fired! Men Down!   *215*

PART 2: MY ENCOUNTER WITH GRACE *241*

10. From the White House to the Potter's
    House *243*

11. Descent into Joy *267*

    Epilogue *289*

    Letter from Jerry S. Parr to the Agents on
    President Reagan's Protective Detail,
    April 3, 1981 *291*
    Acknowledgments *293*
    Timeline *295*
    Notes *309*
    Index *321*

PROLOGUE

There is always one moment in childhood
when the door opens and lets the future in.
GRAHAM GREENE, *The Power and the Glory*

The sun was low in the sky, filtering through the banyan trees as my father walked me down the uneven sidewalks of my youth. The single-storied stucco houses we passed stood snugly on their lots, painted from a palette of pale colors. Green hoses lay in brown yards like snakes uncoiling to sun themselves. At their heads, sprinklers sprayed giggly kids chased by yappy dogs.

This was our neighborhood. Northwest 4th Street, Miami. A mile or so from the Tower.

The Tower Theater was where I went if I wanted to go to other neighborhoods, ones that were years away, like the Old West (if *Stagecoach* was showing), or light-years away (if it was a Buck Rogers serial). Who knew what adventures awaited me at the Tower? Would Beau Geste be off to fight in the French Foreign Legion? Would Mr. Smith go to Washington or Dorothy to Oz?

1

As we rounded the corner, taking a right on 17th, my father reached for my hand and placed it into the strength of his. At five foot eleven he was thin as a rail but just as strong, tempered by years of carrying bulky cash registers from businesses to his car, from his car into our house, then back again. Repair work was slow for the decade of the Great Depression, never steady, never certain.

But because he was often out of work, we were together a lot; this was not the case with my mom, who worked as a beautician, leaving me few leisurely days with her like the one I had today with my dad.

We turned left on 8th, my anticipation quickening with our pace. There on the right it stood—the Tower Theater, with its sleek, art-deco architecture, its forty-foot tower, its glittering marquee:

CODE OF THE SECRET SERVICE

Starring Ronald Reagan and Rosella Towne

My father dug into his pocket, mincing out change. "One adult, one child," he said, and with that, we were in. A ticket taker opened the door that led into the cool lobby and then into the cavernous dark of the theater. We had missed the newsreels, but we were just in time for the feature presentation. We settled into our cushioned seats.

A cone of light flickered from the projection room onto the screen. This time the "neighborhood" was Washington, DC. This time the buildings were not stucco but marble.

The Capitol. The Washington Monument. The Lincoln Memorial. They all loomed on the screen, and my nine-year-old imagination took off.

The camera cut to words on an office door—"Secret Service Division." Through that door bounded the dashing, clean-cut Brass Bancroft, a Secret Service agent played by the young, athletic Ronald Reagan. He flashed an all-American smile as his supervisor talked about a counterfeiting ring the Service had been tracking. He needed a stakeout south of the border. He assigned Brass to go undercover and check it out. It would be dangerous, but duty called.

The next minute Brass was on a plane that we saw dotting across a map of the United States, then landing in Mexico. Brass picked his way through uncertain streets and more uncertain alleys, into a shady-dealing casino, then a shadowy bar, and then a fight broke out. A flurry of fists. Bodies flying through the air, crashing onto tables.

I gripped my father's arm on the armrest.

It was one cliff-hanging moment after another. One narrow escape after another. One plot twist after another. Until at last a beautiful girl, unimpressed by Brass, entered the story. The two were soon captured by the counterfeiters, and the girl was now even less impressed with Brass than she had been.

Before I knew it, the tables had turned. Brass had slipped out of the ropes that tied him to the chair, rescuing the girl and routing the counterfeiters. Suddenly the special agent had the girl's admiration *and* her affection. The music swelled, the credits rolled, and the tail end of the reel threaded through the projector. A splash of white rinsed the screen, followed by the houselights.

When we left the theater, it was dark. My father asked if I liked the movie, and I said I did. With the marquee lights behind us and the streetlights ahead of us, we made our way home. He pulled out a small bottle of whiskey and took a swig, then another before pocketing it.

My father was not Brass Bancroft, not by a long shot. But I loved him. He was kind and good, at least to me. The Depression had taken away his dignity, his confidence, his manhood. But in return, it had given him to me.

I leaned into him while we walked, tired and hungry and quiet.

"How about a lift?" he asked. I nodded. He hefted me onto his shoulders, crossing his arms over my legs so I wouldn't fall off. I took in a chestful of the heavy night air, mingled with the smell of his skin, his hair, his breath.

There was no place in the world I felt more secure, and no place in the world I would rather be.

We walked past neighbors' houses and the suppertime smells that drifted out their open windows. By the time we were home, I was almost asleep.

Yet something was waking in me, drawing me. Was it the selfless service of the agent to his country? Was it the danger? The intrigue? The foreign travel?

Or was it the girl?

MY RENDEZVOUS WITH DEATH

CHAPTER 1

JUST ANOTHER DAY AT THE OFFICE

I have a rendezvous with Death
At some disputed barricade. . . .
And I to my pledged word am true,
I shall not fail that rendezvous.

ALAN SEEGER, "I Have a Rendezvous with Death"

MARCH 30, 1981

It had been almost forty-two years since I saw that B movie at the Tower Theater, and I was a Secret Service agent assigned to protect the actor in that movie, who was now playing the role of a lifetime: the president of the United States. For the past eighteen years I'd worked my way through the ranks in the Service—investigating stolen checks, standing post, working shifts, doing advances—and now I was lead agent for the special detail that protected the president.

When I was younger, I was fascinated by the poem "I Have a Rendezvous with Death," by Alan Seeger. I had even memorized it decades ago and have returned to it often. The poem makes the encounter with Death seem as calm and natural as watching the trees return to life, "when Spring comes back with rustling shade and apple-blossoms fill the air."

Death is talked about not in cold, impersonal descriptions but in warm terms such as "rendezvous" and in personal images of Death taking the poet's hand. For the poet, death is not an encounter to be feared but an appointment to be kept. God is in it. Hope is in it. And so is courage.

There was another man enchanted by this poem. When John F. Kennedy returned from his honeymoon in October 1953, he read "I Have a Rendezvous with Death" to his young wife, Jacqueline, telling her it was his favorite poem. After that, she memorized the poem, often reciting it to him privately. Her soft voice and unhurried accent seemed to calm him, giving him the resolve he needed to face the future he felt awaited him.

In 1963, Jacqueline taught the poem to Caroline, their five-year-old daughter. On October 5, 1963, when the now–President Kennedy was meeting with his National Security Council in the Rose Garden, his young daughter slipped into the meeting and sidled next to him. She tugged at him to get him to notice her. The president dismissed her, but in a way only a young daughter can, she kept trying to get his attention. The president turned to her, smiling. Caroline looked into his eyes and recited the poem. She recited it flawlessly, with perfect diction. When she finished, no one spoke. It seemed not simply a sweet moment but a sacred one. A sense of reverence permeated the silence, touching everyone.

Seven weeks later, this little girl's father made his rendez-vous with Death at the disputed barricade of Dealey Plaza in Dallas, Texas.

A day that has haunted the memory of every American. And every Secret Service agent.

Now, almost eighteen years after that rendezvous, I was an agent, tasked with protecting the president. I was part of the barricade between him and Death. And my sole purpose was to make sure this was the one appointment he would *not* keep.

* * *

March 30, 1981, started for me in the predawn chill, where I jogged around our neighborhood in North Potomac, Maryland. A small, sequestered suburb northwest of DC, it had been carved out of a forest near the Potomac River. The subdivisions had bucolic names like Travilah Meadows, Quail Run, and Mills Farm, and they lived up to their names, forming a quiet respite from the bustling streets of the nation's capital.

It was a spring day, not blue and fair but gray and overcast as I drove into DC. And although the first meadow flowers had appeared in some well-manicured parts of the city, the more than three thousand cherry trees there had not yet blossomed to fill the air with their delicate scent.

The first thing I did when I arrived for work that morning was to sign in for target practice at the gun range in the basement of the old post office building. I was dressed for work in a plain, blue-gray, blend-in-with-the-crowd suit and tie, my gun holstered beneath my unbuttoned coat. As I faced downrange, I spread my feet to square with my shoulders. I relaxed my arms, shaking my hands at my sides to loosen them.

As an agent, I'd had it drilled into me that the one thing I could never do was freeze. In a crisis, an agent doesn't have time to think. Reactions need to be instinctive. So much as a blink or a balk, and I would be a dead man. Or worse—the president would be a dead man.

With a sudden, jarring sound, the target turned from being a thin piece of paper to a man with a pistol. Immediately I flipped open my coat with my right hand, grabbed the butt of my gun with my left, and fired two shots that drilled the paper assassin.

My gun was a stubby Smith & Wesson Model 19, with a six-round chamber that could be changed out in three to four seconds. The impact on the hand was brutal, but the impact on the target was even more so. The .38-caliber bullets burst from the two-and-a-half-inch barrel at a speed of 1,110 feet per second. If the bullet didn't kill you, the blow from the bullet would knock you off balance—if not off your feet. With the Service using hollow points, though, if the bullet did hit you, it would likely be lethal.

When you are protecting the most important leader in the world, lethal is what you want. You don't want to give an assassin a chance to shoot once, let alone a second chance.

You want to drop him the way I dropped that target in the shooting range.

After cleaning my gun, I left for "the office." The office for me was known as W-16, located in the bowels of the White House, directly under the Oval Office. It was the Secret Service's command center, the central nervous system for protecting the president and other key leaders and their families. Intelligence was routed to us there—field reports, surveillance feeds, wiretaps—up-to-date intel on people who were known threats. The Service receives threats every day on the lives of those they are assigned to protect—especially on the life of the president. The lower his approval rating is, the higher the number of threats. And since taking office, President Reagan's approval rating had plummeted.

The president had been in office just seventy days. For the first week after his inauguration, every time the president left the safety of the White House, I stuck so close I could smell his aftershave. But for the next seven weeks after that, others in the management team had been with him while I attended the Federal Executive Institute. Now back at the White House, I felt today would be a good day to spend time with him and get to know him. Although an agent never wants to get on too-friendly terms with the president, you do want to be able to do the best job of protecting him, and that involves knowing him. Knowing how fast he walks or how slow. Knowing how often he stops along a rope line to greet the public and for how long. Knowing whether he is cautious or cavalier. Is he immediately compliant to an agent's suggestions, is he momentarily hesitant, or is he resistant to the point that the agent has to persuade him? In scenarios where every second counts, knowledge like this can be lifesaving.

Johnny Guy was the agent assigned to travel with the president to the Washington Hilton that afternoon, where he was to give a short speech to a labor union within the AFL-CIO. I talked to Guy sometime after ten in the morning to ask if I could take his place. He agreed.

I called my wife, Carolyn, at her office to tell her that I would be accompanying the president to the Hilton and that if she wanted to see him, his motorcade would be across the street. She was a trial lawyer for the IRS at the time, and she had a fourth-floor office in the Universal North Building, with a window that looked down on T Street. She was glad I called and eager to see the president, if only for a moment.

It was a routine route for a routine stop for a routine speech. But that's the rub: routine is the enemy of every agent. With routine comes boredom. With boredom comes distraction and letting down your guard. When that happens, people die.

We had taken presidents and vice presidents to the Washington Hilton 110 times since 1972, and nobody had died. Nobody had even come close. An advance search of the hotel had been done, along with the strategic assignment of agents, sixty-six for this event, plus police. Had we been scheduled for an out-of-Washington trip—say, in Baltimore—we would have used twice that number.

Paul Mobley and Mary Ann Gordon headed up transportation. Both had done the route to the Hilton before, as well as numerous runs to the hospital. They had put the motorcade in place—a caravan of vehicles, each with different duties assigned to those riding in them. There was a lead car that set the pace at twenty-five miles per hour, which would stop for nothing unless it hit someone. There was a tail car, a van with eight agents, and a pilot car, all looking for suspicious vehicles along the route. There were a few ancillary cars, like a spare car with protective support and technicians, a communications car, and a staff car. There was the control car, which would include Deputy Chief of Staff Mike Deaver. Finally, there was the president's limousine, which was code-named *Stagecoach*. Every inch of it was bulletproof, covered in level-4 armor. It weighed six and a half tons and stretched nearly twenty-two feet. There was even an "emergency motorcade" of four vehicles parked at the hotel, should a quick escape be needed. All total, fifteen vehicles.

We had plotted a protected route with police officers assigned to block off intersections along the way. The plan was to arrive at the VIP entrance; otherwise we would have to go to the hotel's basement, where we would have some twelve hundred cars to check out. Then, when the motorcade stopped at the entrance, where uniformed police formed a perimeter of protection, the car doors would open with strategic synchronization, and the president would be whisked away to the hotel ballroom.

It was all very regimented. And all very routine.

In spite of how well rehearsed our responsibilities were, the risks were real. You know that danger is out there—*real* danger—you just don't know where. Absence of evidence doesn't mean evidence of absence. Just because there is no sign of a threat doesn't mean there isn't one. The problem isn't what you know; it's what you don't know. Not what you see or hear, but what you don't see, don't hear. It's the open window you don't notice. Or the sound from a book depository that takes you a second too long to recognize as a gunshot.

Not only do you have to be vigilant; you have to be hypervigilant.

Ever since I joined the agency in 1962, a number of people had died. President Kennedy had been assassinated. Attorney General Robert Kennedy had been assassinated. Governor George Wallace survived an assassination attempt but was paralyzed. President Ford had escaped two attempts on his life. And civil rights leader Martin Luther King Jr. had been assassinated.

President Kennedy, Wallace, and Ford had been under the protection of the Secret Service. The others were not.

In some cases, agents were negligent. In others, they were vigilant.

In all cases, life or death was determined by seconds.

Sometimes split seconds.

★ ★ ★

I had assigned Bill Green to work the advance on the president's trip to the Hilton, which he started on March 25. His job was to draw up a security plan that pinpointed where each agent was to be stationed in and around the hotel. He was to make sure a background check was done on everyone scheduled to meet with the president during his visit, however briefly. He was also responsible for inspecting the ballroom, the hotel basement, the holding room, the stairwells, the elevators, and the VIP entrance.

Though it was the first time Bill had done this at the Hilton, his preparations were thorough, down to the smallest detail. He visited the hotel on Friday for another inspection, then again on Saturday. On Sunday he made a few final calls before finishing his security report, which he handed in first thing on Monday, March 30. He checked the latest intel, and he was told that there was nothing on the radar in terms of threats to the president's appearance that day.

The trip to the Hilton was so routine that I decided bulletproof vests weren't necessary. Besides, it was a muggy day, with rain, and vests were hot and uncomfortable. I sat in the front passenger seat; the president sat behind me. We drove down Connecticut Avenue, got on 18th Street, and made a left onto T Street, which took us to the hotel. When we stopped at the designated entrance, police and other agents were waiting for us. I got out of the car first to pull the coded switch on the president's door—a tricky thing because if you don't do it just right, the system has to be rebooted before you can open the door.

President Reagan, a probusiness Republican, was at odds with the largely Democratic labor unions. But he had been invited to speak and felt a sense of responsibility to come. When Reagan had worked as an actor in Hollywood, he served as president of the Screen Actors Guild, a union under the auspices of the very group to which he was scheduled to speak. And so he felt a certain kinship with the audience.

Once inside, I ushered the president into the elevator that led to the permanent holding room. As we ascended the platform, I picked another agent to stand near the president so I could sit behind him to survey the room. I had a good eye, trained to see trembling hands, darting eyes, sweat on the forehead . . . a disturbed look on the face . . . clothes or shoes that didn't fit in . . . a bulge in an overcoat . . . a purse clutched a little too tightly.

After Reagan was introduced, he stood behind the armored podium to speak. But I wasn't paying attention to the speech; I was paying attention to the crowd, looking with eyes that could cut steel they were so intense. An agent's eyes are weapons, every bit as intimidating as a semiautomatic. I sat with a face as cold and hard as if it had been cut from Mount Rushmore and scanned the ballroom, searching for a face that was every bit as cold and hard as mine, for eyes every bit as intense.

One of the things agents are looking for is a gun. We are trained to shout whenever we see one—"Gun right" if an agent sees someone with a gun to the right or "Gun left" or "Gun in front." Depending on the type of threat and where the threat is, I might push the president down behind the podium, cover him with my body on the stage, or evacuate him from the stage.

When President Reagan finished speaking, the audience rose to applaud. But the speech wasn't his best, and the gesture was more respectful than enthusiastic. With agents flanking his sides, the president stopped to shake a few hands, then we escorted him to the elevator.

In the meantime, Carolyn had lost track of time. She had received a call at 1:45 and became so engrossed that she forgot all about seeing the president. When she suddenly realized what time it was, she looked out the window, and the motorcade was still parked across the street. Even though it was rainy, she grabbed her purse and rushed downstairs to the sidewalk, shortly before the president emerged from the Hilton.

When the VIP elevator at the Hilton opened, the other agents and I surrounded the president in a human barricade we called the "diamond formation." The diamond had four points. Tim McCarthy was positioned in front, Eric Littlejohn in the rear. Jim Varey was stationed at the right, Dale McIntosh at the left. Ray Shaddick and I were inside the diamond on either side of the president. Shaddick was in "POTUS Left" position, I was "POTUS Right," eighteen inches behind the president. Shaddick carried a bulletproof steel slab to protect the president in case of an attack, coated with leather so as not to appear foreboding. Bringing up the rear was Bob Wanko, the gunman with an Uzi in a briefcase, again so as not to appear foreboding.

As we opened the door to the outside, uniformed police in raincoats stood guard on the sidewalk that was wet from an earlier shower. Beyond them was the rope line, where a gaggle of around thirty onlookers and members of the press eagerly awaited an opportunity to shout out a greeting or a question. All my senses were keenly alert, scanning the surroundings for any possible threat—any person that seemed out of place or out of sorts, any door that might be ajar, any window that might be open, any sudden movement, any startling sound. All the while, I was plotting an ever-changing escape route if something did happen. If a threat presented itself as we walked out the door, I would pull the president into the building; if we were closer to the limousine, I would push him into the car.

Carolyn was across the street, standing on the fringe of a small crowd that had gathered there, craning her neck to catch a glimpse of the new president.

As the president approached the limousine, McCarthy got the door, which opened toward the crowd. The president raised his right arm and waved to the small line of spectators that had gathered on T Street. A woman on the rope line called out, "Mr. President! President Reagan!" The president paused a second—only a second—turning his head to the left to acknowledge her, raising his left hand, and mouthing what seemed to be the word *hi*.

In that moment, I moved instinctively to the president's left side to strengthen the barricade between him and the crowd.

CHAPTER 2

INAUSPICIOUS BEGINNINGS

The past is never dead. It's not even past.

WILLIAM FAULKNER, *Requiem for a Nun*

SPRING AND SUMMER, 1962

On a cold Nashville day in February 1962, I dropped into the Peabody College snack shop between classes to warm up with a cup of hot coffee. I was a thirty-one-year-old college senior lost in liminal space, leaving something familiar and, like Abraham of the Bible, "not knowing whither he went."

I was about to graduate from Peabody-Vanderbilt, about to become a father, and about to begin a new career . . . I hoped. Carolyn was eight months pregnant and unemployed. She'd had to stop teaching high school English and Spanish when her pregnancy became obvious. The Nashville School Board thought it unseemly for teachers to show visible signs of pro-creation. I thought, *What a crock!*

Sipping my coffee, I flipped through the student paper, *The Vanderbilt Hustler.* I would graduate in May with a BA in English and a minor in philosophy. English teachers were lucky to make $3,000 a year, and there was no market for students of philosophy. So I was looking for something else.

I saw that Gulf Oil, Mobile Oil, Phillips 66, and General Electric were coming to interview graduating seniors. None of them excited me. I couldn't see myself sitting at a desk.

I was older than most students because of my time spent working as a power lineman and serving four years in the Air Force. I liked working outdoors, in all kinds of weather. In Miami I had worked in fierce storms right before and after hurricanes. In the Air Force I had stood post in Finland, Minnesota, when the temperature sank to minus fifty degrees Fahrenheit. I liked adventure. I liked challenge. The truth is, I was drawn to work that had a dangerous edge.

* * *

I was closing the door on thirteen years as a lineman in Florida, Alaska, and Tennessee, work I had continued through my college years. You might say that during that time I had made friends with Death. I had already been a pallbearer for coworkers eight times, some of the dead having fallen from poles forty-five to fifty feet high. Other coworkers had been electrocuted.

Vigilance was the difference between life and death.

Often the ones who didn't survive had circumvented protocol because they were impatient or too hot. To work the power lines, we donned hooks and helmets, our safety belts and tools. We covered our entire bodies—long pants, long sleeves, leather or rubber gloves—to protect ourselves from getting burned by the hot creosote that coated the wooden poles. Up on the poles we worked with secondary wires that carried from 120 to 240 volts and with primary lines carrying from 4,160 to 13,800 volts. The primaries were lethal. Linemen wore leather gloves to climb or handle dead or grounded wire. But we handled primaries with rubber gloves, rubber sleeves, and "hot sticks." Wearing the wrong gloves could be a life-or-death mistake.

I'd had my own near misses.

In Alaska I worked on a line crew with the 5039th Air Installation Squadron. Some of the six or seven men were experienced; others weren't. One time a lineman on the pole next to me cut a span guy-wire without telling me. That guy-wire was the only thing holding my pole upright—with two transformers of five hundred pounds each attached to it.

Thirty-five feet up in the air, I felt the pole tilt gradually toward a slow-motion death. Thankfully, I spotted a covered walkway below, close enough to jump onto. But I still had to unbuckle my safety belt. There was just enough time—I leaped to the peaked roof of the walkway, slid down, and fell some ten feet farther to the ground. Throwing my arm across my face, I landed facedown. Right beside me a five-hundred-pound transformer crashed to the ground; on the other side sat an enormous one-thousand-gallon fuel tank that could have broken every bone if I'd struck it. Falling in the space right between, I suffered only two black eyes.

Once an electrical fire broke out beneath me, and I had to climb down through it. Another time, on a pole in Key Biscayne, I stood on a pair of double arms (arms that project out on either side of the pole to hold wires) and absentmindedly leaned back in my safety belt, only to discover my belt was not around the pole. I grabbed a cross-arm brace to stop my fall. It wasn't the first or the last time my quick reflexes came in handy.

My mother tried vainly to persuade me to get out of line work. It scared her to death. One morning as I was buckling on my gear to go to work, she sighed, "I know you won't give it up. All I can do is leave you in God's hands." I hoped God wasn't getting tired of rescuing me.

My final near-death lineman experience happened one summer after Carolyn and I had been married a couple of years and I was contracting for Mid-Tenn Electric in Nashville. I was up on an old pole one night, working alone in the spotlights, when another lineman cut some dead lines. The top ten feet of the pole broke off, flipping me upside down in the dark. I found myself staring at the starry Tennessee night sky, clinging to the rocking piece of pole supported only by the new and old wires.

Everyone below was yelling, "Don't move! Don't move!" But I wasn't about to stay there. I got my safety belt loose, grabbed a stable section of pole, somehow turned myself upright, and climbed down to safety. Finally on solid ground, I silently picked up the tools that had fallen out of my body belt. Nobody said a word.

I didn't tell Carolyn until I started twitching in bed and she asked if I was having a nightmare. I hated to tell her because, like my mom, she was praying for me to get another job.

Maybe God was driving home a message: *It's time to hang up the spurs.*

The truth is, I *loved* line work. I loved the feel of my hooks as I climbed, skipping knotholes in the pole where the wood was stronger and might throw me off stride. I loved the view from being up high, and I liked literally being looked up to. I loved working high energy lines. I loved the image E. B. Kurtz used in *The Lineman's Handbook*, calling us "knights of the spur."

I wasn't a thrill seeker; the risks I took had a purpose. Not long ago someone gave me a blue cap with white lettering. It says, "God said, 'Let there be light.' And then God made linemen." We brought light to dark places, often working in severe weather to keep power flowing to hospitals or military bases. I was hoping my next job would also have meaning and would serve others.

* * *

Now, in that snack shop at Peabody College, I knew I'd have a college degree and more choices. It seemed impossible, but

I hoped to find a new vocation with an odd combination: an edge of excitement, good pay, a chance for promotion. But I needed even more than that. I had a wife I loved and a new baby on the way; I wanted to make them proud of me. And I wanted a job that served the common good. I got up to get a coffee refill, and then resumed looking at the list of upcoming interviews. As I skimmed the *Hustler*, my heart began to race. Right beneath the list of corporations, I saw "Central Intelligence Agency" and "US Secret Service." Immediately I signed up to interview for both.

In one of the Vandy Student Union rooms set aside for interviews, the CIA representative spoke to me about analyzing aerial photos of power lines. I could tell how much voltage was going to a particular site, important information in figuring out whether a nuclear bomb was being built and whether a site was developed for a military purpose. The job would involve some travel, and not to tourist destinations. Though the mission appealed to my sense of adventure and patriotism, I still wasn't sure.

Albert Vaughn, a retired agent from the Nashville field office, was the first person who interviewed me for the Secret Service. I knew agents protected the president and, from seeing *Code of the Secret Service* as a kid, I remembered they had something to do with counterfeiting. But I learned more: the Secret Service was part of the Department of Treasury (now the Secret Service is part of Homeland Security), and agents in the field were criminal investigators. They hunted down and arrested suspects for stealing and forging government checks—like Social Security checks from older people's mail—and bonds. They investigated coins altered to look like rare ones. The counterfeiting squads worked undercover under false names—an assignment as dangerous as, or more so, than protection. And agents testified in court to get convictions.

Vaughn leaned forward as if to warn me. "Now, new agents don't get sent to the White House. You have to work your way up. But field agents do get protection experience, especially in an election year. That's because we're called on to supplement the White House guys when a president or vice president—or a major party candidate—comes to town."

He said that field agents also track down threats. They pay a personal visit to anyone who threatens to harm the president. They have a "friendly" chat to determine whether the person is just letting off steam or presents a real danger. Unfortunately, predicting human behavior is not a science. There is room for failure.

My excitement was mounting. Then Vaughn said, "If you're ever in the 'kill zone' around a protectee, you'd be expected to throw yourself between him or her and danger. You might have to give your life for theirs."

That did it! I knew on the spot, *this was the job I really wanted!* I confess, at that moment I didn't consider how such work might affect a wife and family.

The Secret Service invited me to a second interview in Memphis.

With my hair newly cut, I dressed in my only suit and

a crisp white shirt freshly pressed by Carolyn. Bright and early, wearing her favorite navy-blue tie, I drove to Memphis and bounded up the steps to the door of the Secret Service field office. Swallowing hard, I brushed my palms on my jacket so I'd have a dry handshake and went in. The head of the office, Robert Taylor, was expecting me.

Taylor, who later became head of the White House detail, didn't waste any time on small talk. "Why do you want to be an agent?" he asked.

Without thinking, I blurted out, "Well, it's safer than what I've been doing!" He laughed, and I relaxed. Then I told him the rest of the story. I returned home and hoped that I'd hear back from the Secret Service.

Meanwhile, not long after my initial interview at Vanderbilt, the CIA invited me to Washington for a final round of interviewing and fingerprinting, a polygraph, and a battery of tests to qualify me for a top security clearance. But I kept hoping to hear from the Secret Service.

I went to Washington for the final meeting with the CIA. But while I was in town, on an impulse I dropped by the Secret Service office at the Treasury, hoping someone would talk to me about my application. It turned out they were worried about my age—thirty-two was the oldest cutoff—but George Chaney and Howard Anderson thought I was gutsy to drop in and agreed to meet with me.

Later, on an early March afternoon, I came in from class to find two letters had arrived in the same day's mail. Hands shaking, I tore open the envelopes. The CIA offered me a job as an industrial analyst, and the Secret Service wanted me as a special agent. My wish was coming true.

* * *

Until I married Carolyn in 1959, I never imagined myself as a college graduate, even though when we met, I'd already completed the equivalent of a year and a half of college classes between military courses and the University of Miami night school. None of my closest buddies went to college. I was working-class through and through. My highest ambition was to become foreman of a bull gang at Florida Power & Light.

Neither of my parents had finished high school. When I was born on September 16, 1930, in the midst of the Great Depression, they'd already been married ten years—longing for a child the whole time. They were never able to conceive another.

Dad was tall, dark, and dashing. He was ten years older than Mom, a girlish brunette beauty with flirty eyes and an hourglass figure. All her life she attracted men, though not always ones who would treat her well. Patricia Studstill and Oliver Parr met at a USO dance in Alabama. He had just returned from World War I, where he saw combat in France. She was twenty and he was thirty when they married.

The earliest memory that sings in my soul is being held, warm and secure, by my mom in our shiny Model T. The second is running into my father's arms, his front-right gold tooth flashing in the Miami sun. Love and embrace were my first human hints of another kind of love, of a God I didn't yet know.

The Bible says, "Love covers a multitude of sins." During my childhood I absorbed a large share of both love *and* sin. When I look back at the forces that pressed in on my family from without—World War I and the Great Depression—and the inferno of feelings that threatened our family from within, I see Love holding and protecting me. Covering me, you might say. When all was said and done—my father's night fears and drinking, my parents' eventual divorce, a heartbreaking separation from Dad, a lonely adolescence, an abusive stepfather—I always felt the gracious light of my parents' love and the protective sanctuary of God's arms.

For the first eight years of my life we lived in half of a beige concrete block-and-stucco duplex at 1822 and 1824 Northwest 4th Street, down the street from the old Orange Bowl, inhabiting one side and renting out the other. After a Category 4 hurricane struck in 1926, Dad had to rebuild the two other rental units on our property. The frame houses had been completely flattened, leaving only two piles of debris. A detached garage in back sheltered our black Model T on one side and Dad's repair shop on the other. We had—believe it or not—a solar water heater on our roof. Before we got an electric refrigerator, our perishable food went into an icebox on the back porch. Every few days a sweaty, muscular guy from Palmetto Ice Company left a block of ice. We'd use an ice pick to chip off pieces for iced tea or to suck on when the heat was unbearable.

Our yard was alive with bright poincianas, hibiscus, and poinsettias. A white trellis full of red roses ran up the side of one of the frame houses next door. I loved to bury my nose in the roses. Between the small houses, Dad planted avocado trees bearing enormous, mouthwatering avocados. I ate mangoes and guavas from the neighbors' trees. Although meat was expensive, nobody went hungry for fruit. Big banyan trees offered shade and an irresistible temptation to climb.

But hints of something darker also lurked among the houses. I witnessed evil for the first time one sultry afternoon when a vicious dogfight broke out between a reddish-brown Airedale and a tan-and-white pit bull. Men were drinking and yelling and betting on the outcome. Later, I saw the Airedale hanging by its feet, its eyes sunken. Flies buzzed noisily in the end-of-day stillness. I felt wounded by the horror of it. How could these men I knew and trusted be so cruel?

In those early years, I spent more time with Dad than Mom. Except for the few dollars he made fixing machines for small businesses like bars and restaurants, he was out of work. I went with him everywhere.

One of Dad's cash register customers was Skippy's, an open-air restaurant where we shared bowls of vegetable soup with little round crackers. He gave me sips of beer and said, "Don't tell Mama." In the dark, smoke-filled bars where he drank, I felt cool and relieved, sheltered from the terrific heat of a Miami summer in the '30s, before air-conditioning.

Dad and I fished with cane poles in Biscayne Bay or nearby canals. We caught blowfish and ate them fried. We hunted dove and quail in Opa-locka. We ate what we killed because we needed it for food. But Dad had a tender heart.

He was a rescuer, and I became one too. For a while we had a big cage in the backyard where we kept a hawk with a broken wing until it healed and flew away. Together we pulled all kinds of creatures from the road, dead or alive. I was partial to turtles, and to this day I will stop my car to move a turtle out of harm's way. We took in stray dogs, one at a time, and named them all Buddy. Our black cat, Kitty Boots, had to be kept away from my pet mice.

Dad once rescued a three-foot alligator and tied it to an outdoor faucet with a dog leash so it could get water. Its mouth looked big enough to swallow a little boy whole. *Snap!* It lunged at me. That's when Dad put it in the car and returned it to the Everglades.

Mom didn't rescue animals like Dad did, but once she did rescue me. On a sunny Sunday afternoon when I was seven or eight, she took me swimming at Miami Beach. A neighbor boy, Gene, and his mother, Rose, went with us. Gene and I were playing in waist-high water when suddenly I felt myself being sucked farther out. I struggled to regain my footing but couldn't hold it. Gene, about ten, was swimming furiously in the riptide but getting nowhere. I screamed, "Mama!" She came running, waded in, grabbed us both, and tried to drag us to shore, but the current was too strong. All she could do was hold on. My heart was pounding louder than the crashing surf. It didn't slow down until a lifeguard deposited me safely onto shore.

I loved Sundays. Sunday was Mom's day off from the beauty shop where she worked, and we could all do things together. Sometimes we'd just take a ride to Miami Beach in our shiny Ford. My favorite part was coming back across MacArthur Causeway, which was dominated by an enormous neon sign. I'd watch, awestruck, as red paint magically poured out of a Sherwin-Williams paint can and covered a blue-and-green globe. Then the words would appear: "Cover the earth." The paint reminded me, somehow, of love.

Sunday was also the time to snuggle beside Dad, my head resting on his shoulder, while he read me the funnies from the *Miami Herald*: "Dick Tracy," "L'il Abner," "Blondie," "Little Orphan Annie."

I felt safe with Dad. He used to smile and say, "I'd fight a ripsaw for you, Son."

Dad's desire to protect Mom and me sometimes took a frightening turn. When I was around five, I awoke to the sounds of a violent thunderstorm very early in the morning. The fifty-foot-high Australian pine beside our house was swaying and moaning in the wind. Scared, I tiptoed from my little cot in the kitchen to my parents' room and crept into bed with them.

The window was open, and mist was coming in through the screen. The wind was whistling. I was starting to enjoy the sound.

Suddenly there was a terrific clap of thunder. Dad leaped up, screaming, "Shells! Get under the bed!"

Mom cried, "Oliver! Oliver! What are you doing?"

He yelled, "Cover! Cover!"

The terror in his face sucked the air out of my lungs. He threw us violently under the bed and covered us with his body. I could feel his heart pounding hard, and I wriggled to get out from under that bed. But he grasped me tight, and we stayed there until the storm stopped.

In World War I, Dad had served in the 37th Infantry Division of the 116th Regiment of the Ohio National Guard, military police. He fought in the Argonne Forest campaign and at Chateau-Thierry, two of the fiercest battles of the war. He and his comrades had come under intense shelling, and he'd seen many men die.

Dad started drinking in France. Although seventeen years had passed when he threw us under the bed, he was still stuck in the bloody French countryside. Since there was no treatment for what we now call post-traumatic stress disorder, he numbed his memories with the bottle.

Mom worked full-time in a beauty shop and brought home eighteen dollars a week. She stood on her feet all day every day, trying to make cheery small talk with customers while she cut, curled, or colored their hair. Then she dragged herself home and collapsed on the couch. I'd help put her feet up to make her swollen ankles feel better and bring her iced tea. Then I might climb up beside her for a hug. Sometimes she smelled sweet like hand lotion.

Sometimes I noticed the pungent odor of hair-perming chemicals. I didn't mind at all.

But life with Mom could be problematic. She had hoped I'd be a girl. She sometimes treated me like her toy, a doll to dress up. Even though I was a boy, I came with a head of thick, naturally curly, black hair. She loved to play with it, combing it this way and that, making spit curls. I would wiggle away. She trimmed my hair, but I didn't get a real boy's haircut until Dad finally said, "Enough!" and took me to a barber. I was nearly six years old and ready for school.

I fiercely resisted Mom's efforts to tame me, even then refusing to go with her to the Christian Science church because I hated getting dressed up in the little white suit she favored. I played in the dirt and always had a skinned knee or elbow. I climbed everything in sight. I collected turtles and snakes. The more Mom hovered and warned, "Be careful!" the more risks I took.

I used to see linemen from Florida Power & Light working in the neighborhood. I thought, *I'd love to do that.* One day when I was about eight, I practiced on a telephone pole that stood near our neighbor's garage. Starting a few feet up from the ground were horizontal metal rods, "steps" to climb the pole. Ignoring Mom's admonitions to stay out of trouble, I jumped up, grabbed a step to use as a handhold, and struggled into position to climb the pole. Then I scrambled up the pole and stepped onto Mrs. Munden's garage roof. Three wires hung over the roof, and to steady myself I grabbed two wires. I got the shock of my life. I was lucky that day—one of the wires I grabbed was the ground wire. The other two carried 110 volts, and had I grabbed them both, I might have died.

I was a happy child and was not consciously aware of the growing tension between my parents. But I must have been blocking out a lot of stress, because I have no memory of second or third grade, not even my teachers' names. I must have picked up a few cues, however, because one night Mom heard a noise on the back porch and discovered me walking in my sleep. Then one day I saw Dad push Mom down in the driveway.

On a muggy Saturday afternoon in the late summer of my ninth year, Mom said, "Jerry, I want to talk to you about something serious." Her eyes were puffy, as if she'd been crying. My stomach turned. I sensed it was going to be bad. We walked out of the house and turned right onto 18th Avenue, and then took another right on Flagler Street, where the trolley ran. She wanted to get me away from the house to break the news privately.

Though the day was ending, moisture hung in the hot air. It felt menacing. Neither of us said a word.

The trolley ran between downtown and 22nd Avenue, where City Line Grocery marked the western boundary of Miami. As the trolley approached us, I could see sparks fly where it connected to the overhead electric line that powered it. When the trolley stopped, we got on, headed toward downtown, and Mom put two nickels in the conductor's box.

The nearly empty car smelled like cigarettes and human sweat. Windows were open, but the air was muggy, with hardly any breeze. We took hard seats in the back. The trolley rattled as it went along. We passed Stroberg's Grocery on the left, then Bascomb's Pet Store.

Mom said, "I'm going to leave your dad. We're going to get a divorce." In the twilight her face was somber. Twenty years of marriage were coming to an end. The huge sign for Goodyear Tire passed on the right, across from Skippy's. "We still love each other," she said. "But his drinking is wearing me out. He won't work. I just can't take it anymore."

The trolley came to the end of the line, and the conductor walked through the car to the opposite end. We started back toward home. I couldn't say a word.

The sun was going down. "I know how much you love your dad, and I hate to do this," she said. "You'll live with me, but you can still see him anytime. He'll stay in Miami. He'll always be your dad."

For years after, like many children of divorce, I couldn't shake the thought that I was to blame. Decades later a woman in my prayer group said, "I didn't get the mother I wanted, but I got the one I needed." God gave me the parents I wanted *and* needed, and the capacity to absorb the right stuff from each. I could have inherited Dad's love of alcohol and lack of ambition. I might have taken Mom's inability to form healthy relationships with the opposite sex. I could have been violent. But by God's grace I took my work ethic from Mom and my love of nature and living creatures from Dad.

The stability of my first nine years helped me survive some very hard stuff that was to come.

Soon after the divorce was final, Mom married our next-door neighbor, and we moved to another town. But a year later we were back in Mom's duplex in Miami. The second marriage ended when her husband, Everett, kicked me in the face. I still have a scar on my chin.

Around that time I learned how to deal with bullies. Mom had advised me, "Don't fight, Son. Walk away." There came a day when I had to disobey her.

I was in fifth grade. A big, muscular boy named Claude decided I was a safe target: the new kid in town and one of the smallest. He focused on my bag lunch. At the bus stop he regularly grabbed it, threw it in the air, kicked it, and sent it scattering. He laughed mockingly as I collected my baloney sandwich from one end of the sidewalk and my apple from the other. Other kids, afraid of Claude, laughed along with him. I hated going to school.

One day as I was getting off the school bus, I'd had enough. I called Claude a swearword. He lurched toward me menacingly, and I ran up the cement school steps, trying to escape. He followed. About two steps from the top, I realized I was trapped. In desperation, I turned and shoved him with all my might.

He tumbled backward, somersaulting a couple of times on his way down. At the bottom, he lay on his back, spread-eagled. He looked stunned. I glared at him with hatred. He looked away.

Claude never touched my lunch again. Or anybody else's, for that matter.

I tried to stay under the radar so as to not make things worse for Mom. But my inner life was chaos. I never knew what was coming next, from Mom's trolley car announcement, to my separation from Dad, to a new stepfather and stepbrother, to moving to a new house, new school, new neighborhood. Then the stepfather, stepbrother, and new living arrangements disappeared, and we were back where we started but without Dad. All in one year.

My mother used a lot of soap trying to wash out of my mouth all the words I learned from my father. But I was learning there were far worse sins, usually hidden by a thin veneer of respectability. These sins were like the surface of an iceberg, fanged and mortal, most of their mass below the waterline. In only a few years I would come face-to-face with murderous hatred, more than once. And I would feel hatred in return, in the depths of my being.

As I entered adolescence, Mom married a third time, and we moved to Louisville, Kentucky. Unlike Dad and Everett, Jack was not handsome; he was short, bald, and strong. He offered Mom a different kind of stability: he worked hard and was proud of it. He used to tell Mom, "You married one who wouldn't work and one who couldn't work. I work!"

Jack tried to be a good husband and stepfather. He'd never had a child, and he liked me. But he had a violent temper. It didn't surface in all its fury until we moved back to Hialeah, a Miami suburb, in December 1944. With money saved from Louisville and from selling Mom's houses, they bought two beauty shops, and Jack started a car repair business, Cox Motors. I helped him build his garage.

But the stress of starting a business—and my mother's nagging—brought out his anger full force. It terrified my mother. And me.

On Thanksgiving Day 1945, Mom and "Bom," my grandmother, had prepared a beautiful dinner. The table was laid with a turkey, dressing, gravy, mashed potatoes—everything. Jack stood at one end of the table, I at the other. I can't remember what precipitated it. There were words. Jack may have been drinking. None of us had taken a bite. Suddenly, enraged, he lifted one end of the table and turned it upside down. Everything was on the floor, the entire dinner. Salad, cranberry sauce—our entire feast. We stood there stunned and silent. Mom started putting handfuls of food from the floor back on the platters, then realized it was pointless.

Later, Jack got down on the floor with us and helped clean our dinner up, sobbing.

One evening when Jack started on a rampage, Mom and I ran across a vacant lot to a neighbor. We watched from her porch as he wrecked the house. We saw him pacing up and down, a bandanna dissecting his square forehead. We heard the sound of furniture breaking. He threw something out the window that shattered on the concrete. He heaved over the refrigerator on our covered back porch.

Then he was crying and pacing. Spent, he sat on the side

porch and buried his head in his hands. After a while Mom went over and put a tentative hand on his shoulder.

An elderly Hialeah neighbor who had known Jack all his life told us Jack's temper was so bad as a child that his mother chained him to the bed and beat him. He also said people thought Jack had murdered his first wife. I don't know whether that was true, but he had told Mom many times, "I'll kill you if you trifle on me." It was a shadow that hung over their marriage seventeen years, until Jack died.

From 1945 to 1950 (when I left home), I slept with a kitchen knife under my pillow.

I couldn't know then what I know now: those dark, confusing years with Jack, when I flailed through school and life, were preparing me for what lay ahead. I learned to be ever alert. I learned that violence can turn up anywhere, anytime. I couldn't control Jack or my Mom's decision to stay with him, but with self-control and patience, I could keep watch for her and for me. Finally—and I can't explain this except by God's grace—in spite of the hatred I could feel flare up in a crisis, I learned a deep compassion for the perpetrator, to love the sinner and hate the sin.

Even though Mom seemed forgiving, she never put a marker on Jack's grave. After she passed, I paid to have one put on. It said, "Theilan D. Cox, World War I and World War II." He was one of the few Americans who had served in both wars.

My teen years were the pits. All of my contemporaries went to beach parties with girlfriends. The only pretty girl I knew was taken—and four of us were in love with her. All through high school I never had a date. I didn't own a suit. I didn't go to the prom. I didn't make good grades or play sports except for intramural track. Besides, was I going to bring a girl home to meet the resident maniac?

I escaped when the Korean War began. I enlisted in the Air Force.

* * *

With my Air Force commitment behind me, I returned to Miami with a wife, Mary Henry, whom I'd met in Minnesota when she was only seventeen and I was nineteen. We married soon after and were together in Alaska. We settled in Miami, where I resumed line work with Florida Power & Light, and Mary became a flight attendant with Eastern Air Lines. But not long after that, in 1954, the marriage disintegrated. The truth is, we were both too immature to know what we wanted, what we needed from each other, or how to give it.

I was disappointed and buried my pain in work and drinking with friends. I dated very little, perhaps wanting to avoid repeating my mother's pattern of serial marriages and divorces. In 1956 something else happened to distract me from women: my deeply loved father died, leaving me a mission. His final request was a whispered, "Son, take care of Mabel." Mabel was Dad's elderly second wife. I took a room in her house to try to look after her.

When Carolyn waltzed into my life in the summer of

1958, she was a twenty-one-year-old college senior. I was a twenty-eight-year-old power lineman, brown and lined from the Miami sun. On the surface we seemed totally unsuited for each other.

Carolyn and her roommate, Marilyn, had rented a furnished apartment for the summer in a one-story apartment house squatting on a treeless lot in Miami. My best friend, Roscoe, whose mother was Carolyn's new landlady, recruited me to meet the girls. When we knocked at the apartment door, a hazel-eyed brunette with a dazzling smile answered. Inviting us in, she turned to put away her ironing board. I noticed a red rose on the back of her white shorts. I never forgot that rose.

We invited Carolyn and Marilyn to go for a pizza at one of the many drive-in restaurants then springing up in Miami. We surmised that since the girls had just arrived, they probably hadn't drawn a paycheck yet, so a free meal would tempt them. They looked us over, looked at each other, and nodded. "Okay!"

Carolyn and I were drawn to each other right away. Carolyn liked that I was six feet tall and lean. She thought my dark brown eyes looked sad—and kind. She thought I was older than I said, but she wasn't put off by this, or by learning I was divorced. I seemed a little dangerous but intriguing. Later she told me I reminded her of Rhett Butler in *Gone with the Wind*!

When her mother first met me, Carolyn says her only comment was, "He looks experienced."

It surprised Carolyn that a lineman quoted Thomas Wolfe and Plato. That I loved *Madame Butterfly*. That I read poetry by W. H. Auden and T. S. Eliot and Robert Frost. That I was majoring in English and philosophy at the University of Miami night school, not to get a better job but just because I liked ideas. I was happy doing line work.

Carolyn seemed both smart and caring. She was curious about the books I loved and, like me, enjoyed discussing ideas that moved her. Caryl Chessman, a rapist, was about to be put to death, and this disturbed me. I told Carolyn I was against capital punishment. I saw—and still see—life as a precious thing, even the life of a rapist. She wasn't so sure about that.

I liked that Carolyn was spiritual. She was a Christian with Baptist roots and an evolving faith. She said wryly, "I'm still waiting to hear my first sermon that names race prejudice a sin." This was the South in 1958.

I'd had an on-and-off romance with the Catholic church, since I had attended Holy Family Catholic School in eighth grade in Louisville, where Sister Mary Olive told me who I was and where I was going. She was emphatic. As one of only two non-Catholic students, I had to go to daily mass but could not take Communion. However, I loved the mystery of the Latin words, the scent of incense, and the music of the Gregorian chants, which awakened a yearning deep within me. School ended, and Mom, Jack, and I had returned to Jack's house in Hialeah and resumed our normal churchless life. But as a young adult in the Air Force, I read Thomas

Merton's *The Seven Storey Mountain,* and in Alaska I took instruction to become a Catholic.

But now it was 1958, and I was divorced and searching again. Carolyn and I shared honestly where we were in our faith, but it didn't seem like anything we needed to resolve right then. We both wanted to follow Jesus, but we were still figuring out what that meant.

I learned that she, like me, had blue-collar roots. Her father was a carpenter, and I felt comfortable around him.

Carolyn says that on the night of our first date she told her roommate, "That's a man I could marry!" But I questioned my own ability to be a good husband, and it took me awhile to get serious.

Carolyn returned to Stetson University, just north of Orlando, for her senior year, and I drove back and forth to see her. We spent holidays and the summer of '59 together. I dragged my feet, wanting to be engaged but not wanting to set a date. Carolyn tried to be understanding, but she had too much pride to dangle in the wind for long. Besides, she was under time pressure to make another decision. She had graduated magna cum laude and was offered graduate fellowships to six universities, including Yale. She wanted to get a PhD and teach in college. She had to let the schools know her plans.

In light of my indecision, she accepted a three-year fellowship in comparative literature at Vanderbilt. I drove her to the airport, and we shared a tearful good-bye. She left for Nashville.

Six weeks of misery later, I knew I couldn't live without Carolyn. So I gave up my job at Florida Power & Light, where I had ten years' seniority that had accumulated during my service time, four years of which were as a journeyman lineman—no small sacrifice—and drove with Honey, my Alaskan husky-shepherd, to Nashville. Bringing Honey along conveyed "Love me, love my dog." We got married three days later.

Our wedding rings, which we picked up en route to the courthouse, cost ten dollars each. Carolyn was giving a Chaucer seminar that afternoon, so we had a morning wedding. She wore her school clothes: a red-and-gray-plaid wool skirt and a red hand-me-down cashmere sweater. I can't remember what I had on. When we got to the courthouse, I was perfectly calm, but Carolyn's knees were so shaky I had to hold her up. It was October 12, 1959.

Until then it had never occurred to me to get a college degree. The course work I took earlier was for fun. I loved learning, and books opened up the whole universe to me. A college education, I thought, was just for polish. It wouldn't do much besides teach me to say "alternative," not "al-ter-*nate*-tive."

But when Carolyn asked, "Would you like to finish college?" I thought, *Why not?* First, I had to be in Nashville anyway to accompany Carolyn in her education. Second, I could pay my tuition through the GI Bill, since I'd served four years in the Air Force. I could work at night and some days to supplement Carolyn's stipend. And third, I wasn't so sure anymore that I was going to spend the rest of my life doing line work. I was beginning to imagine something different for myself. I just didn't yet know what.

Carolyn completed her master's thesis on "Faulkner's Use of the Christ Symbol" and got her degree in English in August 1960—in less than a year—with straight As. This was to be an interim step toward the PhD; she still had two years remaining on her fellowship. But she began teaching at Hillsboro High, since Vanderbilt refused her request for a year's leave of absence. An extra year would have allowed me to graduate and begin work, and such leave was routinely granted to male grad students. The reason for turning her down? "You shouldn't have gotten married."

The truth is, she didn't mind too much. Her dream of earning a PhD was morphing into another dream. She was already thinking about law school.

After Carolyn taught English and Spanish for a year and a half, Kimberly, our first daughter, was born. Full of dreams of a new life together, we said good-bye to Vanderbilt—and Nashville—and headed to New York. As I held Kimberly close, I whispered in her ear, "Honey, your daddy's going to be a Secret Service agent!"

CHAPTER 3

FROM NEW YORK TO DALLAS: "THE PRESIDENT IS DEAD"

Except the Lord keep the city, the watchman waketh but in vain.

LAST WORDS OF PRESIDENT KENNEDY'S

REMARKS PREPARED FOR TRADE MART

November 22, 1963

OCTOBER 1962–DECEMBER 1963

We arrived in New York City the last week in September 1962, pulling a small U-Haul. Inside were our few pitiful belongings: a portable crib (a gift from Carolyn's high school students), bricks and boards for a bookcase, a lot of books, and a few clothes. The U-Haul also carried Carolyn's Fiat Bianchina, about the size of a golf cart and boasting a 22-horsepower engine. Driving the Fiat was like driving a lawn mower. It was so small that one day, back in Nashville, four ninth grade boys picked it up and carried it into the school, where they set the car down in the hall in front of the cafeteria door. Carolyn laughed as hard as they did.

That minicar would have been awfully convenient in New

York, but our first surprise when we arrived in the city was how poor we were. My starting salary of $5,355 per year yielded about $160 take-home pay every two weeks. We had to sell Carolyn's car because we couldn't afford to pay for the tags and insurance. Everything seemed to cost twice what it had in Nashville. We rented a tiny, one-bedroom, garden apartment in Glen Oaks, a huge development in Queens. Our larger space in Nashville had cost $65 a month, furnished. Glen Oaks was $110 a month, empty. And we were glad to get it.

Money from selling Carolyn's car bought me a second suit and us a little furniture. We couldn't afford a bed and a sofa, so we bought a sofa bed and slept on it the whole time we were in New York. The bedroom eventually held two cribs and a dresser we bought secondhand and painted white; we did purchase new crib mattresses. We dined on a used card table camouflaged with a flowered tablecloth that picked up the pale yellow of the walls of our tiny kitchen.

Our second surprise was that Glen Oaks was as segregated as Nashville. In a development with around ten thousand residents, not one was black. Discrimination in housing was illegal in New York, but when a prospective tenant called, the receptionist would say, ever so sweetly, "We don't have any vacancies right now, but people do move out. Come in and fill out an application, and we'll let you know as soon as an apartment is available." When a white person showed up, they were in luck: someone had just moved out. African American applicants were never called back.

We were disappointed to discover this ruse because we'd

looked forward to having friends across the racial divide. We did learn something about bigotry, though: it wasn't all in the South.

* * *

Raring to begin a new adventure, I reported for duty October 1, 1962, at the Secret Service field office, 90 Church Street in lower Manhattan. Four other new agents started the same day: in time, Ernie Luzania became Special Agent in Charge (SAIC) of Sacramento, Chuck Zboril became assistant SAIC of Chicago; John Joe Howlett retired in Little Rock; and Roger Counts became executive assistant to Director John Simpson. We were all eager to make a good impression and to do well. At thirty-two, I was the oldest rookie. None of us imagined, least of all me, that one day I'd become SAIC of the presidential protective division (PPD) for two future presidents.

A noisy forty-by-eighty-foot squad room was the hub of various activities for around twenty-six agents. It was filled with cigarette smoke, jangling phones, slamming doors, the incessant clicks and metallic sound of carriages being thrown on manual typewriters—and rows of government-issue, gray steel desks arranged back-to-back. Each agent had a phone, but every two men shared an Underwood typewriter.

The squad room was the beating heart of the field office. We left there in the morning with the day's assignments, often returning with suspects or witnesses, sometimes in handcuffs, to be fingerprinted and questioned. There we typed our daily reports. We dictated longer investigative reports to female secretaries, who also worked with four or five other agents. There we also made telephone calls and checked out local threats to President John F. Kennedy, who came to New York frequently.

There were separate small rooms for fingerprinting and interviews. A special counterfeiting unit with five or six agents was very active across the hall.

Although the Secret Service in 1962 was predominantly white and male, the New York field office may have been the most diverse in the country. Charles Gittens, the Service's only African American agent for many years, had been in since 1956. Al Wong was of Chinese descent. Victor Gonzalez was a dark-skinned Puerto Rican. The first female agents would not be hired until 1971.

We new guys met the boss, Alfred E. Whitaker, on our first day. He'd been SAIC of New York for a very long time and in the Secret Service since before I was born. A very, very imposing person with a piercing, no-nonsense gaze and steely character, he was *all cop*. We referred to one-on-ones with him as "going to confession."

George Jukes was second in command. If Whitaker was the stern father, Jukes was more like a big brother. He was conscious of and cared about the stress agents and their families were feeling. He was also an outstanding investigator and a source of advice when an agent was stuck.

In those days we didn't get any formal training until after about six months. On our first day the Service wanted to know whether we could shoot. So they gave us a four-inch barrel, .38-caliber gun and took us to the pistol range in the building. The room was long and narrow, and we had to hit a bull's-eye fifty feet away. The odor of gunpowder invaded my lungs, and the noise was deafening. Ear protectors were not provided in those days: we had to make do with stuffing cotton in our ears, which didn't help much.

A muscular instructor from Customs demonstrated how to load and unload safely. "Turn the weapon sideways so it's not pointing at anyone, push the cylinder toward yourself, and empty the six bullets out of it. Look at the cylinder to be sure all chambers are empty, look away, *and then look again*." We had to look twice to be absolutely certain the gun was empty. Then we reloaded all six bullets—we carried six more in a bullet pouch attached to our belts—and fired. I was relieved to qualify right away.

Then they gave us the gun, a commission book (our identity and authority to make arrests), and handcuffs. That was it for the first day.

The second day we got a huge manual with scarcely any time to read it. A carbon copy list of dos and don'ts, mysteriously dated November 1, 1951 (eleven years before), was also handed out. Its advice included the following:

- "Telephone office every two hours. This in addition to any radio calls."
- "Carry service revolver at all times when on duty. Do your practicing at range; don't fool with guns in offices. Use only in self-defense."

- "Stay out of newspaper photos, give out no publicity."
- "Search prisoners first and thoroughly for weapons, then for evidence. Search includes person, auto, and premises under his control."
- "Don't handle female prisoners without proper assistance."
- "Don't drive alone in car with a prisoner; phone office and assistance will be sent."

There was more, but the warning was clear: *This job is not a tea party!*

The third day was the driving test. Mr. Whitaker put on his gray felt hat, a well-blocked, elegant hat he wore proudly and with authority. Putting on his topcoat, he tossed me the keys to a 1961 Studebaker Lark and growled, "I want to see if you can drive. Take me for a ride." I tried to exude confidence, but as I caught the keys, my hands were trembling. Driving in Nashville traffic was nothing compared to Manhattan. I wasn't really sure how I'd measure up. I drove him along, and he didn't talk. The silence magnified the tension.

"Do a broken U-turn," he rasped. I didn't know what a broken U-turn was, so he said, "Well, just stop and turn the car around and go the other way." In Manhattan traffic.

So I did that, but I was nervous. I felt as if I were starring in a slow-motion scene from a movie: turning left across three lanes of traffic, jerking between fast and slow to avoid being hit by angry drivers. But I made the turn and let out a sigh of relief. We resumed at about 35 mph, when I hit a pothole. There were no seat belts in those days. Mr. Whitaker flew straight up. The force of his encounter with the headliner crushed his hat, pushing it down over his ears.

He didn't say a word. Neither did I. But my thoughts were pounding in my head: *This is the end. I'm ruined. I'm fired.*

Then he said, very quietly, "Son, pull the car over. I want to get out." I stopped the car. We were about two miles from the field office, blocking a lane of Manhattan traffic. Taxi drivers blasted their horns and gave me the finger. People on the sidewalk stared.

Mr. Whitaker stepped from the car and blocked his hat. He put it back on. He leaned in the passenger window. "Reb," he said, "if they'd all been like you, we'd have lost the Civil War." And he walked off. He never mentioned it again.

Being from the South, I took Whitaker's "rebel" remark as a backhanded compliment, but I'm not sure that's how he meant it. Carolyn and I quickly caught on that we were on the wrong side of a cultural divide between New Yorkers and the rest of the country. I took some ribbing about bringing my lunch every day to save money. My cheap, unlined overcoat seemed an object of levity, as well as the fact that I had only two suits. But I started locking up criminals so fast that I soon earned some grudging respect.

Whitaker judged agents not by the elegance of their clothes but by how many people they locked up. He had the "Two-Twenty Rule": in light of the number of unresolved cases, he expected each of us to arrest at least two suspects a month and to close at least twenty cases. "Take 'em off the street!" was his motto. That impressed me so strongly that I didn't even notice I was supposed to write a report on each case until the US Attorney started calling. "Where is the report on so and so?" he'd ask. It took a couple of inquiries for me to realize I'd missed a step. Eager to please Whitaker, I'd already locked up a lot of people, but I hadn't thought to look at the manual.

The derision of New Yorkers was harder on Carolyn. For the first time in her life, she was looked down on. Her Southern accent was one reason; our joint refusal to go in hock for furniture was another. A third was we didn't offer guests anything to drink stronger than beer. We couldn't afford to!

Our neighbors were mostly young couples on their way up, biding time until they could buy a house in Levittown or a similar development on Long Island. The women stayed home with babies and preschoolers. One asked Carolyn, "When are you going to get some lamps and easy chairs? When are you going to get a carpet?"

Carolyn nodded toward her framed diploma on the wall. "There's my carpet." But she soon learned that a master's degree from Vanderbilt carried little weight. Another neighbor actually told her, "You won't be able to teach in New York because you couldn't pass the test. Everyone knows the Southern schools are no good." The saving grace for Carolyn was one new friend, a witty, well-read, red-haired former teacher named Rita Cohen, who had a baby about Kimberly's age. While the kids played, Rita offered Carolyn borscht, matzo ball soup, and an assortment of colorful Yiddish phrases. The women studied piano together, and I bought Carolyn a used upright when I saw how happy it made her.

* * *

Less than three weeks after I arrived in New York, the Cold War with the Soviets got suddenly hot. On October 15, 1962, a United States U-2 spy plane photographed construction of Soviet nuclear missile sites in Cuba. This revelation, which precipitated the Cuban Missile Crisis, became public on October 22. After days of frantic, top-secret discussions with his closest advisers, President Kennedy revealed the sites to the American people. He announced a naval blockade to stop Soviet ships bound for Cuba. The Soviets kept coming, and both nations prepared for nuclear war.

For three days Carolyn's parents, who were in the Florida Keys, witnessed a steady, unending line of heavy military equipment flowing south on US-1 toward Key West. They told us that local residents were lining the highway to watch, unbelieving. None of this was reported on the news.

Nobody doubted New York would be a target.

George Jukes called us into a meeting and grimly read a notice to all agents. The title was "What to Do in Case of Nuclear Attack." Jukes solemnly read, "You will see a flash of bright light. Get under your desk. Bend over. Put your head between your legs. And kiss your a— good-bye."

We needed some gallows humor, because it was terrifying to contemplate.

For days both nations hung on the brink, gripped by terror. Then, on October 28, after the United States agreed not to invade Cuba and the Soviets agreed to dismantle their nuclear missile site, the Soviet ships turned back. It was the closest the world had ever come to nuclear destruction.

* * *

I started out with forty cases in the Bedford-Stuyvesant area of Brooklyn. It was dangerous territory for a guy in a suit. Agents always tried to go in pairs to make arrests. My criminal investigator career began during my first week when I accompanied Harry Gibbs, the office champion at locking people up, to a tenement in Bedford-Stuyvesant. On the way he warned, "Only three kinds of guys in suits come here: preachers, social workers, and insurance collectors. The locals know the preachers and social workers. If they think you're an insurance collector, they may jump you, because those guys carry cash."

He added, "So pull your jacket back so they can see your gun. Then nobody will mess with you."

At our first stop of the day we threaded our way through a group of unemployed men loitering in front of the tenement. I pulled back my jacket. The urine stench near the stairs put me on edge. But then, as Gibbs and I climbed the stairs, I smelled something else, something familiar: frying fish and

. . . something that reminded me of my grandmother. Then I recognized the scent of collard greens and relaxed a little.

Gibbs demonstrated how New York cops knock on a suspect's door: with a billy club. This was clearly not the South! A man opened the door and peeked out through the chain on it—a chain just long enough for his rottweiler's head to stick out. I talked him into unchaining the door and soon learned I had a gift for talking to people. I could usually coax them to come without a struggle. These were check forgers, after all, not murderers.

Since Mr. Whitaker liked his agents to lock people up, I did it with wild abandon. But even I had my limits. Once I tracked down Myrtle S., a woman with a long record of forging Social Security checks. When I knocked, she yelled, "Come in, the door's unlocked!" I wondered if I was about to be ambushed. But there was Myrtle lying in bed . . . giving birth to her sixth child! I did not arrest Myrtle that day. Even Whitaker understood.

Will Rogers said, "I never met a man I didn't like." It's a funny thing, but I never arrested a person I didn't like. How I felt about the people I arrested was similar to the way I'd felt about my stepfather Jack. Certainly I disliked what they had done, but after I talked with them awhile, I began to see their human faces and issues.

Finally, after several months, the Service sent me to a six-week course at Treasury school in Washington, DC. Kimberly was only eleven months old, and we'd just discovered Carolyn was pregnant again. To save a little per diem money, I was staying at a cheap boardinghouse called Ma Bouma's. There was a pay phone in the hall, but—again, to save—I was trying to ration calls to one a week.

When I called home the second week, Carolyn sounded despondent. "Kimberly is so sad. I think she's grieving for you. She won't eat, won't smile, just stares at the door." Her voice broke. "I don't know how to make her happy." Then she really started to cry. "*I* miss you too!"

So I began hitchhiking from DC back to New York every weekend. Kimberly—and Carolyn—started to smile again. It was our first hint of the immense sacrifices we would make as a family for my work in the Service.

★ ★ ★

Not all my work involved stolen checks. As Albert Vaughn had promised when he interviewed me in Nashville, whenever the president or his family came to New York, our field office worked protection, supplementing the White House detail. A scant month after I was sworn in, I got my first protective assignment. On November 7, 1962, former first lady Eleanor Roosevelt died of bone marrow tuberculosis. President Kennedy and Vice President Lyndon Johnson were coming to the funeral in Hyde Park, New York. The Service needed some back-up agents, and I was chosen. George Sershen, a wizened, older agent, and I went to Stewart Air Force Base, where a helicopter was scheduled to land. Then the president would take a limousine to Hyde Park. As a brand-new agent I had the humblest of jobs: to guard the empty helicopter until the president returned.

I'll never forget seeing Jack Kennedy walk off the chopper on that crisp autumn morning with Agent Roy Kellerman behind him. At six foot four Kellerman was an imposing figure, taller than the president. The agents who followed also appeared to be at least six feet tall, in their thirties, and in superb physical condition. They looked sharp and confident in their tailored suits and perfectly shined black shoes, some carrying London Fog trench coats.

I had no aspirations to get on the White House detail. I didn't think I was sophisticated enough. I still ordered wine by the color, and all I knew was that the bottles with corks cost more than those with screw-off lids. Except for my Air Force experience, I'd hardly left Miami. These were really magnificent guys, I thought. You had to be special to be doing that.

Throughout 1963 Jack Kennedy came to New York often. He was more exciting than a movie star. He glowed with charisma. He glittered. He lit up the space. People would wait in ten- to fifteen-degree weather out at the airport just to glimpse him as he drove by. If he touched them, they wouldn't wash their hands! Women especially went crazy when Jack Kennedy entered a room or worked a crowd.

One day I covered the president at the Waldorf, bringing up the rear of the phalanx surrounding him. But he saw a crowd behind a rope line and walked back to greet them, right where I was. For a minute or two I was the only agent close to the president, so I started working the line in front of him, telling the crowd, "Take your hands out of your pockets where I can see them," as I'd seen the PPD agents do. The PPD agents rushed back and took over, but I had one moment of glory. And I was close enough to see a quality in President Kennedy that you don't find in many political leaders—something like an electrical field of energy surrounded him. But I could also see something else, something I have a gift for seeing. I saw a lot of pain. I saw suffering in the way he held his body, leaning slightly forward and stiff when he wasn't "on."

Every time the president or Mrs. Kennedy came to New York during 1963, I was assigned to work them—either at the airport or the speech site or up at the Carlyle Hotel on Madison Avenue, where they maintained two suites. As a rookie agent, I got to know the Carlyle well, especially the hallway where I stood guard between their two enormous suites, 34A and 34B, which encompassed the entire thirty-fourth floor.

I'd never seen anything like the Carlyle. From the lobby to the roof, it combined the most luxurious appointments with understated elegance. Guests enjoyed fine art, furnishings, carpets, and linens accompanied by sweeping views of Central Park. Although I was too lowly to be invited into the presidential suite, I was told it came with private terraces and a grand piano.

Jacqueline Kennedy loved to come to New York, sometimes with her sister Lee Radziwill, to shop or attend the

Metropolitan Opera. One of the agents would hold the door, while Clint Hill and other agents accompanied her. If she stayed in the Carlyle and wasn't going out, they only needed one agent on post in the hall, and I was sometimes "it."

One day Mrs. Kennedy decided to go shopping in Manhattan and found herself a little short of cash. "Oh, Agent," she began, not knowing my name, "do you have $800 on you that you could lend me?"

"No, ma'am," I gulped, trying not to look as stunned as I felt. It had been a long time since I'd seen $800 in one place, let alone in my pocket! But she didn't hold it against me. She was very kind. I showed her a snapshot of Kimberly, and she autographed it for me.

Besides physical protection, we investigated an increasing number of threat cases: individuals who seemed to be focused on the president. Some were harmless. One woman told me she was Kennedy's wife and her address was 1600 Pennsylvania Avenue. We had a lot of that—many people passionately loved or hated Kennedy.

Of those who disliked Kennedy, some held him responsible for the failed invasion of Cuba at the Bay of Pigs and the raising of the Berlin Wall in 1961. In addition, the nuclear arms' race was a nightmare waiting to happen. By 1962 both the United States and the Soviet Union had resumed nuclear testing in the atmosphere. The Cuban Missile Crisis had caused both Khrushchev and Kennedy to recognize the dangers inherent in a game of international "chicken." So in June of 1963 Kennedy made a speech announcing ongoing talks with the USSR, together with Great Britain, to limit nuclear testing. This announcement was popular in New York but not everywhere in the United States.

Also in June the president proposed civil rights legislation to ban discrimination in public accommodations, housing, and jobs. All these major changes in the status quo created enemies. It seemed as if every announcement brought increased threat activity. The Secret Service stayed on edge. And the threat level in New York continued to rise.

Most of Kennedy's critics were law-abiding citizens. But others were more deadly. I had to pull a gun only once in my entire career, not while on protection or on a counterfeiting or check case; it was a threat investigation. And the gun I pulled was not my own.

A sixteen-year-old was spewing threats against the president, and Joe Gasquez and I decided to bring him in for an interview. He was very, very muscular for his age. We sat him down in the field office, when suddenly he jumped up, yelling, "Yes! I threatened the president, and I'm going to kill the s.o.b.!" Gasquez got one handcuff on him, but he flung Gasquez off. He ran into the hall, one handcuff dangling and Gasquez in full pursuit.

The suspect turned into a blind alley where the door was blocked. Gasquez had taken off his coat, so the gun in his holster was exposed. The kid turned to confront Gasquez and grabbed for Gasquez's gun. Gasquez was fighting him off. I came up behind and snatched the gun—Gasquez's gun—and stuck it in the kid's ear. That calmed him down.

Gasquez put the other cuff on him, and we took him back.

My rookie year in the service was a blur. I worked so hard to please Whitaker that I closed the third-most cases in the office (out of twenty-six agents), and that was with six weeks out for Treasury school in DC. I confess I was a little bit proud of myself. My teacher, Harry Gibbs, again won first prize: a bottle of whiskey.

Many years later, just before I retired from the Service in 1985, out of curiosity I looked up my personnel file. In my sixty-day evaluation, I discovered Whitaker had written, "An excellent, aggressive field agent but doesn't appear to be White House detail material." At the time I would have agreed.

In late September the Nashville field office had an opening, and the SAIC, Paul Doster, requested me. Our second child, Jennifer Lynn, had just been born the day after my thirty-third birthday, September 17, 1963. I loved the challenge of working in New York, but our living expenses were killing us. I later learned we'd been eligible for food stamps on my starting salary! We were eating pancakes and chicken wings to stay alive. The same money in Nashville would put us into a house of our own. I took the transfer, effective November 12, 1963.

Near the end of my time in New York I went out to Idlewild Airport to work President Kennedy's arrival and departure for his visit to the United Nations. It was late September. When he climbed out of his limousine and walked to the plane, I had an ominous feeling. I thought, *I'll never see him again.* Something about the way he walked to that airplane gave me a sense of foreboding.

* * *

Anyone who was five or older on November 22, 1963, remembers where they were and how they heard that President Kennedy had been shot. In the Nashville motel room where we'd been living since my transfer, Carolyn and I were munching on ham and cheese sandwiches and trying to keep the babies entertained, waiting to move into our new house. Our furniture was already there, and I'd taken the day off. But here it was lunchtime, and we were still stuck in the motel.

We were waiting for a call from Bob Gaugh, the Secret Service agent I was replacing. We'd bought his house, a one-year-old brick split-foyer with a big yard at 4818 Sunlight Drive. Gaugh had run into a snafu with his own mover, and we didn't want to move in until he had moved out.

Though my transfer to Nashville was a lateral move, it felt like a promotion. I'd soon advance from a GS-7 government grade to GS-9, with a $2,000 raise. But the main benefit was that it cost so much less to live in Nashville than in New York. The three-bedroom, two-bath house with a garage and rec room seemed enormous compared to our one-bedroom garden apartment in New York. We were about to move up from the working poor to the middle class!

It was twelve thirty Nashville time, and I was absently surfing TV channels. When I hit CBS, an invisible voice-over interrupted a soap opera, *As the World Turns*, for breaking news. Suddenly Walter Cronkite was on the screen. He tried to keep his voice calm, but in the newsroom behind him, I could see that chaos reigned. He said, "There has been an attempt . . . on the life of President Kennedy. He was wounded in an automobile driving from Dallas Airport into downtown Dallas, along with Governor Connally of Texas. They've been taken to Parkland Hospital there, where their condition is as yet unknown."

Like so many people who heard those words that day, Carolyn and I began to pray for the president. Then Cronkite switched to the Dallas Trade Mart, where a group had gathered to hear President Kennedy speak. Reporter Eddie Barker of Dallas WKRLD started talking:

As you can imagine, there are many stories that are coming in now as to the actual condition of the president. One is that he is dead. This cannot be confirmed. Another is that Governor Connally is in the operating room. This we have not confirmed.

Perhaps picking up our vibes, Jenny started to cry. Carolyn gave her a bottle. I grabbed my gun and ran outside. *Am I crazy?* I thought. *There's no enemy to shoot.* Back inside, I paced like a caged lion, a sick feeling in my stomach.

More details were coming in. "He is now in the emergency

room at Parkland Hospital in Dallas. He is remaining in the emergency room because Secret Service aides say that the facilities there are as good as elsewhere. They have moved Governor Connally . . . to the operating room at Parkland Hospital. Mrs. Kennedy . . . was not injured but was said to be in a state of shock. . . . The president slumped into her lap with . . . a bullet wound in the head."

I couldn't believe what I was hearing. In my mind I started to bargain with the news. *Maybe he was grazed. Maybe it wasn't fatal.*

Cronkite said, "We have just been advised from Dallas that blood transfusions are being given to President Kennedy." A staffer in the newsroom then handed Cronkite a note.

Back to the Trade Mart, where people were praying. Eddie Barker of WKRLD said, "The report is that the president is dead. This is not confirmed. . . . Word just came to us a minute ago. The word we have is that President Kennedy is dead. . . . He was shot by an assassin at the intersection of Elm and Houston Street just as he was going into the underpass. . . . A doctor on the staff of Parkland Hospital . . . says that it is true. He was in tears when he told me just a moment ago."

I thought, *A doctor would not be crying if it weren't true.*

The shot was fired at 12:30 p.m. central standard time. The president was pronounced dead thirty minutes later. The world was informed shortly after that.

Carolyn and I just looked at each other, too stunned to speak, struggling to absorb what we were hearing. In addition to shock and grief, I felt a primal sense of failure on behalf of the Secret Service. I determined right then and there that nothing like this would happen on my watch. I'd give my best gifts—intellectual, physical, emotional, spiritual—to be certain. This would not happen on my watch.

The jingle of a phone broke our silence. Bob Gaugh said, "Our movers have come and gone, but we can't tear ourselves away from the TV. Why don't you just come on over, and we'll watch it together." So we did.

I've often wondered what Bob must have been feeling on this, his last day as a Secret Service agent. He and I were watching every agent's worst nightmare unfold in real time. His wife had persuaded him to take a commission in the Army, which she thought would be better for the family. Little did they foresee that Bob would be deployed to Vietnam only a few months later.

We huddled together in the basement amid untouched boxes, eyes riveted to the TV as scene after scene unfolded. Parkland Hospital announced that Governor Connally was seriously wounded but would survive. A single bullet had struck him in the back, an arm, and a leg. Doctors speculated he may have been pierced by the bullet that passed through the president.

Cameras showed people still standing, frozen along the parade route. Maybe if they didn't move, the scene could be replayed with a different ending. Now a casket was being carried from Parkland and loaded into a borrowed hearse to be driven to the airport. Mrs. Kennedy got in the back and rode with the body.

Two hours after the shooting, Vice President Johnson was sworn in as president of the United States with Lady Bird Johnson on one side and Jacqueline Kennedy on the other, still wearing her blood-stained pink suit. On Air Force One, where John F. Kennedy's body rested to be flown to Washington, federal judge Sarah Hughes wept as she administered the presidential oath of office.

The trauma was being shared by the entire country. As happened later on September 11, 2001, the whole world, in fact, was watching.

Now a suspect, Lee Harvey Oswald, was in custody. He'd also shot and killed a young police officer, J. D. Tippit, as he tried to flee.

Long after dark, the Gaughs finally tore themselves away.

Though I was on annual leave that Friday, I called Paul Doster, my new SAIC. He said, "Come in to work on Monday. But you'll probably be going to Dallas in a few days." In fact I didn't go into the office until Tuesday, because Monday was declared a national day of mourning for the president's funeral. The public wept before TV sets all over the United States as we saw Jackie Kennedy covered in black, with Robert and Ted Kennedy leading the funeral procession from the White House to St. Matthew's Cathedral. Heads of state and dignitaries from more than ninety countries followed. They included Charles de Gaulle and Willy Brandt.

Every heart broke at the sight of two-year-old John-John saluting his father's casket.

As I watched, my thoughts were a little bit different from the public's. I shared in the outpouring of grief, but I was also thinking about the security nightmare of that event—and my heart was going out to the exhausted and heartbroken agents working it. They were now protecting President Johnson, Jacqueline Kennedy, and her children. They were coordinating security for the entire event with ninety international security details and the State Department, which was then responsible for the visiting heads of state. Police, special agents from other federal agencies, FBI, and military all had a critical role in keeping participants and the public safe. A bomb in St. Matthew's during the requiem mass could have decapitated the governments of the entire Western world—and more.

Added to their personal pain of losing the president, those agents must have been feeling the burden of massive failure. I was. An agent's professional life has one mission: to protect the principal. When that mission fails, it fails utterly. There's no silver lining, no learning for next time. There are still agents today who can't talk about the Kennedy assassination. Many of the guys in Dallas that day drank their way to retirement, defeated and weakened by losing the president. At that time many of us wondered whether the Secret Service itself would survive. A Congress disgusted with the assassination could have transferred presidential protection to the FBI or the military. I wasn't sure I'd still have a job six months from then.

Before I could leave for Dallas, a police groupie named Jack Ruby shot and killed Lee Harvey Oswald while Oswald was in custody of police officers in the basement of the Dallas police station. Again on live TV. Was this part of a conspiracy to silence Oswald? Were the police involved? There was so much death in the air, so much pain.

I'm now convinced that the Warren Commission, which President Johnson appointed to investigate Kennedy's assassination, was correct: Lee Harvey Oswald was a lone gunman. But at that moment there were many unanswered questions.

I flew to Dallas the following Friday, November 29. To my surprise there seemed to be a lot more grief in *me* than I sensed as the pervasive mood in Dallas.

Many people in Dallas did not like the president. The Democrats themselves were deeply split between liberals and conservatives, who threatened to bolt the party. Unhappiness focused on the same two issues: foreign policy and civil rights.

Though Kennedy had partially redeemed himself with a trip to Berlin, where he declared, *"Ich bin ein Berliner"* ("I am a Berliner")—and with ending the threat of missiles in Cuba—conservatives were still smarting about his handling of Khrushchev in Europe. They feared we had given away too much power in the test ban treaty that Kennedy had signed on October 7, 1963. Many Americans did not trust the Russians to abide by it.

Kennedy's civil rights stance had also evoked fear and

hatred, especially but not solely in the Southern states. In the South ministers and students, white and black, were joining hands in peaceful sit-ins, eat-ins, teach-ins, and voter registration campaigns. In the North Malcolm X was urging a more active kind of resistance to de facto segregation of schools, workplaces, and neighborhoods. On June 11 two African American students, James Hood and Vivian Malone, walked through the doors of the University of Alabama, escorted by the federalized Alabama National Guard. In a speech announcing this action President Kennedy had named integration—both north and south—as "a moral issue." A week later he'd sent proposed civil rights legislation to Congress.

As a result, the Dallas air had been thick with tension as the president's visit approached. Less than a month before, UN Ambassador Adlai Stevenson had a frightening experience in Dallas. As he left the Memorial Auditorium Theater, where he had just received a standing ovation from 1,750 people, a woman struck him in the face with a sign, just missing his eye. And a young man spat on him. This happened on October 24, 1963.

Embarrassed, Dallas city leaders rushed to assure the world that Dallas was a hospitable city. The mayor, chamber of commerce president, and many conservatives signed an apology to Stevenson—with a copy to President Kennedy—for "a minute group of uninvited irresponsibles." Governor John Connally, the leading Democratic conservative, called the troublemakers "a handful of people who let their emotions run away with them" and asserted they "are not representative of the people of Dallas." The *Dallas Times Herald* apologized in a front-page editorial: "Dallas has been disgraced. There is no other way to view the storm-trooper actions of last night's frightening attack on Adlai Stevenson."

But I learned that not all the violence came from the right wing. Some had come from the left.

I recently asked Roger Warner, who had been an agent with the Dallas field office at the time of Kennedy's assassination, how he viewed the atmosphere in Dallas before and after the president's murder. He said, "Jerry, here's what you were seeing: in April a sharpshooter tried to kill General Edwin Walker, a right-wing hero, by shooting into his house. People were already on edge because the shooter was loose and still unidentified. Then we had the Stevenson incident. And now it was the *president*!

"Then Jack Ruby shot Oswald. Every day seemed to bring more shock, more trauma, more drama. Rumors were flying. People were afraid we might be going to war with Cuba. What you were probably sensing in Dallas, Jerry, was fear."

But the truth remained: whatever I sensed in Dallas was very different from the adulation I'd seen in New York.

My first couple of days in Dallas I "backed up" autopsy pictures of Oswald; that is, I wrote up all the details of the autopsy report on the back of each photo: his name, the time of the autopsy, the hospital, doctor, pathologist—that kind of information.

Then I was assigned to Marguerite Oswald, the assassin's mother.

There were two reasons to protect her. First, there had been enough killing. Oswald's mother; his wife, Marina; and even his brother Robert had received threats. How many more Jack Rubys might be lurking, seeing themselves as avenging angels for the death of the president? The cycle of vengeance had to stop.

The second reason was that the FBI wanted to question Oswald's family, to see what they knew about Lee's motive for going to Russia, marrying a Russian woman, and seeking asylum there. When the Russians wouldn't take him, Oswald was forced to return to the United States. It was known that he had gone to Mexico in September 1963, where he visited the Cuban embassy and sought permission to travel to Cuba. Permission was denied. The FBI wanted to know more, and specifically whether others were involved.

As it turned out, Marguerite and Robert didn't really know anything, and after a few weeks their protection was dropped. But we kept a detail with Marina until the Warren Commission report came out in September 1964.

For now, I was driving to Fort Worth to begin my assignment protecting Marguerite Oswald, who lived in a modest house with a porch. I was greeted by Marguerite, a grandmotherly nurse who appeared to be in her early sixties, with thinning gray hair pulled back in a bun. She wore large glasses with dark rims, pointed at the sides. She enjoyed getting protection because it made her feel important, but it was really more like house arrest. Four of us took turns with her: Bob Camp, Carl Hardy, Gary Seals, and I. She drove us all nuts.

As we'd say in the South, Marguerite Oswald was a piece of work. In a nasal, grating voice she insisted—loudly and repeatedly—that Lee was an agent of the CIA, sent to Russia by the US government. She referred to herself proudly as "a mother in history." I never heard her say she was ashamed or even embarrassed by the fact that her son had murdered the president of the United States. On the contrary, she reveled in the attention she was getting. Her son was said to have hated her, and after a short time I could understand why. I was with her only four days, December 1 to December 4, but I spent every minute possible out on the porch.

On a Sunday afternoon some kind women from a Baptist church came to visit and brought Marguerite a bouquet of lovely pink and white calla lilies. One of them said, "We were thinking how upset you must be about what happened, and we wanted to tell you we're praying for you. We thought you might enjoy these flowers from the altar today."

As soon as they left, she angrily threw the flowers in the trash. "I don't want no *used* flowers!" she huffed.

By the time I was assigned to Marguerite Oswald, her son had already been murdered and buried. According to Roger Warner, getting him in the ground had not been a walk in the park. After the autopsy the family managed to get him embalmed, but then no cemetery wanted him. Finally, the Secret Service prevailed upon Rose Hill Memorial Burial Park in Fort Worth.

A funeral was out of the question because of the danger of a riot. But Oswald's wife, Marina, would not agree to bury him unless a minister was present, and no preacher in Dallas or Fort Worth would do it. So the FBI found someone from outside the area who agreed to come in and say a prayer for the family.

The next problem: no one wanted to act as a pallbearer to help lower the casket into the ground. Secret Service agents couldn't do it—they needed to have their hands free. Some guys from the press eventually pitched in.

Just before the casket was lowered, both Marguerite and Marina wanted to look at Oswald's body one more time. So the casket was opened and they each kissed him. Roger saw Marina lay her wedding ring on his chest. Maybe she wanted to get rid of it.

Marguerite harped on the idea that "Marina's going to get rich, and I deserve some of that money." Allan Grant, a *LIFE* magazine photographer who tried to take Marguerite's picture, said she demanded $2,000. (He could not get authorization from his managing editor to pay her.) She alternated between hating and loving Marina, but since Marina spoke no English, she blessedly didn't know it.

Marguerite also obsessed over the thought that someone would steal her son's body. Unlike most of her notions, this was a real possibility. Unconfirmed ghoulish rumors were flying. (One was that an employee of the embalmer wanted to cut off Oswald's trigger finger as a souvenir!)

One night I overheard Marguerite yelling on the phone.

The guy on the other end was from the Tarrant County Sheriff's Department. Marguerite screamed, "I don't care if it takes every policeman in Tarrant County. I don't want Lee's body dug up!" They couldn't keep a guard there all the time, so finally they covered the casket with poured concrete to make it hard to steal.

A postscript: like everything else surrounding the Kennedy assassination, conspiracy theories abounded about Lee Harvey Oswald's burial. A British lawyer, Michael Eddowes, was convinced that Oswald's body had been switched with a Russian agent's. Finally, to quell the rumors, Oswald's body was exhumed on October 4, 1981, and examined by Baylor University. Dental records conclusively proved that the coffin did indeed contain the remains of Lee Harvey Oswald.

After my few days on Marguerite's porch, I was relieved to be transferred to Marina, a pale brunette with large, frightened eyes. She lived in a house with the Paines, acquaintances of Oswald's who had taken her and the children in. Young and terrified that someone would try to kill her and her children, Marina never smiled. She spoke no English and had two babies almost the exact ages of mine. I was surprised that, unlike my kids, her children almost never cried.

From what I learned, Marina's life with Oswald had been miserable. Her lack of English and her two babies had kept her trapped. She never knew what to expect from her husband: he'd disappear and not come back for days, which was a relief from his harsh temper and occasional blows. They were living apart at the time of the shooting.

Marina later told investigators that Oswald had bragged to her that he was the shooter who had tried to kill General Walker. Like many assassins, Oswald did not discriminate left wing from right wing. He was a killer, looking for a victim—and personal fame.

When the FBI brought Marina to Washington to be questioned by the Warren Commission investigators, she would not talk to the police or the FBI. But we had a Secret Service agent who spoke Russian. My job had been to keep her alive and to help win her trust of the Secret Service so that when the agent arrived, she would talk to him. I did . . . and she did.

✷ ✷ ✷

Shortly after President Kennedy was assassinated in Dallas—maybe one or two days later—a movie of the actual killing appeared on TV news stations. Secret Service agents, young and old, have committed those scenes to heart.

The gentleman who took the film was Abraham Zapruder. Here's how it goes: Zapruder is standing on the grassy knoll high ground as the motorcade moves toward the underpass at a slow rate of speed, from left to right on the screen. As the film begins, President Kennedy and Jackie are in the backseat of the presidential limousine, code-named "100X." Texas governor John Connally and his wife, Nellie, are in the jump seat. Agent Roy Kellerman (deputy chief of the White House detail) is in front, and Agent Bill Greer is driving.

Suddenly President Kennedy jerks both fists to his throat

as Jackie responds to the sound of the gun behind them. Then the president's head explodes, spewing his skull, hair, blood, and brains into the air in a pinkish gray mist that drifts to the rear. The president falls forward into Jackie's lap.

In the meantime Agent Clint Hill from the follow-up car sprints to the rear of 100X, trying desperately to get to the left running board and handhold on the side behind the first lady. As Clint takes his closest step to the car, he misses, then hurls himself once more, gaining access with a good grip on the hold. He stops Jackie, who is now on the trunk of 100X, trying to retrieve pieces of her husband's skull and hair. Clint pushes her back to her seat and sees the president with a palm-size cavity just above his right ear.

Clint is now seen covering both Jackie and the dying president with his own body. Mr. Zapruder stops his camera as the motorcade disappears in the underpass.

For me personally, and for every agent in the Secret Service, the horror of this scene remains vivid. The president's exploding head became an iconic memory embedded deep in my psyche, waiting, waiting for that terrible moment agents pray never comes to them.

Jack Kennedy kept his rendezvous with Death on November 22, 1963. Like all other agents in the Service on that day, I prayed to do everything in my power to see that no one I protected would keep that rendezvous on my watch.

CHAPTER 4

VIETNAM: GOING FROM BAD TO WORSE

Experience is a hard teacher because she gives the test first,
the lesson afterwards.

VERNON SANDERS LAW

1964–1967

As we circled the Washington Monument, my eyes were wide open. Lights illuminated the imposing Capitol dome on one end of the National Mall and the Jefferson Memorial on the other. From this suspended viewpoint, I could take in the grand expanse of monuments and government buildings all at once. *Beyond these facades*, I thought, *are the corridors of power.* These were the buildings where our nation's history was continuing to unfold. Though my family and I had recently moved to Nashville on January 28, 1964, I flew to the LBJ ranch for a few days and then to Washington to fill in temporarily on the presidential detail. Trying to absorb the panorama through the chopper window, I wondered, *Is this really me? Can I really be going to the White House—to guard a president?*

Climbing out of the helicopter, my colleague Sam Sulliman and I went straight to the White House, where I was going to stand post with the four o'clock to midnight shift. I'd never been to the White House. I looked up at the looming, two-story columns, feeling smaller than usual. Trying not to look like a rube, I copied Sam: I greeted uniformed White House Police Force officers at outside entrances, showed my commission book, and walked right in.

Agents in the White House were responsible for two inside posts: one in the hallway leading to the Cabinet Room and one by the door to the Oval Office. A third post was outside, by the door to the Rose Garden. To keep everyone alert, we "pushed" (rotated posts) every thirty minutes. Each post had a letter and number. Sam said, "Stand here—at E-6." I was alone and trying to get my bearings. Then I realized E-6 was the president's door to the Oval Office. I felt really important . . . for about a minute.

Suddenly the door opened, and President Lyndon Johnson towered over me—all six foot four inches of him. Sounding annoyed, he demanded, "Come in here and help me turn these lights off!" It was now early February. Though he'd been president for more than two months, Johnson had spent the Christmas holidays at the ranch and was slowly transitioning from his vice presidential office at the Old Executive Office Building. He still didn't know how to turn off the lights.

I took a couple of steps into the Oval Office. I would later have time to notice the details of that room. The red carpet and floor-to-ceiling blue-trimmed white drapes were literally brand new, chosen by Jacqueline Kennedy and installed while she and her husband were in Dallas. President Kennedy never saw anything but the drawings. President Johnson left them unchanged.

But that afternoon I had a job to do for the new president, and unfortunately I had no idea how to do it. *Where would the light switch be?* I thought, scanning the room fruitlessly. Embarrassed, I confessed, "Mr. President, I'm at a loss. I don't know where the switches are."

He called me an obscene name. In utter disgust, he spat out, "Secret Service don't know nothing, and some of them never will know nothing!" And he stomped out.

I was supposed to follow him. Shaken, I found some other agents, and we followed him back into the mansion. I told Sam Sulliman about the encounter, and he said, "Oh, don't worry about that, he does that all the time." Later I learned I was lucky he didn't fire me. He habitually fired agents. But not even the president can fire a civil service employee without cause. The fired agents were back the next day, and he'd say, "Didn't I fire you?" They'd say, "Yes, sir." He'd curse and mutter "Secret Service" under his breath. President Johnson never knew our names. He and his detail understood (and tolerated) each other well. Nobody took it personally. We'd share Johnson stories and laugh it off.

I returned to Nashville on February 19 less starry eyed and

a little more seasoned. In Nashville I was getting accustomed to my new duties tracking down check forgers and adjusting again to the Southern culture. Not long after my return, I tracked down a check forger I'd been hunting for months and found him in a dentist's chair. Flashing my credentials at the suspect, I said, "Sir, I'm Jerry Parr, US Secret Service." I showed him the evidence. "Did you forge this check?"

He said, "Yes, sir." (Note: this was in the pre–Miranda warning days.)

The dentist yelled, "What are you doing? You can't just barge into my office like this! Get out of here!"

Ignoring him, I told the suspect, "You're under arrest. I'll wait for you in the hall." When he came out, I cuffed him and took him away.

The furious dentist called my boss, Paul Doster, to complain. When I got back to the office, Doster spoke to me like a patient teacher of a young child. "Jerry . . . Son . . . This is not New York. This is Tennessee. We're a little more polite here. Next time stay in the waiting room and let the dentist finish—and then arrest the s.o.b.!"

In May 1964 Lyndon Johnson came to Knoxville to make a campaign speech. It's hard to believe now, but the Presidential Protective Division (PPD) had sent only one agent, Ron Pontius, to do the protective survey, which agents called "advances." The field offices provided support. So Doster sent Bill Hudson and me to Knoxville to help Pontius. I'd never done any kind of advance before, and I didn't know where to start.

Pontius didn't like to waste words. Here's how he instructed me to cover the speech site, a cavernous hall big enough to hold fifteen thousand people: "Secure it. Do a report." That was it.

Then he took Hudson, also a rookie, over to the University of Tennessee and said the same thing. He told us, "I'll come in ahead of the president, but you'll tell me where the posts should be and how many agents and police officers we'll need to cover them."

So my first advance wasn't the first lady or one of the president's children. It was a *presidential* advance . . . in this huge place, all by myself! And that's where I came up with the notion that an agent has to think like an assassin.

Walking all over the auditorium, I inspected every place the president was going to stand and work and sit and do his thing. And I thought about how many ways a killer could take him out. Then I tried to think of ways to neutralize them all.

It took me all day, and I wrote it all down. I probably overcovered it. The detail didn't have enough agents—even with local cops—to cover my plan. But despite only partial implementation of my plan, Johnson came and left alive, and Hudson and I could breathe again. I didn't know it at the time, but the Service was seriously considering me for a spot on a protective detail. I had passed the first test.

Right after that I spent a month in Washington at my second Secret Service school. Carolyn and the kids came along at our own expense, but I was so exhausted by the rigorous training, I wasn't very good company. We practiced swimming rescues in the dark. (Scenario: downed helicopter upside down in the water. Practice getting the passenger-protectee out alive.) I learned to cover and evacuate a president under attack. (Don't look for the assailant. Don't shoot back. Shield the principal with your own body, and get him or her out of there. Agents and police on the outer perimeter will take care of the assassin.) The trainer would shout, "Cover! Cover!" until it became automatic. We practiced shooting in the field with pop-up targets, learning when to shoot and when to hold our fire. (Some pop-ups would be children or priests.) We learned "Ten Minute Medicine": how to stop a bleeding wound, how to keep a heart attack victim alive for ten minutes—enough time to get medical help.

I hoped I'd never need to put this training into practice, but if that time came, I prayed I'd be able to perform.

Nineteen sixty-four was an election year. Johnson's running mate was Senator Hubert Horatio Humphrey of Minnesota. Republican candidates were Senator Barry Goldwater from Arizona and Representative William Miller from New York. In those days there were no candidate details; only President Johnson had protection. But for the first time, the new vice president would get protection. In November, I was again called out of Nashville—this time to Minneapolis to wait with Humphrey for the election results. If Johnson won, I would become part of Humphrey's brand-new vice president–elect detail.

As the results rolled in showing that the Johnson-Humphrey

ticket had won, red, white, and blue balloons floated to the ceiling. Corks popped. Cheers resounded with each positive announcement. Campaign workers threw confetti and danced with joy, ecstatic. Everyone was giving me high fives, as if I were part of the team. I liked it. And I learned something: politicians live and breathe politics. They attach to friendly faces. It's easy to get caught up in the giddiness of the moment. *Be careful,* I told myself. *This isn't about you.*

Getting sucked into politics is not healthy for an agent's career, for the person being protected, or for the country. If an agent is looking adoringly at the principal, he or she is not looking at the crowd where an assassin may be lurking. I used to say that if an agent's eyes start to glaze over when he or she hears "Hail to the Chief," it's time for a transfer.

Agents have to understand that our job is to protect the office of the president, regardless of who holds it. Whether we like the person is irrelevant. We're there to protect the constitutional right of Americans to choose who will govern them. We can't allow a bullet to cancel the vote of millions of people. If an agent doesn't get that, he or she should not do protection.

It takes some maturity for agents not to let the activity around them go to their heads. Young people are especially vulnerable. George Reedy, President Johnson's press secretary, once said nobody under forty should work at the White House.

On December 2, 1964, Carolyn and I packed our things again—now we actually had furniture—and moved from

Nashville to Arlington, Virginia, just outside Washington. My official start date on the Vice Presidential Protective Division (VPPD) detail was December 6, 1964.

Glenn Weaver became Special Agent in Charge (SAIC) of the VPPD, and Walt Coughlin was his deputy. They came from the White House to run the permanent detail, and I was flattered that they wanted me to join it. I'd been in the Service for two years. Honored and excited to be on my first protective detail, I could not have foreseen that the Humphrey years, 1964–1968, would be the most challenging of my Secret Service career.

★ ★ ★

Today a spacious, elegant Victorian home serves as the official vice-presidential residence. Located on the grounds of the US Naval Observatory, where 34th Street dead-ends at Massachusetts Avenue, it housed admirals from 1893, when it was built, until 1974. Beautiful and expansive, the grounds afford space for a helicopter to land and take off safely.

But Humphrey never lived there. Neither did vice presidents Agnew or Rockefeller. As had previous vice presidents, they lived in their own local homes, which were hard to adequately secure and afforded no space for official entertaining. In 1974 Congress recognized that an official vice-presidential residence was needed. In 1977, Walter Mondale was the first vice president to occupy the house; all subsequent vice presidents have followed suit.

We initially set up our command post in the basement of Humphrey's very ordinary, two-story suburban home on a small lot at Coquelin Terrace, a quiet, tree-lined street in Chevy Chase, Maryland, five or six miles north of the White House. Outdoors, an agent sat inside a car parked in an open carport, from which he saw clearly anything that moved out front or on the right side. The other post, a glass-enclosed cubicle the size of a phone booth, guarded the rear and left sides. Mercifully it was heated, sheltering us from the cold wind and rain of winter. We kept this arrangement until the Humphreys moved to a high-rise condo on the Potomac River a couple of years later.

As a rookie on protection, I rotated shifts every two weeks: 8:00 a.m. to 4:00 p.m., 4:00 p.m. to midnight, or midnight to 8:00 a.m. Shifts were often extended to ten or twelve hours—or worse—depending on the vice president's activity. Shift work challenges agents physically and mentally, especially at night. While sitting was permitted, we had to stand if the public was around. Agents could see each other, a critical element in staving off lonesomeness and inattention. Still, midnights at the residence were the pits. Boredom was the enemy. We were all drilled, "You *must not* sleep! Dozing will get you thirty days 'on the beach'—or fired." We had a supervisor who was always trying to catch someone asleep. One morning at about two o'clock, in total darkness, he crept up on the booth, hoping to surprise another rookie agent. Then the boss heard the unmistakable sound of a shell being cranked into the chamber of a shotgun—which was pointing right at him. He gave up that game. And we all gave the new guy two thumbs-up.

At times, in the dark of night-morning, my mind would drift toward home. I imagined my little girls asleep in their canopy beds. Picturing Carolyn's face, I wished I were beside her, especially at the end of a twelve-hour day. As at the White House, we pushed posts every thirty minutes to stay grounded. But what really kept me awake and sharp was the image of JFK's head being blown apart.

We were all still vibrating from Kennedy's death, and remembering that some crazy might want to kill the vice president helped me keep my edge.

We also stood post at Humphrey's home in Waverly, Minnesota, where he retreated once or twice a month and on every holiday. I used to joke that I spent so much time in Minnesota I could have voted there.

A brown, four-bedroom rambler standing on seven or eight acres near the shore of Lake Waverly, Humphrey's house was surrounded by tall firs and other evergreens. Maple, walnut, and oak trees flamed into color in early autumn, and the air smelled fresh and piney. Beautiful in summer, the lake was clear, dark, and deep; in winter it turned to ice. The family's boats were tied to a dock; a boathouse with windows doubled as a post. But I wasn't there to enjoy the beauty. I was looking for danger. I never wanted to forget that.

The command post was a converted house trailer parked near the front gate. Besides a coffeepot, it contained chairs where agents could rest a few minutes, a table and a manual typewriter for daily reports, and a small refrigerator for food we'd brought from our hotel in Minneapolis or picked up en route. We drove the forty miles back and forth from the Sheraton Ritz to Waverly in a leased Ford station wagon.

Also in the trailer were telephones and a radio system with handheld P33s with antennas for use on post and in a boat in case we had to call for emergency help. We kept arctic gear there, extra shotguns . . . and gas masks. We were prepared for anything.

Standing post outdoors in the Minnesota winter was brutal, but I thrived on the challenge. Better prepared than most, I knew what to expect from my time in the Air Force. On the base in Finland, Minnesota, where I had guarded radar sites in 1951, the temperature once plummeted to minus fifty-eight degrees. Guys spit to watch their saliva freeze before it hit the wall. I found Anchorage to be warmer—only minus twenty-six there! Though I had grown up in a tropical climate, neither hurricanes nor thunderstorms nor cold frightened me. I had relished working on power lines in the teeth of threatening weather, and for some reason known only to God, I was at my best when nature showed its might.

We covered three outside posts including the boathouse—two in back on the lakeside and one in front. In winter the ice on the lake was so thick we drove a car out on it and used it for an extra post facing the opposite shore. If too many of our people were on advance, temporary details filled in from the Minneapolis field office or the White House Police Force (later called Executive Protective Service—EPS—and now known as the Secret Service Uniformed Division). Each post had a 12-gauge, pump-action shotgun, which we handed off to our replacements. On winter nights the moon and stars shed light on the snow; we also used flashlights and our ears—the crunch of dead summer leaves underfoot warned if anyone approached. Normally we stood post for thirty minutes at a time. But as the temperature approached zero, we'd put on arctic gear—fur-lined parkas with big hoods—and limit our outside exposure to fifteen minutes at a site, rotating between an outside post, the boathouse, another outside post, and the command post to warm up with a cup of coffee.

There was a swimming pool in the side yard, enjoyed by the Humphrey children and grandchildren in the summer. I thought how my little Jenny, a fearless swimmer at age three, would love to play with them. And how Kim, a four-year-old climber like I was, would be scooting up a tree. For long stretches, I enjoyed family life only vicariously, through the Humphreys. Their daughter and son-in-law, Nancy and Bruce Solomonson, frequently stayed in a guesthouse on the property with their three children. Humphrey loved all three, but the vice president particularly doted on Vicky, a little blonde girl with Down syndrome. His face lit up when he saw her. She'd laugh out loud as he swung her around. "More, Papa! More!"

One Thanksgiving the snow was so deep that walls of it eight feet high lined the cleared paths between the house and posts, like a system of canyons. The family was together in the house, enjoying a feast. Just thinking about it made my stomach—and my spirit—growl. Carolyn and the kids were having their Thanksgiving back in Washington—without me, again—and I imagined the turkey and dressing, the mashed potatoes and gravy. The nearest food the agents might find was at the local delicatessen miles away, but it was closed for the holiday. Hungry and lonely, I fantasized someone from the house would come out and offer us turkey sandwiches. But nobody did. We stood vigilant and invisible.

* * *

Early in the 1960s John F. Kennedy had sent a few military advisers to help our ally South Vietnam combat a threat from the Communists in the north, and in August 1964 a US Navy ship clashed with North Vietnamese forces in the Gulf of Tonkin. Johnson asked for and got a resolution from Congress, which he treated as permission to deploy troops. During the 1964 presidential campaign Johnson promised not to get us more deeply involved in Vietnam. He said, "We are not about to send American boys . . . to do what Asian boys ought to be doing for themselves." He defeated Senator Goldwater of Arizona with an ad showing a little girl picking petals off a daisy in a lovely meadow with a mushroom cloud looming in the distance, painting Goldwater as a dangerous warmonger. Johnson was elected as the peace guy.

But on April 7, 1965, President Johnson made a speech at Johns Hopkins University that changed everything. He said,

Viet-Nam is far away from this quiet campus. We have no territory there, nor do we seek any. The war is dirty and brutal and difficult. And some 400 young men, born into an America that is bursting with opportunity and promise, have ended their lives on Viet-Nam's steaming soil.

Why must we take this painful road?

Why must this Nation hazard its ease, and its interest, and its power for the sake of a people so far away?

We fight because we must fight if we are to live in a world where every country can shape its own destiny. And only in such a world will our own freedom be finally secure.

The message meant one thing: more American boys were indeed going to Vietnam, now as troops, not advisers. Who could have foreseen then that the names of more than fifty-eight thousand dead Americans would finally be engraved on the Vietnam Veterans Memorial Wall?

And Humphrey's role would take an unexpected turn: he was to become the administration's point man on Vietnam.

The East Room of the White House is full of history and ghosts. A huge chandelier and a full-length portrait of George Washington, the oldest possessions in the White House, dominate the room. Dolley Madison saved that Gilbert Stuart portrait from a fire set by British troops in 1814, quickly removing it from the frame and fleeing as the

British approached. In November 1963 President Kennedy was the seventh president to be officially mourned in the East Room, and the following year President Johnson signed the 1964 Civil Rights Act there on live television.

Now it was 1965. Shortly after the Johns Hopkins announcement in April, the president summoned Humphrey to a briefing in the East Room, and I accompanied him. The room was packed with all the highest-ranking leaders of the House and Senate. They were there to get the inside story on the Vietnam War.

Secretary of State Dean Rusk and Secretary of Defense Robert McNamara had starring roles. The president said, "I've given Dean Rusk one hundred days to finish this war on the diplomatic front and Robert McNamara ninety days to finish it militarily."

I'll never forget Secretary McNamara getting out his map of Vietnam. He showed the North and the South. He planned to put divisions in the Delta, in the highlands, on the Ho Chi Minh Trail, at the DMZ, at Haiphong Harbor. It was a plan!

At the time I made no judgments about the viability of this plan. That wasn't my job. But when I think about it now, I see what they were missing. No one in the room could imagine that a North Vietnamese guy who weighed less than a hundred pounds would be able to carry a hundred pounds of rice, ammunition, and guns . . . and be sick . . . and walk a thousand miles . . . and then, at the end of the trail, fight to the death. Nobody picked that up. Everybody in the room thought it would all be over in three months.

* * *

Humphrey began to travel incessantly. This was partly because President Johnson sent him everywhere he didn't want to go and partly because Humphrey was an irrepressible extrovert who loved people and loved to talk. At the beginning, we had no idea how this would affect all of our lives for the next four years.

Because of so much travel, every agent on the detail learned to do advances. Roger Warner, Jimmy Taylor, Roger Counts, Jack Giuffre, and I did the most. Our leaders— Glenn Weaver, Bob Burke, and Walt Coughlin—stayed with the vice president all the time. They were the ones we had to please, because if we fouled something up, they'd be sure to notice.

Doing an advance is like eating a chicken gizzard: the more you chew it, the bigger it gets. It's impossible to cover every hypothetical uncertainty, but agents try. The drumbeat of self-questioning can wear a person out. For four years the stress never lightened up. In fact, it got worse.

I started with domestic visits and graduated to leading foreign advances. I was good at it, and at first I loved the challenge. Each site was unique. Some were dangerous. It was edgy and kept me on my toes.

I scrutinized airports, ran routes, sanitized speech sites,

and secured hotels where my protectee would spend the night. I learned where the closest hospitals were and how to work with local police and fire authorities. I liked going into a town and running meetings with the local folks. Making sure they got thanked, I'd line up the police officers who supported us so they could shake the vice president's hand. They appreciated it and welcomed us back.

But there was a dark side nobody had warned me about. I soon came to understand that leading an advance was a wounding experience. Psychologically and emotionally. We were playing a deadly game. The stakes were very high, and no one could put a price on what agents had to do.

Every time I looked at Win Lawson, the advance agent for President Kennedy's trip to Dallas on November 22, 1963, I thought, *There but for the grace of God go I.* He had done everything right, but it had all gone terribly wrong. Here's the thing: there's no advance that can be done, has been done, or will ever be done that can't be defeated. But we were determined that we would die trying.

When Johnson started sending Humphrey around the globe on trips he himself wanted to avoid, the VPPD had to carry more of the burden that normally would have gone to the president's agents. The Presidential Protective Division (PPD) carried a force of nearly one hundred men, but we were only eighteen guys. We worked five to a shift plus three supervisors, the bare minimum needed.

Our days extended twelve to sixteen hours back-to-back. If we weren't traveling, we were home in DC, working shifts. If we took whichever two days a week off we were supposed to get, that left maybe one person available for advances. Our overtime shot through the roof. From 1965 to 1968 it was common for agents, as I did, to log more than one thousand hours overtime each year. And—because of Public Law 763 then restricting overtime pay for federal workers—most of it was unpaid. Not only that, travel time that exceeded a normal shift didn't count toward overtime unless you were actually accompanying the protectee! Walt Coughlin accumulated two and a half years' worth of overtime in seven and a half years.

Every day I learned something new, often from a mess up, like a principal's car that ran out of gas because the gas gauge was defective. I learned my own limits—and then went beyond them. I learned I was no longer an only child: I became part of a brotherhood bonded by shared adversity and mutual commitment to a larger goal. Although we carried guns, our goal was to save life, not take it.

I learned to trust my own instincts. We all had to improvise because we never had enough men, enough rest, enough time to plan ahead. We learned to make do with what we had.

We learned to forgive each other's mistakes born of exhaustion; we had each other's backs. Beyond that, the inner sense of safety I carried from my parents' love helped me continue to feel safe, even in very unsafe circumstances.

And we all learned that the women we loved were stronger than we could have imagined—because, like us, they had to be.

Love is what kept us going.

When I was transferred permanently to the VPPD detail in December 1964, Kim and Jenny were toddlers. For the next few years, Santa arrived whenever I could be with them—sometimes before, sometimes after, but almost never on December 25. Carolyn kept the kids inside, monitoring the TV so they wouldn't know that other children had not received presents yet or had gotten them the previous week.

The agents' wives formed a sort of village, pitching in to help one another. Older women mentored the younger ones. They babysat for one another. They attended (and in one case coached) one another's children's Little League games. Several gave birth while husbands were on the road. A Secret Service wife would fill in for the labor, holding the mother-to-be's hand and coaching, "Breathe! Push!"

Missing such moments was a terrible loss for the men, too. We all felt torn—and guilty.

Carolyn would drive me to National or Dulles Airport. She and the kids would kiss me good-bye and not see me for a week or two. One day Carolyn overheard our three-year-old tell a neighbor, "My daddy works at the airport."

My travel vouchers and daily reports tell the story. Here's January 1966, a typical month:

On January 1, 1966, my day began at 6:00 a.m. in Manila, Philippines, where I finished an advance and worked the vice president when he arrived. I had not been home since December 23 at 8:00 a.m., when I left Washington for Chicago, then Anchorage, then Tokyo, then Manila, where I arrived at 2:30 p.m., December 25, 1965. Merry Christmas. (That year Santa had come on December 22.)

After seeing the vice president off to the next stop on January 1, I was homeward bound. I flew to Tokyo, arriving at 11:40 p.m., and spent the night. (Fifteen hours)

January 2—9:00 a.m. at the airport, standing by to fly home. Got an 8:00 p.m. flight to the United States. After crossing the international date line, stopping in Seattle and New York City, I arrived at Dulles at 1:40 a.m., January 3. (Seventeen hours) When I left home, I had lived in Virginia; I returned to a house in Maryland. We'd bought a house, and to save state taxes, Carolyn moved the family into it on New Year's Eve, by herself.

After one day off, I started working midnights until January 11, when I unexpectedly flew to New Delhi with the vice president. Got home January 15 at noon. (Forty-six hours overtime plus thirty-two regular—seventy-eight hours total) After regular days off I started working midnights, made a quick trip to Lincoln Center in New York City, then to Chicago for five days doing an advance plus a day of working protection when the vice president arrived.

Total time for January: 109 hours in DC, 182 hours away. A regular forty-hour week would be 173 hours per month. *I'd worked 291 hours! Not counting travel time!* I was a walking zombie. We all were.

* * *

Where two or three were gathered together, Humphrey could be found in the midst of them, making a speech or telling a joke at the Republicans' expense. One of his favorites went like this: "A man needed a heart transplant, and three hearts became available. One was from a twenty-six-year-old Olympic marathon runner; one was from a thirty-year-old Jesuit priest; and one was from a fifty-year-old Republican. The man said, 'Oh, I'll take the fifty-year-old Republican heart. I want a heart that's never been used.'" The Democratic crowds loved it.

When Humphrey got going, he couldn't stop. On a speech circuit, we typically ran later and later as the day progressed. Once on an advance in Nashville, we arranged to close down a major highway that went to the airport, telling the local sheriff we'd notify him when the precise moment came. I knew Humphrey was going to shake hands and talk to people after his speech for at least fifteen minutes, so I advised, "Sheriff, you'd better not close the highway down until we *really* leave."

He replied, "Son, I run this county, and I'll do it the way I want to do it."

The sheriff closed the highway when he heard that the speech was done, without waiting for word from us. And sure enough, we didn't leave for another fifteen minutes. As we made a right turn onto that highway, I saw four lanes of headlights into infinity. There was no telling how far that traffic went. The sheriff had stopped an interstate at seven thirty at night! People were standing on their cars, waving fists, shouting obscenities. It reminded me of Manhattan. You could have landed a 747 on our side of the police blockade. There was nothing in front of us.

Humphrey was so busy talking, he never turned around to look, and he never found out about it. But I thought, *That's how you lose votes.*

Sometimes emergencies came up when there was no time for an advance. Then we improvised as we went. This was the case on the January 11, 1966, trip to New Delhi.

On that day Prime Minister Shastri of India died of a heart attack in Tashkent, where he was meeting with Soviet Premier Kosygin. The funeral would be in New Delhi twenty-four hours later. Of course, Humphrey would represent President Johnson.

I came to work on the midnight shift and found myself at one o'clock on an airplane—with no extra underwear, no toothbrush, no razor. I'd barely had time to call home. "Honey, I won't be coming home in the morning," I had to say. "I'll be gone three or four days. I can't tell you where I'll be." (I couldn't tell her because the trip was unplanned and there would be no advance security.) All that came from the other end of the phone was a deep, resigned sigh.

My shift got on the plane with nothing but what we had on our backs and in our pockets. We flew all the way to India, along with the day shift and the four-to-midnight shift, who brought in extra things. I ended up with Rufus Youngblood's underwear and somebody else's toothbrush.

On landing at the airport in New Delhi, we found about fifty cars already lined up in the motorcade for the funeral. Our follow-up car, critical for protection, was twelve cars back from the vice president's limo! We coaxed the Indian drivers—this was not easy—to let us drive that car up into proper position behind the vice president.

Ten million people lined the funeral route. We couldn't do a thing to improve security except pray. We saw Indian police with long, thick sticks mercilessly beating people who were trying to climb a fence. I thought, *I'm glad I live in America. Our cops never act like that.*

As we rode along, I noticed people waving and smiling. They were calling out something I couldn't quite catch. Humphrey was waving back, surprised and pleased to be recognized. Then we all heard the words. They were chanting, "Bob Hope! Bob Hope!" The agents were all laughing, but Humphrey's face fell and he stopped waving. After all, he was the vice president of the United States! But they didn't know him from Adam.

* * *

The travel got even more intense. I worked 305 hours in February, when Humphrey went to Southeast Asia. My stops were Honolulu, Saigon, Bangkok, Manila, and Seoul.

That was my first of six visits to Vietnam, three with Humphrey and three with Vice President Agnew, never on advance. Saigon was still a beautiful place in February 1966, when we first arrived with Humphrey. We dined elegantly on the top floor of a French hotel, the Caravelle. But behind the string quartet's dinner music I recognized the sound of fire-fights: American-made artillery trying to interdict Vietcong in the Delta, not far away. I thought about the total dedication of the troops, the Green Berets—and tried not to think of the reality that human beings on both sides were dying as I savored my *boeuf bourguignon*.

We used to joke that when Humphrey arrived in Vietnam, there'd be a forty-two-gun salute: twenty-one from the South to honor him and twenty-one from the North trying to kill him! At Tan Son Nhut, the US Air Force base at Saigon, stood a huge sign you couldn't miss: "Pilots . . . climb to five thousand feet as rapidly as possible." Planes needed to avoid small-arms fire coming out of the jungle nearby. The battle was coming closer to the city.

In 1967 Humphrey flew into Vietnam to attend the inauguration of South Vietnam's President Thieu. That evening, as cars lined up in a circular driveway in front of the presidential residence, Glenn Weaver got a queasy intuition that they had been sitting there too long. He ordered the driver, Rick Barbuto, to pull out and go the other way around the circle.

Furious and embarrassed, Humphrey cursed at Weaver, shouting, "We can't act like that! That's very arrogant!"

A minute after Barbuto obeyed the order, two cars right in front of where the limo had been were hit by a mortar, and a driver was killed. It was clearly intended for the vice president. Humphrey apologized to Weaver.

✳ ✳ ✳

Clark Air Force Base, near Manila, was the closest military hospital for Americans wounded in Vietnam. Medics stabilized the wounds as best they could in field hospitals, then flew the wounded soldiers directly by C-141s to Clark. Humphrey wanted to visit the base after our first Vietnam visit in 1966. We went in the aftermath of Operation Double Eagle, a joint Army and Marine Corps effort that culminated in a ferocious battle between one of the big airborne units or cavalry units and, for the first time, a North Vietnamese regular infantry division. Our side killed about 2,300 North Vietnamese that one battle, but we lost more than 200 of our own troops, and hundreds were wounded. They poured into Clark, week after week.

I watched the choppers land and unload their cargo: shattered men, just hours from the battlefield, many still in uniform. Humphrey and I saw them arrive with missing legs, missing genitals, missing arms, missing eyes, brain damaged. The pain on Humphrey's face was reflected in my own. They were my age, or younger. *What will their lives be like when they get home?* I wondered. *Will they be able to work? Will their wives still love them?*

We walked room to room, speaking to the men. At the door of a darkened room, Humphrey asked a male nurse, "May I come in?"

The nurse said, "I'll have to ask him," and nodded toward his young patient lying in bed. In a minute the nurse returned, apologetic but firm. He said, "I'm sorry. He just lost both eyes in a concussion grenade blast and can't bear to talk about it yet."

We saw some of the most terrible wounds, including one marine who had caught a machine-gun round right through his throat. He saved his own life by using his bayonet to perform a tracheotomy on himself. He lived because he opened an airway in his own throat.

The Clark Air Force Base hospital reminded me of a scene in *Gone with the Wind*, the one with a huge panoramic view of all the wounded from the Battle of Atlanta in the US Civil War.

Right there I witnessed a change in Hubert Humphrey, a dramatic change. He and I had talked about Vietnam before, intellectually. It was always head stuff. But that hospital tour got the war out of his head and into his gut. Mine, too.

I observed from then on that Humphrey did what he could to change the course of the war, but he only succeeded in alienating President Johnson, who punished him by cutting him out altogether. We agents heard him say, in the car, "I detest this war! I detest it!" Then he'd add, "But I have to support my president."

Tom Wells tells this story:

In 1967, I was a shift leader at a meeting in the vice president's office to go over with staff some appearances he was scheduled to make that day. As we were speaking, he got a call to come to the

Cabinet Room, and as the senior supervisor on duty that day I accompanied him. Johnson was meeting there with several cabinet members. I'm pretty sure Secretary of Defense McNamara was there; not sure who else. I did not go in but waited outside the door.

I kept getting phone calls from Humphrey's staff: "Any movement yet? When will he be leaving? He's way behind schedule!"

No movement. The meeting lasted at least two hours. Then people started to come out. Everybody but Humphrey. He was in there alone with the president.

After a while he bounded out, clearly uptight. He and I took the small elevator in the west basement lobby. We were alone. He looked at me, red faced. "If that man gets another bite out of my a—, there won't be anything left but bones!" I couldn't say anything, of course. He glared at me. "I mean it!" And then he repeated himself to be sure I understood.

While most of the public protests we ran into involved Vietnam, racial protests were also getting more intense and were no longer relegated to the South. In the Watts section of south central Los Angeles, a riot began on August 11, 1965, when a white policeman stopped an African American man suspected of drunk driving. It's unclear whether the police officer behaved inappropriately or not, but a crowd gathered and began to heckle him. Alarmed, he called for backup. When more police arrived, a riot erupted and raged for six days, resulting in thirty-four deaths, more than one thousand reported injuries, almost four thousand arrests, and property damage estimated at more than forty million dollars. It took fourteen thousand California National Guard troops to quell the riot.

The civil rights alliance between liberal whites and blacks forged by Reverend Martin Luther King Jr. was shredding.

Black anger was not directed toward Humphrey—he was known to be friendly to the cause of civil rights. But as Tom Wells reminded me, the immediate aftermath of fires and riots is not comfortable to be in. Humphrey visited areas like Detroit right after control was reestablished. He met with city and civil rights leaders, trying to mediate calm and peace. But peace was fragile. It seemed as if we agents could never relax our vigilance, even for a moment. As Wells put it, "The fires were out, but the heat was still there."

When Humphrey left the United States on a multinational trip in March 1967, Europe had not yet seen any violent antiwar demonstrations. The first one happened in Rome, and it was on my watch.

Jack Giuffre, Rick Barbuto, and I had arrived in Rome on March 22, 1967, to do the advance for a three-day Humphrey visit with Italy's prime minister and the pope. The vice president arrived on Thursday, March 30. As a member of the advance team, my piece was the first event: a performance of

Verdi's *Ernani* at the Rome Opera House. I expected this to be a routine event.

The first hint of trouble was when I saw someone trying to rip the American flag off the vice president's car. Then, driving past Rome's ancient Colosseum, I noticed a huge Vietcong flag flying from a pole in front. As we approached the elegant columns of the opera house, a small group of long-haired young people in jeans stood in front, handing out anti-American leaflets. There was some heckling. Still, I didn't expect a real problem.

The vice president's car pulled up in front of the Teatro dell'Opera, where the manager waited to greet him. I opened the door for Mr. Humphrey. He got out smiling, as usual, and I said, "Mr. Vice President, this is your host for the evening, Mr. Angelo Carlucci." Angelo Carlucci was elegant in his perfectly tailored suit and a full head of perfectly coiffed gray hair. Both men smiled, and just as they were shaking hands, a bag of bright yellow paint arched out of the evening sky and struck Mr. Carlucci a glancing blow on the top of his head. I wondered if it was Sherwin-Williams paint, said to "cover the earth" in my favorite boyhood neon sign.

Yellow paint spattered everywhere—on Carlucci, on the vice president, on me. Never at a loss for words, Humphrey spat out paint and asked pleasantly, "Does this happen to you often, sir?"

We agents shoved both men into the lobby. Then I heard a scream. Other agents and the carabinieri (Italian police) had captured a young Communist named Gianni Buzzan.

I read in the paper that he and seven others, including an American, were held overnight, charged with something minor, and released. I was told but never confirmed that the district chief was relieved of duty.

After his meeting with the pope, Humphrey took a train to Florence, and I rode in a NATO helicopter with an AR-15 rifle to cover the route. Chickens scattered as we flew low over the farms along the way. I understand this affected egg production for weeks.

In Florence the "Flying Carabinieri" went into action. These were police on motorcycles and jeeps brandishing long sticks. They drove up onto the sidewalk where they thought the crowd was getting too big or too rowdy, flailing their sticks in every direction. It was pretty effective crowd control.

My assignment was the vice president's arrival in Florence. We were surrounded by what seemed like four thousand police—who in turn were surrounded by about thirty thousand hostile demonstrators. The smell of pot hung in the air. Some hippies were strung out on drugs. Hal Thomas saw a guy take a bite out of a live chicken, just to gross people out.

We got the vice president in and out—alive. I didn't see much art. But I knew without a doubt that Vietnam had come to Europe.

* * *

In November 1967 Humphrey again visited Southeast Asia, spending time in Saigon before a visit to Indonesia. In Vietnam the vice president had an up close experience of the enemy's spirit. Hal Thomas took Humphrey to a field hospital where wounded Vietcong were being treated along with Americans. As the vice president passed one Vietcong soldier's cot, the soldier, who had just lost a leg, raised himself on one arm and spat on Humphrey.

The vice president's next stop was Indonesia. Some of us fanned out to do advances: Roger Warner went to Jakarta and Tom Behl to Bali. My responsibility was a place called Semarang.

Semarang, in central Java, was then very primitive. A wall of burning humidity hit us as we climbed out of the Navy DC-9. I couldn't wait to take a shower.

I quickly discovered that this was a bad idea. Local US State Department employees warned us that not only was it dangerous to drink the water, it was dangerous even to shower or shave. After a day, we began to dehydrate and to worry. We got permission to drink a beer on duty and ate canned meat—Spam—for breakfast, lunch, and dinner for five days.

Bill Skiles, my colleague, gave his suit to the hotel for cleaning. I was outside and heard a slapping noise. Bare-breasted women were beating Bill's suit on a rock beside a stream where we had observed people defecating in the water and water buffalo lumbering and drinking.

The minute the vice president arrived, we guzzled the water his staff brought.

I overheard one of the vice president's aides tell him as he was leaving the plane, "Don't forget to thank the agents."

But he was off to another adventure. I shrugged to myself and thought, *Sic transit gloria mundi.* "Thus passes the glory of the world!"

However, to my surprise, I received copies of three letters shortly after we returned home. One was from Rufus Youngblood, assistant director of the Secret Service, addressed to the VPPD detail boss, Glenn Weaver, thanking each of us for our work on the Vietnam visit. Next was a letter to James J. Rowley, Secret Service director (the *big* boss), commending the entire detail for the trip to Southeast Asia. In the final paragraph, the writer said,

> *An additional mission that deserves special attention is that of Special Agent Jerry S. Parr and Special Agent Jerry [sic] Skiles, who prepared my visit to Semarang, Indonesia, and lived under extremely adverse and difficult conditions and yet were able to prepare a flawless visit to that economically backward area.*

It was signed, "Sincerely, Hubert H. Humphrey."

Finally, the third letter was from Director Rowley, commending me and saying, "A copy of this letter is being placed in your personnel file as a permanent record of your achievement."

So I felt more than adequately thanked after all.

✷ ✷ ✷

As the war in Vietnam was going downhill on the battlefield and in public esteem, we were heckled or attacked with flying debris almost everywhere the vice president went. Protesters were getting meaner, and so were police. Vice President Hubert Humphrey, despite his sympathy for the protesters, would become their prime target.

CHAPTER 5

1968: THE YEAR FROM HELL

No one in human history has ever set out to do something evil. Instead they
believed what they were doing was right and proper. . . . But in truth more
often than not they have only taken the evil into themselves.

LAWRENCE KUSHNER, *Eyes Remade for Wonder*

1968

From the twenty-sixth floor of Chicago's Conrad Hilton
hotel, Hubert Humphrey and I looked down on a scene
from Dante's *Inferno*. A chaotic mix of police, horses, and
National Guard struggled to prevent a crowd of demonstrators from bursting out of Grant Park onto Michigan Avenue
and entering our hotel. The twin scents of marijuana and
tear gas invaded the lobby and wafted up through our open
window. It was August 28, 1968. Both demonstrators and
police were exhausted and very angry. When a demonstrator
tore down an American flag, furious police, who had been
holding back for days, finally broke under the stress.

I'm still haunted by the crisp *rat-a-tat* sound, like galloping horses' hooves striking pavement, horses that did not slow down, horses that kept coming without a pause. This was the sound of police clubs hitting demonstrators' heads. A sound rising up twenty-six floors and spilling into Americans' living rooms through their television sets on the nightly news.

Humphrey turned pale. No one could have plumbed the depth of dismay that showed in his face. He looked heartbroken at what was happening to those young people. And he must have known the scenes of violence would be played and replayed, over and over, on national television. I think he intuited that what was happening below—what he was helpless to prevent—had already doomed his candidacy.

I asked myself, *How did we ever get to this place?*

Antiwar activity had begun in earnest with passage of the Gulf of Tonkin Resolution on August 7, 1964, which President Johnson took as a blank check to use military force in Southeast Asia, and the subsequent deployment to South Vietnam of major American ground, air, and naval forces in the first months of 1965. With Johnson's speech at Johns Hopkins in the spring of 1965 announcing that we would make a stand in Vietnam, the antiwar movement gathered strength.

The early protests were dominated by peaceful idealists making speeches, marching, or kneeling to pray at the White House, Congress, and draft centers around the country. They sang "We Shall Overcome" or "Give Peace a Chance." Sometimes they picketed sites where Humphrey was speaking. My only worry about them was that a violent person might hide in their midst, using them for cover.

Churches and clergy were divided. Conservatives such as Baptists and Mormons generally supported the war; they saw the United States helping a weaker ally repel an invasion. Liberals such as Unitarians and some mainline Protestant leaders opposed it; they thought we were intervening in a civil war that had nothing to do with us and that was killing innocent civilians. Catholics were split: because South Vietnam was heavily Catholic and Ho Chi Minh was a Communist, America's Cardinal Spellman described Vietnam as a "war for civilization" and "Christ's war against the Vietcong and the people of North Vietnam." But Dorothy Day and the Catholic Worker Movement, as well as Pax Christi, were pacifists. For the first time Pope John XXIII decreed that pacifism was a Christian stance but also that "just war" in self-defense was permitted. (He did not say Vietnam was a just war.) Yale's William Sloan Coffin and other college chaplains, along with many black clergy including Martin Luther King Jr., opposed it. Muslims refused to serve. To punish heavyweight champion Cassius Clay (renamed Muhammad Ali) for resisting the draft, the Boxing Commission stripped him of his title.

Young men over age eighteen were vulnerable to be drafted, and college campuses became centers of resistance. Some counseling focused on how to postpone or avoid the draft legally: by entering certain exempt careers (such as teaching special education) or by attending a religious seminary.

Conscientious objector status was limited to Quakers, Mennonites, and a few others, and then only to longtime members. In some states joining the National Guard was safer than gambling on the draft lottery. Some young people chose imprisonment for refusing to serve. Others spoke with their feet: they fled to Canada or Mexico.

In the years preceding 1968, prominent baby doctor Benjamin Spock and celebrities such as Joan Baez and Jane Fonda were actively encouraging draft-age youth to resist. Civil disobedience became progressively more provocative: blocking traffic, burning draft cards, invading draft centers and pouring blood on records, burning flags, heckling or harassing anyone in uniform, calling policemen "pigs." Protesters chanted in front of the White House: "Hey, hey, LBJ, how many kids did you kill today?" Some carried the flags of the Vietcong.

Police and students, nuns and military leaders—all thought they were the ones who were right. And righteous. Many behaved much worse than they ordinarily would have because they were part of a crowd and because they were convinced that the people on the other side of the barricade were evil. The biblical command to "love your enemies" seemed to have vanished from American consciousness—and mine. Though by now I thought of myself as a committed Christian, I stashed the part about enemies into a separate compartment.

As opposition to the war grew and Vice President Humphrey carried more water for Johnson, we agents were increasingly thrown into the teeth of demonstrators. In every city Humphrey visited, back-to-back, day after day, it never let up. The most active area was the Upper Northwest: Seattle, Portland, and San Francisco.

Protesters came up with clever ways to make the police look bad. Agent Tom Wells recalls trying to leave an airport in a car with Humphrey and being blocked by people in wheelchairs. Police in the lead car had to move them out of the road. Cameras rolled, of course.

Not every agent supported the war, but as fellow law enforcement officers we all sympathized with the police. For one thing, we needed their help—and always got it. Initially some police chiefs were naive about demonstrators. Hal Thomas had a formal-looking folder, which he solemnly placed on the desk of police chiefs the first time they met. On the cover it said, "Introducing . . ." and inside was Hal's card and the words, "The smart a— from Washington who knows it all." Everyone would laugh, and any defensiveness vanished. A little mood lightening was needed. When we showed up, officers had to work twelve-hour shifts, give up their days off, and even be called back from vacation. We owed them some loyalty.

Another bond we shared with police was our ages. Most of us grew up during World War II. We'd been taught to respect the president and the military—and police officers. Who did these kids think they were, giving the finger to authority figures? When our country needed us, we had been ready to serve. It was hard for us to understand these angry, flag-burning kids with long hair.

Long hair. That was the feature that most clearly distinguished protestors from guys like me. Long hair symbolized rebellion, antiwar protests, drugs, sex. It was also a class symbol. Cops didn't have it. Military guys didn't have it. Union members didn't have it. College students had it. Agents were college graduates, but most of us were first-generation graduates. We grew up working class and went to school on scholarships or the GI Bill. We respected working-class people and their values.

I remember a bumper sticker that made me smile: "Next time you get mugged, call a hippie."

I developed a visceral reaction to guys with long hair.

Humphrey's traditional supporters had been labor, blacks, liberals, and youth. Labor stuck with Humphrey, but the Watts riots in 1965 and those that followed in several urban areas had destroyed the positive racial alliances that prevailed in the early 1960s. Humphrey had been a college professor, and he loved young people. Until the war they had loved him back. Hoping to regain their support, during his tenure the vice president visited seventy-six colleges and universities. It was a quixotic effort. Humphrey was heckled in all but the military academies and two church-related schools: Baptist Wake Forest College, in North Carolina, and Mormon Brigham Young University, in Utah.

As more American soldiers rendezvoused with death in the jungle, protests at home became fiercer. Agents' advances grew more critical and tense. Berkeley and Harvard were two of the worst places. Those folks were not holding hands and singing "Kumbaya." To try to predict what a crowd might be planning, young-looking agents infiltrated student planning meetings and fed us information. At each school we met with the head of campus security, faculty leaders, and the dean to try to take the temperature of the campus. And we coordinated with local police, the FBI (to learn if any of the leaders had a record), and our own Intelligence Division.

In Oakland, California, word came to us that a woman was planning to *lay her baby in front of Humphrey's car* to force us to stop. Her cohorts intended to rush us and turn the car over. This may have been nothing more than an inflated rumor, but as the lead advance agent I took it seriously. I came up with a strategy to thwart this and similar behavior.

Agent Hal Thomas used to say, "The secret is not to fight 'em but to fool 'em." Using a dummy motorcade or some other subterfuge, we would sneak Humphrey in. Whenever we got close to a speech site, normally a hotel, demonstrators crowded together, waiting to rush us as we got out of the car. Armed with paint, urine, nail-studded foam balls—whatever they could think of—they posed a very real physical threat. We kept as much distance as possible, with police lined up to hold them at bay.

One of the tricks we devised to avoid the threatening crowd involved the vice president's press corps, which traveled in four big Greyhound buses. Dennis Lacey, agent in charge of the press, sat in the lead bus with a radio. About a minute before our arrival, I would radio him: "Okay, make your move."

The motorcade would move slightly to the right, and the press corps buses would drive up bumper to bumper, stopping right in front of the demonstrators waiting across the street from the site. We would pull in beside the buses, which blocked the crowd's view and allowed us to rush Humphrey in.

When the crowd realized what was happening, their rage would increase. They would furiously attempt to rock the buses, which didn't budge. Sometimes they broke windows. It was a pretty fine technique for getting Humphrey in and out safely. For some reason, the reporters on the bus were never amused.

Nineteen-sixty-eight was arguably the most turbulent year in American history, other than the years of the Civil War. It was certainly the worst year of my life as an agent, and every man I know who was in the Secret Service in 1968 will say it was the year from hell. Some guys left their families and didn't come back home to stay for eight months.

* * *

As the year began, I found myself on advance in Nairobi, Kenya. Humphrey's last foreign trip as vice president took us to thirteen cities in nine African countries. In Europe and everywhere we went, we were pummeled verbally and sometimes otherwise. In Kinshasa, Congo, a Peace Corps worker hurled a rock at Walt Coughlin. The layers of irony were not lost on us.

Seventy thousand North Vietnamese launched the Tet

Offensive on January 31, surprising the South Vietnamese and US forces. The offensive lasted several weeks and, although our side eventually prevailed, we paid a heavy price in American lives and public support. In a single week in February 543 Americans perished in the steamy jungles of Vietnam; 2,547 were wounded. Walter Cronkite, America's most respected journalist, broke his neutrality on February 27 in a report from Vietnam, where he'd gone to see for himself the aftermath of Tet. He criticized American leaders for deceiving the public, predicted the war could not be won, and advocated negotiation "not as victors, but as an honorable people who lived up to their pledge to defend democracy, and did the best they could."

Only one politician was willing to challenge the sitting president: Senator Eugene McCarthy. Toward the end of 1967 McCarthy announced he would enter primaries as an antiwar candidate. He did not think he could possibly win but just wanted to keep the issue before the public. On March 12 the New Hampshire primary shocked the political scene when McCarthy came within 230 votes of defeating President Johnson. McCarthy had little money and no campaign workers except students who had shaved and gotten haircuts to be "clean for Gene" so as not to scare off independents. The near loss in a primary for a sitting president's reelection revealed Johnson's surprising vulnerability. Less than a week later Senator Robert Kennedy entered the presidential race. McCarthy reportedly felt Kennedy had betrayed him and was furious.

Later that month, on March 31, President Johnson announced the United States would stop bombing 90 percent of North Vietnam, including all populated and food-producing areas. He urged Ho Chi Minh to join in peace talks. And he closed with these surprising words: "I shall not seek, and I will not accept, the nomination of my party for another term as your President."

For the rest of his term, except for trips to the ranch, Johnson basically stayed in the White House. It fell to Vice President Humphrey to speak for the president as well as for himself. And even more than in the busy prior years it fell on twenty-seven men to carry the travel and security burdens that the presidential detail, with many more resources, would normally have borne.

Walt Coughlin, our assistant SAIC, was riding in the right front seat of the vice president's car headed to the Washington Hilton when he heard on his earpiece that Rev. Martin Luther King Jr. had been shot and killed. He had to turn around and tell Humphrey the terrible news. Humphrey was distraught. All his life Humphrey had fought for equal rights for all, and Martin Luther King was a strong symbol of hope. It was April 4. A white man, James Earl Ray, had murdered the civil rights leader in Memphis. As Americans expressed their grief and rage, some sixty cities burst out in flames and riots. Among them were Baltimore, Boston, Chicago, Detroit, Kansas City, Newark, and Washington, DC, where the vice president and his wife, Muriel, now lived on the Maine Avenue waterfront.

Along with the entire VPPD detail, my days off were canceled, and I went on emergency duty. For a couple of days no one was allowed into the city without identification and a very good reason to be there. Driving in from Maryland, where I lived, I was stopped at Chevy Chase Circle by the National Guard. I showed my commission book and was allowed to proceed. Forty-six deaths across the country were blamed on the riots.

Then a university campus erupted. Beginning April 23, angry students occupied five buildings at Columbia, including Hamilton Hall, where they kept the dean from leaving his office. They also invaded President Grayson Kirk's office. The siege lasted six days while faculty tried unsuccessfully to mediate issues involving race and war. Demands included an end to the university's relationship with the Institute for Defense Analysis, for which Columbia did weapons research; prohibition of draft recruitment on campus; and cessation of plans to build a gym on land used by kids in Harlem but that would now offer limited access to them. Other students wiped out a construction fence at the gym site and struggled with the cops who tried to stop them. On the seventh day President Kirk called in New York City police. The police came on campus, beat demonstrators (as well as bystanders and faculty), and made more than seven hundred arrests. For all practical purposes, the anger that followed closed the university for the rest of the semester.

While all this was happening, Humphrey announced his candidacy for president on April 27. He shot to the top as the leading Democratic contender, with Robert Kennedy a strong second and gaining.

The protest activities in the streets and on campuses flowed into every area of American life, including the arts. The resulting increase in public sympathy made our job harder. A prime example occurred in April 1968. *Hair: The American Tribal Love-Rock Musical* opened on Broadway and ran for 1,750 performances. Simultaneous productions in cities across the United States and Europe followed. A London production ran for 1,997 shows. The actors looked like the wild-eyed, long-haired folks we were meeting on the barricades. It painted them as harmless kids being victimized by brutal police.

Two months after the musical opened, on June 5, after winning the California Democratic primary, Senator Robert (Bobby) Kennedy was shot by Sirhan Sirhan. The motive was Kennedy's support for Israel. Had Kennedy survived, that victory might have put him in the lead. He died the next day.

It fell to Walt Coughlin, who had passed the terrible word of Martin Luther King Jr.'s death, to pass the word again. He and Hal Thomas were staying in guest quarters at the Air Force Academy, where Humphrey was to make a speech the next morning. At two o'clock in the morning Coughlin got the call. He and Thomas went together to wake up Humphrey. Thomas recalls, "When Coughlin told the vice president, he visibly aged ten years in front of us. He turned the color of ash."

As Coughlin remembers, the next morning a general

showed up to take the vice president to the speech site. Humphrey told him, "Robert Kennedy has been shot. I have to go back to Washington."

The general misunderstood and said, "Oh, you can stay here and give your speech. You don't have to be afraid."

Humphrey recoiled in fury. "I'm not afraid of anything!" he spat. "You give the speech. I'm going back to Washington!" He immediately returned to DC and suspended his campaign for two weeks. Humphrey said, "I wanted to win, but I didn't want to do it this way."

Bobby Kennedy did not have Secret Service protection. That was rectified overnight. Now we had agents on every candidate, including Senator McCarthy; "Dixiecrat" Governor George Wallace of Alabama; and Republican contenders Richard Nixon, Ronald Reagan, Nelson Rockefeller, and Harold Stassen. In 1968 the Secret Service had a total of only 575 agents to cover physical protection and advances for all these candidates, plus counterfeiting, forged checks, and threats throughout the country. It was impossible.

All the murder and mayhem and hatred loosed in the country spewed onto the Secret Service. It had to. Death was in the air we breathed.

Not only the vice presidential detail but all agents in the country were lacerated by the anger and hostility and disorder we saw on the nightly news. We felt it in our guts as well as in our heads. This was only five years after John F. Kennedy's death, and we were still shaken from that. We were still not healed. And in 1968 we had to work till we dropped. It was like a war.

What I remember most are the eyes of the demonstrators glistening with hatred and rage at us, the police, and the political leaders we were trying to protect. Not to put too fine a point on it, it was my colleagues and me they were calling "pigs." Down deep I began to hate them and secretly hoped they'd attack us physically so we could respond with nightsticks and fists.

I know now I'd have been sorry the rest of my life if I'd really hurt someone.

Though I secretly fantasized revenge, Agent Don Bendickson actually got it. An incident happened not on the West Coast but at the Illinois state fair in the summer of 1968. Hal Thomas was running along the right side of the vice president's car, and Don Bendickson was jogging on the left. The crowd lining the street seemed friendly, and the car was moving slowly so Humphrey could wave and be seen. Suddenly a man from the crowd leaned forward and put something in Bendickson's hand. Don looked down to discover a handful of human dung. The car was already a block past the perpetrator, but Don heaved it at a long-haired guy in that direction. Then, shouting, "Get back!" he wiped his hand on the T-shirts of hippies crowding in beside the car as it passed.

The Republicans nominated Richard Nixon and Maryland governor Spiro T. Agnew in an uneventful convention in Miami. As street violence grew, Democrats considered moving their convention site from Chicago to Miami also. A meeting on Key Biscayne could have been easily isolated by a checkpoint on the Rickenbacker Causeway, the only way to enter or leave the key other than by boat. But President Johnson didn't want to offend Mayor Richard Daley, who swore to maintain law and order. Daley was a powerhouse in the Democratic Party, and Humphrey would need Illinois votes. So the Democrats stayed in Chicago.

We flew in on Sunday, August 25. Along with Senator McCarthy, the vice president, and their entourages, we stayed at the Conrad Hilton, the favorite hotel of Democratic bigwigs when they came to town. The Hilton entrance was on Michigan Avenue, facing Grant Park.

A story Walt Coughlin tells illustrates Mayor Daley's power: The day before Humphrey arrived, Coughlin met with the mayor's can-do guy, Colonel Riley, a man in his seventies who wore an eye patch. Coughlin noticed that all hotel exits led to the street where crowds were gathering. He said, half to himself, "It would be a lot easier to get him in and out through the alley, but there's no hotel door there." The next day, there was a door to the alley.

The weather was near perfect: highs in the low seventies, lows in the fifties. Though protests started building in Lincoln Park before we arrived, police seemed to have the situation under control. But by Wednesday, August 28, chaos reigned, both inside and outside the convention. Crowds trying to get to the convention site had been forced back and were filling an already-crammed Grant Park. Humphrey wanted to go down into the park to speak to the crowd, but SAIC Glenn Weaver wouldn't let him.

Coughlin did go into the park. The crowd was unarmed except for rocks and sticks, and perhaps the majority were nonviolent. But many members were clearly trying to provoke police. Some carried North Vietnam flags. Walt saw a young woman walk up to a policeman, take a puff from her boyfriend's joint, and blow marijuana smoke in the officer's face. Then she spat on him.

The air was filled with the acrid smell of tear gas thrown by police and stink bombs thrown by the crowd. When word came from the convention hall that the peace plank had been defeated, a demonstrator tore down the American flag and replaced it with a bloody shirt. That act seemed to be the match that lit the tinder. Police charged into the crowd, swinging billy clubs. By then, the fifth day of demonstrations, they didn't care who they hit. A cacophony of screams and grunts and epithets rose twenty-six floors to the open windows where the vice president and I stood and watched.

A few floors below us was Senator McCarthy's headquarters. In McCarthy's absence the "clean for Gene" kids tried to help the demonstrators. They threw ashtrays, lamps, and trash baskets on the cops below. I saw a policeman look up to the source of the improvised weapons. I saw his lips move and realized he was counting floors. Then he and his brother cops rushed up sixteen flights of stairs to McCarthy's suite—and beat everyone in there, guilty or not.

As Humphrey and I watched the melee below, all he could

say was, "Oh my. Oh my. Oh my." His eyes welled with tears. Both of us stood rooted to the spot, looking out, horrified and helpless. I flashed back to the scene in India of police beating the fence climbers, and suddenly I understood the Indian police better. A secret part of me felt the satisfaction of revenge. The police officers' anger had invaded me, too. What I most deeply wanted at that moment was to be home, holding my girls and knowing Carolyn would understand my conflicted emotions, even the ugly ones.

The head knocking below went on and on—seventeen minutes according to some reports—until most of the demonstrators had fled or had been arrested and thrown into paddy wagons. Walt Coughlin saw people pushed through the plate glass windows of hotel shops on the Michigan Avenue sidewalk. Bloody McCarthy workers and young people injured in the street staggered into the Hilton lobby and huddled together, weeping and hugging one another. As dusk fell, exhausted police were replaced with National Guard troops. By midnight the fury on both sides was spent.

Around two o'clock in the morning we deemed it safe enough for Humphrey to speak to the injured young people, who once had followed him. He would be the Democratic nominee—but his candidacy was mortally wounded.

Miraculously, no one died. Numbers are not exact, but according to the South Loop Historical Society, the police department reported 192 officers injured. The Medical Committee for Human Rights estimated medics treated more than 1,000 demonstrators in the streets. Hospitals reported

111 demonstrators and 49 police officers went to emergency rooms. Approximately 668 protesters were arrested.

I'd seen a lot of demonstrations in the previous four years, but nothing approached the violence in Grant Park. The police overreacted, but I understood. I did. Just as love is contagious, so is hatred. I knew in my heart I could have done what they did in a moment of exhaustion and rage. The thought made me tremble.

Blessedly, the violence on August 28 and 29 seemed to be a catharsis. A boil had been lanced. Never again were we confronted with the hostility and anger that had dogged us earlier. In September Humphrey called for a Vietnam cease-fire, and McCarthy endorsed him. On October 31 President Johnson brought the bombing to a complete halt. But it was too little, too late to save Humphrey against Nixon's law-and-order platform.

By the end of Election Day, November 5, Humphrey knew it was over. He had made a valiant effort. He had only 19 percent of the popular vote when the convention ended, but, always positive, he had believed he could win. Although Nixon won decisively in the electoral college, 301 to 191, the popular vote was much closer: 43.4 percent for Nixon to Humphrey's 42.7 percent. Wallace received forty-six electoral votes, all in the Deep South.

I was with Humphrey in 1964 when he won the vice presidency, and four years later I saw his pain at losing to Nixon. As we left the Minneapolis hotel to helicopter to Waverly, Muriel Humphrey was weeping. The vice president put his arm around her. "I gave it my all," he said. "The American people have spoken. We don't need to talk about it anymore."

Mrs. Humphrey whispered to Hal Thomas, perhaps thinking of Bobby Kennedy, "Well, at least now he'll live."

I had observed the full gamut of emotions in a man who won, who suffered by winning (because he had to support a war he really opposed), and who suffered by losing. I would see the pain of losing again, with Vice President Spiro Agnew as he resigned and with President Jimmy Carter when he lost to Reagan. Regardless of my own political views, I couldn't help absorbing some of the pain of those who lost.

Humphrey wanted to go to Waverly to meet a friendly hometown press and lick his wounds. But when we disembarked the helicopter, nobody was there. Instead sat five hundred empty seats where media would have been. The cheering had turned to silence. Humphrey was suddenly as interesting as yesterday's breakfast. He had become the invisible man.

But then a wonderful thing happened. A little blonde girl with Down syndrome came running toward him, arms wide. "Papa! Papa!" With a huge smile Humphrey picked up Vicky, his beloved granddaughter, swung her around, and hugged her tight. He was home.

CHAPTER 6

TWO DEATHS

The mass of men lead lives of quiet desperation.

HENRY DAVID THOREAU, *Walden*

1968-1973

The vice president's limousine sped toward Baltimore on a sunny October afternoon, bound on a sad mission, each of the occupants lost in his own thoughts. Spiro T. Agnew and his chief of staff, Art Sohmer, rode in the rear; I sat in the front passenger seat next to Agent Billy "Grits" Williams, the driver. We were headed toward a secret destination, the United States District Courthouse in Baltimore, Maryland, where Agnew would make history, but not in the way he'd have wished.

Only a handful of people—Sohmer; President Nixon; my boss, Sam Sulliman; Agnew's lawyer; and I—knew this day, October 10, 1973, would be the vice president's last day in office.[3] Not even Mrs. Agnew knew. When Sulliman confided in me around eight o'clock that morning, I could hardly believe the news.

"Jerry, the vice president is going to resign today." Sam's voice broke. "He's going to plead no contest to one charge of income tax evasion. He begged us not to tell *anyone*, not even our own headquarters, until it's all over. I said I'd keep the secret. Will you?" In shock, I agreed.

★ ★ ★

As soon as the votes were counted in 1968, I had moved over to the new vice president, Spiro T. Agnew. The transfer became permanent on January 20, when he was sworn in. The reduction in stress from the Humphrey days was dramatic, like surfacing after a long deep-sea dive. We now had forty-eight agents to do what twenty-seven had previously been doing. Except for some continuing foreign trips, my overtime dropped way down. And, though I would make three more trips to Vietnam, peace talks were ongoing and the war appeared to be winding down. The violence at home seemed to have spent itself at the Democratic Convention, and the demonstrators we now met were usually peaceful, though protest activity did pick up after April 30, 1970, when Nixon extended the war into Cambodia. But it was nothing like the Humphrey years had been. And when the Agnews wanted to leave Washington, they traveled three hours away by car to their condo in Ocean City, Maryland, not to Minnesota.

Although I continued to work shifts, in April 1969 I was promoted to shift leader (assistant to the special agent in charge, or ATSAIC), a management position. I was in terrific company: the other leaders were Clint Hill, Sam Sulliman, and John Simpson. Clint had been SAIC of PPD for Johnson, Simpson would become director of the Secret Service, and Sam would take over as SAIC of the Agnew detail when I was deputy. I learned from each of them.

Now I was able to enjoy family time again. I enjoyed it so much that, on October 3, 1970, our third daughter, Trish, was born. In fact, eleven agents who moved from Humphrey to Agnew had babies in the fall of 1970. I was proud to say that Trish was the first!

From November 30, 1970, to December 9, 1972, I served as a leader of the brand-new Foreign Dignitary Protective Division, where I would serve two terms. I went there as Assistant SAIC. After the Nixon-Agnew reelection in 1972 I returned to Agnew and rose to Deputy SAIC of VPPD on July 22, 1973, second in command under SAIC Sam Sulliman.

When the Watergate break-in of Democratic headquarters surfaced during the '72 election, it seemed like a minor burglary by minor criminals, a blip on the election scene. Nixon defeated Senator George McGovern by a wide margin, and Agnew stayed on.

During Agnew's first four years, the VPPD agents' time

had been relatively uneventful. On January 23, 1973, Nixon announced a cease-fire between North Vietnam and the United States, and we visited Southeast Asia for the last time: Singapore, Saigon, Manila. South Vietnam had not yet surrendered, but the writing was on the wall. As far as the United States was concerned, the war was over. No more protesters to fight.

But a new stew of domestic dissent was brewing. The Watergate scandal had not gone away—it was growing in intensity. On May 17, 1973, the Senate began to hold televised hearings that ran until August 7. The public was mesmerized at first, then infuriated as more and more "dirty tricks" designed to subvert the election were revealed. *Washington Post* reporters Bob Woodward and Carl Bernstein wrote stories tying funding for the break-in to Republican campaign funds—and the trail led to US Attorney General John Mitchell, who would eventually serve nineteen months in prison. The president and his inner staff were spending all their time doing damage control. President Nixon himself was not yet implicated but was under constant and increasing pressure.

Then, beginning August 9, 1973, the curtain began to descend on Spiro "Ted" Agnew. Unrelated to Watergate, reports surfaced that the Justice Department was investigating corruption in Maryland that might involve the vice president's prior tenure as governor. News stories hinted at kickbacks from state contractors, which Agnew vehemently denied. Like the other guys on the detail, I believed him. But

(TOP LEFT)
Mama loved my
three-year-old curls.

(TOP RIGHT)
Ready for school
with short hair

(RIGHT)
With my stepdad,
Jack Cox. At twelve,
I was small for
my age.

Florida boy in a typical cold Minnesota winter

Private Jerry Parr, 20

Newlyweds Carolyn, 22, and Jerry, 29

I liked heights. Note the size
of the transformer.

Working the lines with gloves

Building a family—Carolyn, Jennifer, Trish, Kim, and Jerry

Scanning parade bleachers with Vice President Humphrey; his wife, Muriel; and their granddaughters Vicky and Jill Solomonson, c. 1965. Agent Walt Coughlin is in the front seat.

President Carter liked to ride on top of cars, waving at the crowd. My left hand is holding him by the belt.

Surprise fiftieth-birthday cake on Air Force One as President Carter looks on

Behind President Reagan right before John Hinckley Jr. fired. Tim McCarthy, who was hit, is at the right.

Relying on my training and quick instincts, I pushed the president into the limo as shots were fired.

Leaving George Washington Hospital on April 11, 1981, the Reagans smile at applauding nurses while I look grim. Patti Reagan is on the right.

To all the Parrs - With every good wish & Warm Regards
Ronald Reagan

Trish, Kim, me, President Reagan, Carolyn, and Jennifer (right after I retired)

Carolyn, now a lawyer, and me

I checked out the bus bound for El Salvador.

Amparo Palacios and me, in love with Salvadoran orphans

OFFICE OF NANCY REAGAN

October 21, 2012

Dear Jerry,

As friends and colleagues gather today to sing your praises and pay tribute to the contributions you have made to the Secret Service over the years, I want to add my own sincere congratulations to their chorus – along with my personal gratitude.

It hardly seems possible that thirty-one years have passed since the attempt on my husband's life. That day is frozen in my memory and every detail is as clear – and as terrifying – as if it were only yesterday. There were several people who, like you, put themselves in harm's way to protect Ronnie, and I am forever grateful to all of you. And if not for your own quick thinking and your decision to go straight to the hospital instead of back to the White House, I would have lost him.

On that day you not only performed a valuable service to your country, but thanks to you, I had twenty-three more wonderful years with the man I loved.

I hope you have a wonderful afternoon and enjoy all the well-deserved praise that you are receiving today.

Fondly,

Nancy Reagan

Mr. Jerry Parr
Tribute Luncheon
Crofton Country Club
Crofton, Maryland

(ABOVE)
A grateful hug from
First Lady Nancy Reagan

(LEFT)
Letter I received from
Nancy Reagan, October 2012

With four presidents—Reagan, Carter, Ford, and Nixon—and two first ladies

a steady stream of leaks continued to wound his image like death by a thousand cuts. There was no indictment, no talk of impeachment, just daily damaging leaks. Cries for Agnew's political hide grew more strident day after day.

The staff suspected the leaks came from a White House eager to distract attention from Watergate. Agnew refused to resign and denied everything.

Conservatives including Senator Goldwater rushed to Agnew's defense, but he had a lot of enemies. He loved to play with words and relished inventing comical names for groups he deemed too liberal. He called the press "nattering nabobs of negativism." Supporters of women's liberation were "radiclibs." Academics were "pointy-headed intellectuals." Democrats he deemed soft on demonstrators were "pusillanimous pussyfooters."

Now the tables were turned. The press was staking out a deathwatch across from Agnew's home in Kenwood. Mrs. Agnew couldn't open the door to pick up the morning paper without seeing them. When I asked a female television news reporter why she was there every day, she said matter-of-factly, "We want to be first with the story when he either resigns or commits suicide." Everywhere he went, he was hounded with shouted questions.

Suffering showed on his now-haggard face. Already trim, we could see he was losing weight. As summer passed into autumn, I frequently heard sighs and groans coming from the backseat of the car; sometimes the soft sound was Mrs. Agnew weeping as her husband tried to comfort her.

We agents liked the Agnews personally. To a unique degree the vice president and his wife, Judy (whom we called "Mrs. A"), recognized our humanity and appreciated our service. They asked about our families and looked at photos of our kids. In late October 1970 the vice president took a vacation to Hawaii, and seeing the Air Force plane would essentially be empty, he and Mrs. A invited the agents to bring their wives along. That would be unheard of now, but it didn't cost the government any extra money—we paid our wives' expenses except for the flight—and seemed to all of us an incredibly generous gesture. Carolyn couldn't leave our two-week-old baby behind, so she didn't go, but she was disappointed.

Mrs. A was completely unpretentious: she cooked the family's meals, packed the vice president's suitcase, did needlepoint. She called the agents "my boys," and none of us seemed to mind. If it started to rain and one of us was standing post outside, she'd ask Sulliman to let us move into the carport. If we looked hungry, someone from the house would offer us a sandwich. She also reached out to our wives in a special way. She attended their luncheons. She visited women with new babies. If someone was in the hospital, she'd be there.

One Christmas the Agnews even came to our home in Silver Spring. Carolyn and I hosted a party for the detail agents and their wives. Worried that the shift who would be working the vice president would have to miss the party, the Agnews asked if they could come as guests. Mrs. A held Trish;

the vice president played the old piano in our still-unfinished basement, challenged the guys to a game of Ping-Pong, and admired "big sisters" Kim and Jennifer. The Agnews stayed until well after midnight. No reporters were in sight.

To them we were people and not furniture that came with the job. So the other agents and I unconsciously did something I'd always warned against: we moved from professional, detached concern to personal affection for our protectees.

Because we cared about their feelings, we also personally absorbed a lot of the family's pain. One day in late summer Jack Kippenberger and I were driving the vice president from his home in Kenwood to the White House. Noting the press camped out across from the house as we started the car, Agnew said something like, "They want to put me in jail."

I thought a little humor might lighten the mood and suggested we agents could accompany him to prison. I joked, "Well, Mr. Vice President, we'll find someone to smuggle us a hacksaw blade in a lemon meringue pie so we can get out."

He leaned forward on the seat so Jack and I both could clearly hear him. He swore and said, "That wasn't funny!"

But Jack, who was driving, couldn't stifle his laughter. Then the vice president began to laugh. Then I burst into guffaws. We passed the reporters in a state of uproarious hilarity. I think it made Agnew's day. He knew, even though we still did not believe, that jail was a real possibility.

But in the car speeding toward Annapolis on October 10, 1973, there was no laughter. Desperate to stop the stories, Agnew's lawyers had subpoenaed certain reporters and newspapers to force them to reveal their sources, and the subpoenaed parties moved to quash. The judge set a hearing in Baltimore on October 10 for lawyers' oral argument on the motion. No one expected the vice president to attend.

Agnew asked to be taken first to his office in the Executive Office Building, where I later learned he had arranged for letters of resignation to be hand delivered to Secretary of State Henry Kissinger and to President Nixon. Then we climbed into the car for the forty-mile drive from Washington to the Federal District Court in Baltimore.

As we entered the courthouse, a handful of reporters, there to hear the subpoena arguments, turned in surprise when Agnew walked in. The wood-paneled, high-ceiling courtroom was only half full. Agnew joined his lawyers at the table on the defendant's side. On the opposite side was the team of prosecutors from the Department of Justice, headed by Attorney General Elliot Richardson himself.

"All rise," said the clerk. We all stood as a black-robed, distinguished older gentleman entered and took his place behind the bench. Judge Walter E. Hoffman, sixty-six, was not familiar to the Baltimore crowd. Appointed by Eisenhower, he was finishing up a twelve-year term as Chief Judge of the US District Court for the Eastern District of Virginia. He had been brought in to prevent any appearance of a conflict of interest with the Maryland lawyers and potential witnesses involved.

That's when I learned the details. After months of flat denial, Agnew and the prosecutors had reached a plea agreement the night before, and the vice president had informed President Nixon around six o'clock in the evening that he would admit to one incident of failing to report income tax in 1967 while he was governor. However, Agnew would not plead guilty; the plea would be *nolo contendere* (no contest). He would deny everything else, and all the other charges would be dropped. Prosecutors would recommend probation without prison and a $10,000 fine. But Agnew would have to resign as vice president.

There was a risk. Regardless of what the US Attorney recommended, the final sentence would be up to the judge.

In the courtroom Attorney General Richardson alleged that if the vice president was indicted and brought to trial, the evidence would establish "a pattern of substantial cash payments [to Agnew] during the period when he served as governor and in return for engineering contracts with the state of Maryland." However, Richardson indicated that with Agnew's plea the Justice Department did not intend to press further charges.

Hands trembling, Agnew then read from a prepared statement. He began, "My decision to resign and enter a plea of *nolo contendere* rests on my firm belief that the public interest requires swift disposition of the problems which are facing me. . . . I am aware that witnesses are prepared to testify that I and my agents received payments from consulting engineers doing business with the state of Maryland during the period I was governor."

He then denied, with one exception, any assertions of

illegal acts that might be made by government witnesses. His language was carefully crafted. Agnew did not deny receiving the payments; he denied that it was illegal to do so. He admitted that the persons who made the payments did receive state contracts and that he was aware of such awards. But he stressed that no contracts were awarded to incompetent contractors, and in most instances state contracts were awarded without any arrangement for a payment. He said, "I deny that the payments in any way influenced my official actions" and averred that he never enriched himself at the expense of the public trust.

There was a sole exception: he admitted he received payments of $29,500 during 1967, "which were not expended for political purposes and . . . were income taxable to me in that year, and that I so knew." To this count he pleaded *nolo contendere*.

Agnew also mentioned what he felt was his real justification: "My acceptance of contributions was part of a long-established pattern of political fund-raising in the state." Agnew never apologized.

Though "everybody does it" is a dubious ground for accepting bribes and kickbacks, subsequent reports proved Agnew's "established pattern" language to be true. The Maryland governor's salary in 1967 was $25,000, up from only $15,000 the year before. But the governor and his family were expected to live a lifestyle far above what would have been possible on that income. In setting the salary, the state legislators expected governors to augment their income from grateful citizens. In an interview with Ben Bradlee for the Center for the Study of Democracy published in fall 2006, award-winning *Washington Post* reporter Richard Cohen named eleven Maryland political officials who were convicted on corruption charges while he was covering Annapolis.

Judge Hoffman reluctantly accepted the agreed sentence; he said in open court that he would have imposed a prison sentence were it not for Attorney General Richardson's personal intercession on Agnew's behalf.

Riding away from the courthouse, in the silence of the car, Agnew began to recite softly the speech from *As You Like It,* by William Shakespeare:

> *All the world's a stage,*
> *And all the men and women merely players;*
> *They have their exits and their entrances;*
> *And one man in his time plays many parts. . . .*

Agnew's sad day was not over. The body of Roy Pollard, Agnew's half brother, lay in a Baltimore funeral home waiting for Agnew to make arrangements. When the four-to-midnight shift showed up to relieve us, I was more than ready for my day to end.

I felt shocked and disappointed. But, as had been the case with other wrongdoers in my life—my stepfather Jack, check forger Myrtle S. giving birth—my heart went out to Mr. Agnew. I reflected that life is paradoxical. Good people sometimes do bad things. That doesn't make it okay. But the Bible tells us that God loved David, an adulterer and a murderer. Jesus loved prostitutes, Roman soldiers, even tax collectors who cheated the people. I'm not sure what Jesus meant when he warned, "Judge not, that ye be not judged," but as I get older I realize that life is not lived out in black and white but in the complexity of the gray.

I learned that three people telephoned Agnew that evening: his longtime friend Frank Sinatra, who offered money to pay the fine; Billy Graham; and Governor Jimmy Carter, who knew Agnew from the Governors' Conference. I don't know what Graham and Carter said, but I can guess it was something about forgiveness, redemption, and second chances.

The minute the news of Agnew's resignation broke, Deputy Assistant Director Paul Rundle called me on the radio, furious. "Why didn't you let Headquarters know what was going on?" he demanded. "We had to hear it on the news! Now we're scrambling to get a team over to Carl Albert! Something could have happened!"

Carl Albert of Oklahoma, Democratic Speaker of the House, was next in line until a vice president could be confirmed under the never-before-used Twenty-Fifth Amendment. The process is set out in Section 2:

> Whenever there is a vacancy in the office of the
> Vice President, the President shall nominate a Vice
> President who shall take office upon confirmation
> by a majority vote of both Houses of Congress.

Within two days Nixon nominated House minority leader Gerald Ford, who was soon confirmed.

All I could tell Rundle was the truth. "Mr. Agnew asked us to keep it a secret, and Sulliman thought if Headquarters knew, you'd put a detail with Speaker Albert right away, and that would tip off the press. They were already watching Albert's house." Sam was correct, but so was Rundle. We had allowed ourselves to be drawn in, to the possible detriment of a protectee (Albert), the country, and our careers. As a result of keeping Headquarters in the dark, my rise in the Service took a detour for a while, but I weathered the storm.

Agnew's political demise was painful enough. But earlier in 1973 something else had happened that caused me to think about leaving the Secret Service entirely. Near the end of August, Jim Connolly, an agent I knew from the Humphrey detail, shot himself at home with his service revolver.

Jim was tall and angular with a friendly smile and a firm handshake. I resonated with his Irish fatalistic sense of humor. He was a loyal friend. He loved a good party but didn't know when to quit. We all laughed at his clowning and knew he drank too much, but no one wanted to confront him. Back then we didn't really know how. The Service frowned on anything that hinted at psychotherapy, even marriage counseling, so a lot of situations that could have been helped went untreated.

The day Jim died, he called into his field office three times, each time increasingly incoherent. His speech was slurred, and he wasn't making much sense. People were trying to work, and they were annoyed. Assuming he was drunk, the SAIC sent two men to get Jim's car keys, gun, and commission book. Taking the commission book meant he probably would have been fired. When the agents arrived, however, what they found was a human tragedy.

Jim had carefully turned the air-conditioning down as low as it would go to prevent a smell if he weren't found quickly. Then he sat down in his comfortable leather chair and shot himself with his service revolver. There was no suicide note, but the Maryland police had no trouble determining the wound was self-inflicted.

Jim left a lovely wife and several young sons who didn't deserve this. Fortunately they were in Boston at the time, visiting family. The agents and Tom Wells, an inspector, did something that was not in their job description: they worked all night with a cleaning crew to remove the blood and bits of bone and flesh that speckled the wall, carpet, chair, even a lamp shade. They didn't want Jim's wife to have to see what they were seeing.

I probably made some unfair assumptions, but I blamed the Secret Service for Jim's death. At the time we had no employee assistance programs; the Service was totally "mission" focused. And we loved that mission. But as an organization the Service had a hard time dealing with *pain*. We had not yet found a voice for dealing with the human suffering of agents. We did all the "right" things: we went to the funerals, we sent flowers. But when it was over, we expected agents to make a quick recovery. Well, Jim obviously did not recover from his alcoholism or whatever personal demons may have lurked behind it.

I was enraged. I believed the agents who spoke to him on the phone should have recognized his calls as cries for help. I thought they cared more about Jim's car than they did about him. I was so angry I thought seriously about resigning. I kept asking myself, *How could they be so callous?*

I know now that I had absorbed entirely too much pain. It was a perfect storm for a midlife crisis. I was the right age: forty-three. I had just come out of four years of nonstop hypervigilance, danger, lack of sleep, family separations, and other hardships to rival battlefield conditions. To some extent every man on the Humphrey detail was a wounded warrior. Maybe Jim's invisible wounds were too deep for tears.

Agnew's disgrace was another blow I took personally. He was a father figure to me, and grief from my own father's death seventeen years earlier came rushing back. I lost my appetite and found it hard to sleep. For the first time since childhood I felt vulnerable. But I never told anyone at work. The men I worked with never knew. I soldiered on, putting up a strong front.

The anger and grief lasted several months, but by talking to God, to Carolyn, and to a friend I trusted, I gradually came through it.

I had been a friend to many agents over the years, one

they could trust with their hidden feelings, and I knew I had helped some of them. I wished I'd known how to help Jim. I knew I had a gift for listening nonjudgmentally and for resonating with the pain of others. But if I was going to be the person whom hurting people could come to, I would need training.

I wondered, *Could my own vulnerability become the germ of a new calling when my days as a Secret Service agent end?*

At least partly in response to Jim's death, in September 1973 some of us put together a little school for agents who were going to do protective advances. I was now Deputy SAIC of VPPD and had been doing advances from 1964 to 1973, with either vice presidents or foreign dignitaries. At the school, I spoke off the cuff and from the heart, unaware that Bob DeProspero was recording my remarks. Others would speak about the nuts and bolts of advances, but I asked to introduce the topic. And I said something nobody expected: I talked about suffering.

I said doing advances would maim them, but with each success they would gain self-confidence. I said they'd see more holes in their advances than anyone else. I warned that they should expect to be criticized and second-guessed but not to feel guilty about small things.

First of all you go there and you create an organism.
It's nothing. You and the political advance man,
and the [local] SAIC, the committee man—you
create this organism from nothing. You use your

enthusiasm, your judgment, your intelligence. You get a lot of people to work for you. You sell the idea that it's worthwhile to protect the president or vice president. You create this thing from nothing, and as "the Man" lands, it is big and complicated and you have involved so many people. They're connected by radio, by telephone, transported by boats, cars, helicopters, airplanes. It's an organism in itself. . . . It may last as long as the inauguration, but it's temporary. . . .

You can expect human failure. When you organize something as big as an advance, there will be somebody who doesn't get the message. I often say, to myself and others, "I'm mildly surprised when the thing works at all." . . .

You always want to leave a good deposit when you go, not a deposit of ill will. I've gone to stops, and the first thing the Man says to me is, "You didn't bring that s.o.b. with you, did you?" . . . His ego has been hurt by some young, brash advance man who thought he knew it all.

It's like Don Bendickson used to say: "You can muck up a counterfeiting case, but when you muck up the president, they write thirty-two volumes [the Warren Commission Report]." So you do a good job—and the Man leaves. It would be better if he left happy and alive, but certainly *alive*. It's a great relief to have completed a good advance and done the best you could. It has only been in the last couple of years that I've really understood what President Kennedy meant when he said, "A good conscience is your only sure reward." Because that's all you're going to get out of it—the knowledge that you've done a good job.

I told them they might not understand what I was saying for a while, but I knew the five men in the room who were running the class would know what I meant.

Three years later I was surprised by a note from Tom Quinn, who was present that day. He said, "Your words on September 13, 1973, have always meant a great deal to me, but you were right in that it's only been the past year . . . that I completely understood their full meaning. I have played the tape of that day often, and it has given me something extra to rely on when doing advances." I had not even realized my speech had been taped, but Tom had had copies of the tape made and distributed to other agents who were there and to the training division. He also had it transcribed. With his note Tom enclosed a framed copy, titled "Words of Wisdom by Jerry Parr." Like an underground newspaper, it had been passed from agent to agent, almost secretly, for three years!

I'm not sure how wise they were, but I think my remarks resonated with so many because I was someone with earned credibility, and I was unashamed to talk about pain.

I wish Jim Connolly had been there.

CHAPTER 7

SINNERS AND STATESMEN: WATERGATE AND THE WORLD

Don't be so humble—you are not that great.

GOLDA MEIR

1970–1976

A scant two days after Vice President Agnew resigned, on October 12, 1973, Nixon nominated House minority leader Gerald Ford to take Agnew's place. I moved over to protect him. While all the world's attention was on Nixon (with a slight distraction to Agnew), my five months with Ford were deceptively peaceful—like the eye of a hurricane. Ford was an affable man with kind eyes, a friendly smile, and a firm handshake. He was minority leader of the House, whose only ambition was to become Speaker should Republicans gain control. He never sought or expected to be president. His brunette wife, Betty, had been a professional dancer with choreographer Martha Graham. She was down to earth and refreshingly candid. I liked them both.

Since Ford was reputed to be ethical, competent, and well respected by leaders of both parties, his confirmation as vice president was virtually assured. But before Congress could vote, President Nixon himself provoked a constitutional crisis that came to be known as the "Saturday Night Massacre."

Like an angry sea, Watergate swirled around both Agnew and Ford, rocking each in very different ways. But I was focused on the sharks—the physical danger to my charges—and relatively unaware of the political currents tugging at them. Unlike the anger over Vietnam that had directly threatened Humphrey's safety, the lapping of Watergate seemed to me like white noise.

Only later did its true significance dawn on me.

The Watergate saga began on June 17, 1972, while I was still with Agnew. Five men were arrested at two thirty in the morning trying to bug the offices of the Democratic National Committee at the Watergate hotel and office complex. A GOP security aide was among them. In a burglar's possession detectives found the White House phone number of the Committee to Reelect the President (derisively called "CREEP"), controlled by Attorney General John Mitchell. Then investigators discovered a $25,000 cashier's check in a burglar's bank account, earmarked for the Nixon campaign and traceable to CREEP. These discoveries led *Washington Post* reporters Bob Woodward and Carl Bernstein to begin an investigation that uncovered a secret Republican fund used to finance sabotage and spying on the Democrats.

Pursuant to a leak, the *Post* reported on October 10, 1972, that FBI agents believed the break-in was the tip of a massive iceberg of intelligence gathering and "dirty tricks" on behalf of the Nixon reelection effort.

Nevertheless, by election time none of this had yet been linked to the president or his inner circle. He and Agnew were reelected by a wide margin on November 7, 1972.

Rapid-fire disclosures began to surface a couple of months later. On January 30, 1973, former Nixon aides G. Gordon Liddy and James W. McCord Jr., in addition to five others, were convicted or pleaded guilty to conspiracy, burglary, and wiretapping. The sentencing judge was John Sirica. Then the *Washington Post*, Judge Sirica, and members of a Senate investigating committee started to dig deeper. Aided by an informant nicknamed "Deep Throat" (later revealed as Mark Felt, deputy director of the FBI), Woodward and Bernstein continued to investigate and write, and the scandal grew. Nixon aides were rumored to have tried to get the CIA to impede the FBI investigation, a clear misuse of presidential power and an obstruction of justice if true.

Nixon's closest aides, H. R. Haldeman and John Ehrlichman, resigned on April 30. So did Attorney General Richard Kleindienst, who was not involved but felt he could not prosecute a friend. Suspecting that White House counsel John Dean was talking to investigators, Nixon fired him.

The Senate Watergate committee began its nationally

televised hearings in May 1973. Attorney General–designate Elliot Richardson chose former Solicitor General Archibald Cox as the Justice Department's special prosecutor for Watergate.

On June 3, 1973, the *Post* revealed that John Dean had told investigators he discussed the Watergate cover-up with Nixon at least thirty-five times.

Shortly thereafter, Alexander Butterfield, former appointments secretary, testified before Congress that since 1972, Nixon had recorded all conversations and telephone calls in his office. The Senate committee and Cox immediately asked for the tapes, but Nixon refused to turn them over.

Because of Nixon's troubles, Vice President Agnew, next in line to become president should Nixon resign or be impeached, started to draw attention. He had nothing to do with Watergate, but beginning in August, it became clear that Agnew had his own problems. His resignation in disgrace did not deflect attention from Nixon's troubles for long.

Just ten days after Agnew's resignation, on Saturday, October 20, 1973, the president tried to decapitate the Justice Department, which he believed had become his enemy. In what the *Washington Post* called "the most traumatic government upheaval of the Watergate crisis," Nixon ordered Attorney General Richardson to fire special prosecutor Archibald Cox. Richardson refused and resigned. Deputy Attorney General William Ruckelshaus also refused, and was either fired or resigned (Nixon said each at different times). Solicitor General Robert Bork, third in line, did the deed.

The immediate and overwhelming public outrage at the firings took Nixon and Capitol Hill by surprise. Within hours thousands of telegrams, letters, and calls from angry constituents flooded Congress. They poured in from Republicans as well as Democrats, conservatives as well as liberals, demanding that the president be impeached. The "Saturday Night Massacre" did not end the Watergate crisis, but it may have been the single most important event that doomed Nixon's presidency.

If Nixon had expected Bork to protect him, he was soon disillusioned. The acting attorney general quickly appointed a new special prosecutor, Leon Jaworski, who, on March 1, 1974, convened a grand jury that indicted seven of Nixon's former closest aides on various charges related to Watergate. In its report the grand jury referred to Nixon as an "unindicted coconspirator."

Although Nixon eventually released edited transcripts, it was too little too late. On July 24, 1974, in *United States v. Richard M. Nixon*, the United States Supreme Court ruled unanimously that the president must turn over the actual taped recordings of sixty-four White House conversations. A scant three days after receiving them, the House Judiciary Committee passed the first of three articles of impeachment: abuse of power, obstruction of justice, and contempt of Congress.

On August 8, 1974, Nixon became the first US president to resign. And, with his hand on the Bible, Gerald Ford swore to "protect and defend the Constitution of the United

States." In light of what had just occurred, these words hung heavy with meaning.

But by the time Ford became president, I had moved on.

⭑ ⭑ ⭑

I served with the Foreign Dignitary Protective Division (FDPD) twice. My first deployment, from November 30, 1970, to December 10, 1972, was sandwiched between two periods with Agnew. And now, around the time of the Watergate grand jury indictments, I returned to "foreign digs," this time as Deputy SAIC.

FDPD was born in 1970 after a French president was roughed up in Chicago and someone unsuccessfully tried to kill Taiwanese Vice Prime Minister Chiang Ching-kuo in New York. Alarmed that poor security could cause an international incident, Nixon transferred foreign dignitary protection from the State Department to the Secret Service. It began with a special detail for a United Nations gathering. I was one of four experienced agents charged with the safety of all visiting heads of state when they were on US soil. It was a major responsibility.

Ken Balge was the first SAIC, Dick Roth was Deputy SAIC, and Bill Payne and I were ASAICs. One of us would always act as detail leader; agents temporarily pulled from field offices filled in the shifts.

To accompany heads of state from so many different countries—each with its own diplomatic and security staff—demanded flexibility and openness to cultural differences. US State Department representatives, trained in protocol, accompanied us. I watched them carefully, trying not to make a faux pas—although I secretly believed that their emphasis on protocol over security was the reason Nixon had taken security away from them and given it to us. Protocol and security had to be parallel concerns, but like oil and water, they did not mix easily.

Our every action also required political sensitivity. Rigidity was the enemy of security. As I learned on my very first assignment, shades of gray were the order of the day.

King Hussein of Jordan was friendly to the West, spoke perfect English, and had a beautiful English wife, Princess Muna. (As I write, Jordan's current monarch is the son of this union.) The king was small in stature but large in importance to the United States. He was likable, easy to protect, and seemed to appreciate our work.

On his last day in the United States, at around six forty-five in the evening, a top member of the royal staff asked me to come to his room in the Waldorf Towers in New York. He wanted to present gifts to the detail agents.

I was prepared for this. Headquarters had decided that FDPD would follow normal State Department procedure, which allowed for the exchange of small gifts, tokens of national pride. I was told this was expected and acceptable in diplomatic circles. We could accept gifts worth no more than fifty dollars (later raised to seventy-five dollars). But we absolutely could not accept cash.

The Jordanian official said, with an apologetic smile, "His Majesty ordered gifts to be purchased for the agents, but there has not been time. So he would like to express his appreciation with cash gifts for each one." He held out three envelopes.

I took a deep breath, then patiently explained that I appreciated the thought but could not receive monetary gifts because Treasury regulations forbade it. But the official, perhaps frightened now by his own failure to follow the king's orders, insisted that the gifts were personal in nature from His Majesty and that to refuse them would be a serious breach of diplomacy.

The king's flight was going to take off soon, so I had to act fast. All I could think was, *Please don't let me cause an international incident!* None of my superiors was instantly available—this was before cell phones. Trying to look as if I knew what I were doing, I excused myself and found the Jordanian ambassador to the United States and a Jordanian brigadier general I'd met who were still in the hotel. Both insisted that the king would be offended if the gifts were refused.

In desperation I thought of a third way. I agreed to accept the envelopes if the ambassador himself would write a letter explaining the circumstances surrounding this gift. He complied on the spot, and I accepted the envelopes, expressing appreciation. I finally reached Deputy Assistant Director Clint Hill, who agreed that to refuse the money would have caused an awkward situation.

The envelopes contained traveler's checks in the amounts of three hundred dollars for me, two hundred dollars for my number-two man, and twenty hundred-dollar traveler's checks to be distributed to the troops. That was a lot of money in 1970 (three hundred dollars then was equal to about eighteen hundred dollars in 2013), but I was not in the least tempted. I loved my job and wanted to keep it!

As soon as the king's entourage took off, I sat down and wrote a memorandum to my boss, Ken Balge, with copies to Assistant Director Boggs and to Hill. I attached all envelopes with original contents to the report, together with the ambassador's letter.

The men on the shift never knew about this (nor, perhaps, did the king). It was the first time in my knowledge that a protectee had ever tried to tip an agent—but it would not be the last, especially with Third World leaders. (An African leader once tried to give me five hundred dollars.) King Hussein came to the United States many times after that, and the agents would receive cuff links or some other memorabilia, but no one from his party ever again offered us cash.

During my first round with FDPD I led protection for fourteen heads of state. Aside from King Hussein (whom I guarded several times), some of the others included Prince (now king) Juan Carlos and Princess Sophia of Spain, Prime Minister Lynch of Ireland, President Léopold Sédar Senghor of Senegal, Marshal Tito of Yugoslavia, Willy Brandt of West Germany, President Echeverria of Mexico, and various high

Israeli officials including Prime Minister Golda Meir, Deputy Prime Minister Yigal Allon, and Foreign Minister Abba Eban.

Some were persons of world-shaking stature and power. Some were petty tyrants. Some were cruel, some corrupt, some ruthless. (I was shocked to hear a Latin American leader refer to his people as "monkeys.") Some were US allies; some were enemies. And some were spiritual giants.

Léopold Sédar Senghor, first president of the Republic of Senegal, was such a man. I knew very little about him until I led his security, but almost immediately I felt honored to be in his presence.

Senghor was the founding father of independent Senegal, winning independence from France not by revolution but by persuading Charles de Gaulle to peacefully cede control. Senegal became a republic in 1960 and Senghor its first president. He was reelected four times until 1980, when he voluntarily retired. A Roman Catholic, he led a predominantly Muslim country. He was a poet, professor, philosopher, and chief theoretician of *Négritude* ("blackness"), a term for the common culture and spiritual heritage of the peoples of black Africa. (He gave me an autographed copy of his book by that title. Though I don't read French, I treasure it.)

Senghor studied at the Sorbonne and respected Western literature and political thought. When African rivals criticized his friendly relations with colonialist powers, he said, "I wear European clothing and the Americans dance to jazz . . . from our African rhythms: civilization in the 20th century is universal. No people can get along without others."

From several advances to African countries with Vice President Humphrey, I knew that the country of Senegal was unique in its stability. I asked President Senghor how he managed that.

"Tribes are very important in African thought and culture," he told me. "When I became president, I called together leaders of every tribe in Senegal, and we agreed upon a power-sharing arrangement. It has held. Most other African leaders favor their own tribe, but that's not what I did. That's why Senegal has peace."

Because protection is always high-tension work, we agents often joked around to relieve stress. So when the opportunity arose on my first tour, I couldn't resist trying my hand at satire. I wrote the following tongue-in-cheek memo to my former boss, who was still with Agnew:

To: SAIC Sulliman—Vice Presidential Protective Division, Dec. 2, 1971

From: ASAIC Parr—Foreign Dignitary Prot. Div.

Re: President Maga of Dahomey

It has come to my attention that the Vice President will be staying at the Park Lane Hotel in New York City at the same time as President Hubert Maga of the Republic of Dahomey.

Inasmuch as a President has precedence over a Vice President in all matters, I would appreciate it if you would comply with the following:

1. *That your Detail not interfere with my elevator operation.*
2. *That your Detail not get the best parking area in the hotel and not block our parking entrance to the hotel.*
3. *That your Detail not interfere with the Foreign Dignitary Protective Division radio frequencies.*
4. *That your Detail not start false rumors with my Detail.*
5. *Inasmuch as my Detail will be using the permanent lapel pins with the green down, it is necessary for you to obtain other identification for your agents.*
6. *Advise your agents to keep the noise level down in the hotel as my principal likes complete solitude and silence.*
7. *Please check with me daily for any other restrictions that might develop on the scene.*

If the above items are adhered to I will see that the Vice President, you and DSAIC Simpson receive an autographed picture.

Jerry S. Parr
Assistant Special Agent in Charge

Fortunately, Sam got a kick out of my parody of the privileges that the PPD sometimes claimed.

Sometimes the principals themselves provided the humor. There were endless opportunities for foul-ups. In New York I was once stuck in a Waldorf Hotel elevator with Golda Meir, prime minister of Israel. She was headed for a banquet upstairs, and everyone was waiting to hear her speak. And waiting. And waiting. I radioed for help, but it seemed to take forever to get us out of that elevator. My feet hurt and my stomach rumbled. Hearing that familiar sound, Mrs. Meir turned to me and asked, "Mr. Parr, do you think we could send out for a kosher pastrami on rye?"

Mrs. Meir was my first female head of state to protect, a large woman in her seventies with steely gray hair pulled back in a bun, strong features, and plenty of power. She was good natured. She once said, "Not being beautiful was the true blessing. Not being beautiful forced me to develop my inner resources. The pretty girl has a handicap to overcome." Feminists were proud of her achievements, but she wore them lightly. She said, "Whether women are better than men I cannot say—but I can say they are certainly no worse."

The women's movement arrived at the Secret Service on September 15, 1970, when our Executive Protective Service appointed its first female officer, followed quickly by others. (We led federal law enforcement agencies in this regard.) In December 1971 five EPS female officers became special agents. Several of those women hired in the first few years would work with me at FDPD: Shawn Campbell, Kathy Clarke, and Mary Ann Gordon.

As the father of three girls, I absorbed this culture shock more easily than some of my colleagues. I wanted the world to be open to my daughters. And there was another reason: for a few years Carolyn had been subtly breaking me in about the women's movement. In fact, she was still thinking about law school. In the late 1960s she had enjoyed work as an assistant to a K Street lobbyist, but when we discovered our live-in nanny had a drinking problem, Carolyn resigned to stay home. When Trish was born in 1970, Carolyn put her long-deferred dream of law school on hold yet again, but her career clock was ticking. She was already thirty-three years old, and law school would take at least three years. While I worried a little about how this change would affect the family, I was not about to try to stop her. Carolyn had always encouraged my dreams, postponing her own. When she was ready, she could count on my wholehearted support. I never doubted she would succeed. And I knew our love would make a way.

Beginning in May 1972, I yo-yoed back and forth between foreign digs and temporary assignments to the Agnew detail and to various other individuals who needed protection. Nixon ordered security for Senator Ted Kennedy and House Speaker Wilbur Mills when they started to get threats. In May

I put in 172 hours of overtime, reminiscent of the Humphrey days. Advances for major heads of state also ate a lot of time, especially if they planned a long visit. In the single month of August, I also led advances for Agnew's detail to Miami, Arkansas, Phoenix, Los Angeles, and Palm Springs, which totaled 176 hours of overtime. Still, these periods were rare, and there was time to recuperate between them.

I returned to Vice President Agnew in November 1972 and then moved to Ford in October 1973. My second tour at foreign digs, now as SAIC Bill Barton's deputy, began March 17, 1974.

* * *

The bicentennial of our nation's founding was coming up, along with another United Nations meeting. A flood of dignitaries poured into the United States, among them Emperor Hirohito of Japan, making his first and only visit to the United States. Others returned and specifically requested me: President Senghor, Prince Juan Carlos, and King Hussein. In 1976, after I moved to the Inspection Division, I was called back to protect Queen Elizabeth and Prince Philip.

Two protectees, Emperor Hirohito and Yasser Arafat, leader of the Palestine Liberation Organization (PLO) and sworn enemy of Israel, would require special handling.

My introduction to the Hirohito assignment was unusual and a little awkward. It was cherry blossom time in Washington in 1975, and Maseo Tachibana, Japanese embassy security officer, looked embarrassed. "Mr. Parr," he said, "please don't be offended, but I have to ask you a question." Tachibana and three other security officers, including Mr. Katsuta, chief of security, were visiting my office six months before the emperor's planned visit. Normally, the only security forces who came more than a week or two ahead of time were Israelis and Palestinians. In this case, the Japanese planned exceptionally early. I understood: they wanted to learn how we did security. I didn't mind because we were building relationships that would help us when we came to Japan in the future.

And they wanted to look me over personally.

I was puzzled at Tachibana's diffidence. "Of course," I said. "Ask me anything you like."

"Mr. Parr, do you remember Pearl Harbor?" *Oh. That was it.* Indeed I did remember when the Japanese drew us into World War II by bombing our naval fleet anchored in Pearl Harbor, Hawaii.

"Yes. I was eleven years old."

Unaccustomed to speaking so directly, he looked down at his feet. "Um. Mr. Parr, how do you feel about it now? Would you be able to protect our emperor?"

I hesitated, because his question deserved a serious, truthful answer. Many people don't understand that the identity of the person we protect and how well we do it do not depend on our personal feelings. It is in America's interest to assure the safety of foreign leaders—whoever they are—when they are guests in our country. As I write this, we've never lost one, although some (presidents Tolbert, Somoza, and Anwar Sadat) were murdered later in their own countries.

But I also recalled how violently my friends and I all hated the Japanese between 1941 and 1946, my formative years. I remembered a movie cartoon of Popeye the Sailor Man crushing a can of spinach, pouring its contents down his throat, instantly sprouting huge muscles, then punching out a cartoon caricature of Hirohito. It's no exaggeration to say that anyone who had killed Hirohito in those days would have been an American hero.

But that was 1941, more than thirty years in the past. This was 1975. I certainly didn't feel that way now.

"Well, like many Americans, I was shocked, then angry," I responded. "But that was a long time ago. Most of our agents weren't even born then." I flashed what I hoped was a reassuring smile. "I don't hold any anger. Your emperor will be safe with me." Tachibana returned my smile and visibly relaxed. Putting their hands together, he and his men bowed. I bowed back. We had reached an understanding.

I took Tachibana and the other Japanese security officers to every site the emperor would visit in Washington, including the monuments, Arlington Cemetery, and Blair House, where he would stay. I showed them where our people would probably set up posts, and invited them to have their men double up with us if they wanted to. They began to trust me, asking and taking my advice. I told them that if the emperor were threatened, we would "cover and evacuate." I warned, "We might have to handle him roughly. But as soon as the crisis passes, you can take over." At first the thought of anyone throwing their emperor to the ground or in a car was shocking. But they quickly agreed to prepare him for this possibility and explain the reasons.

The Japanese visit was not a small operation: an estimated two thousand policemen and security personnel would protect Emperor Hirohito and Empress Nagako on their monthlong, eighteen-thousand-mile itinerary. We started the actual advance about a month before their arrival in late September. Seven or eight security officers—a big contingent for a foreign visit—showed up a couple of weeks ahead of the principals and shadowed our advance team. When the emperor arrived, his team worked right alongside our own.

I had to prepare my agents for some cultural differences. I told them to watch the protocol officers from the State Department who accompanied our guests and to do as they did. The emperor was small in stature and unaccustomed to being touched by strangers, so no backslapping or hand shaking unless the royals initiated it. It was okay to bow. The empress customarily walked behind her husband at a respectful distance, so we had to adjust our usual formations to accommodate that. I learned to bow and say, "Ah, so," to indicate agreement.

In spite of their ages (he was seventy-four, she seventy-two), they were indefatigable tourists, and every stop had to be advanced. They explored colonial Williamsburg, where the emperor rode on an open car with me beside him holding his belt (with his permission) to keep him from falling off. A Japanese agent told me that a photo of this caused a stir in Japan. He said, "Jerry, everyone is trying to guess your identity. They say you must be a very important person to be allowed to touch the emperor!"

President and Mrs. Ford entertained the royal couple at a White House state dinner. They toured Washington, then Manhattan, from which we helicoptered out to Vice President Nelson Rockefeller's Japanese-style house on his Pocantico Hills estate. The laboratories at Woods Hole on Cape Cod fascinated the emperor, himself a marine biologist. In Chicago he toasted Mayor Daley and made a side trip to inspect a corn and soybean farm. In San Diego the couple visited the Scripps Institute of Oceanography. In San Francisco they visited Japan Town, and in Los Angeles they greeted Mickey Mouse and watched a bicentennial parade in Disneyland and, at the emperor's request, lunched with John Wayne. Large crowds of excited Japanese Americans greeted them everywhere, especially in Hawaii, where they ended their tour.

The emperor visited Pearl Harbor without public comment. Thirty years before, he had accepted full responsibility for Japan's role in the war, and his humility at Japan's surrender convinced General Douglas MacArthur, leader of US occupying forces, to spare his life and even to allow Hirohito to remain in place. The only condition was to tell his people he was not divine, which he did.

Although the crowds were friendly and happy—not angry and threatening, as with Humphrey—it was never safe to relax. The absence of evidence is not evidence of absence: an audience member could have been a survivor of the Bataan Death March or a Japanese prison camp.

As in the 1960s, we all worked long hours and got little sleep on airplanes and buses. But one agent, John Pforr, went above and beyond. He was assigned to the Japanese press corps. In Williamsburg on September 29 he mentioned a dull pain in his left leg but said, "It's not too bad," and kept working. Back in Washington three days later, I sent him to Bill Voss, Agnew's former doctor, who gave him the option of returning home or continuing with the detail. John said, "Being with the press doesn't require much physical activity. I'll keep going."

Pforr continued to work from October 2 to October 10, traveling through DC, Cape Cod, New York, Chicago, Los Angeles, San Diego, and San Francisco. But at eight thirty in the morning on October 10, Agent Jim Beary called me. He said, "John Pforr can't walk. He's in terrible pain. An ambulance is on its way to the Hilton." I radioed Marty Haskell at San Francisco's field office. He accompanied Pforr to the hospital, then put him aboard a plane for New Haven. Pforr had worked fourteen days with a herniated disc!

When the visit was over, I was still bowing and saying, "Ah, so." Carolyn had to tell me to stop or the neighbors would wonder if I'd gone round the bend.

If working Hirohito was *Battlestar Galactica*, Yasser Arafat was *The Twilight Zone*. As chairman of the PLO, Arafat was the sworn enemy of Israel. Not only that, the PLO was widely blamed for the Munich Massacre two years before at the 1972 Olympic Games, when terrorists kidnapped and murdered eleven members of the Israeli Olympic team. Jews—and many others—passionately hated Arafat.

Palestine had no standing as a state, and our State Department considered Arafat an international terrorist. Nevertheless, the United Nations invited him to speak on November 13, 1974, and the United States had to let him come to New York City. Although our government did not officially recognize Arafat's presence, President Ford ordered the Secret Service to protect him. Outside of Israel, Manhattan may have been the most dangerous place in the world for him. We had to keep him safe. If he were killed in the United States, the whole world would believe we colluded in his death.

Arafat would be in the States for only eighteen hours, but his second in command, Farouk Kaddoumi, came early and stayed ten days. When he arrived at JFK Airport, Bill Duncan and I went there to greet him. We didn't have his photo, so I boarded the plane and called, "Farouk Kaddoumi, Farouk Kaddoumi." A hand went up, and I said, "Follow me." He was working his prayer beads. We took him to a mobile lounge, and he sat down. He was wide eyed and trembling. I asked, "Are you Farouk Kaddoumi?" and he shook his head. We had the wrong guy! The real Kaddoumi was still on the airplane!

Fortunately, the foreign passengers had not yet been allowed to disembark. Back on the plane, I again announced,

"Will the real Farouk Kaddoumi please come with me?" I don't know what he expected, but he came along. As Arafat's deputy and designated successor, he was number two in the PLO hierarchy. He had attended American University and spoke perfect English. As it turned out, we got along well.

More than sixty agents were assigned to the detail. Don Edwards from the Foreign Dignitary Division coordinated the advances. Ham Brown from Chicago headed transportation. Drivers were agents Ernie Graves and Jack Cliff. We had a first-class detail: guys with White House experience like Chuck Zboril, Bill Duncan, George Opfer.

Arafat would fly in on November 13, address the United Nations, and fly out before dawn the next morning. I had to figure out how to get him in and out of the airport, his hotel, and the UN building without public exposure. We wanted to keep Arafat off the New York streets as much as possible. I recalled Hal Thomas's mantra from the Humphrey days: "Don't fight 'em, fool 'em."

With Kaddoumi, the team leaders and I brainstormed a plan. We lined up hundreds of New York City police to run a motorcade from JFK to downtown Manhattan. We would put *Kaddoumi* in the motorcade and *Arafat* in one of eight helicopters that all looked alike. They were olive-drab, combat-style Army "Hueys."

Arafat arrived with five bodyguards of his own. The leader was Abu Hassan ("The Red Prince"). He was very, very tall and handsome. Suave. Debonair. He spoke English. I later learned Abu Hassan was not his real name. He was the PLO's answer to James Bond.

Arafat, on the other hand, was swarthy, short, and bald under the headdress he always wore. Personal charisma, not looks, was the source of his power. As soon as he landed, Kaddoumi told him, "You're going by helicopter. I'm going by motorcade to throw people off. We'll mix the helicopters up in the air. There will be eight; no one will know whether you're in a car or one of the helicopters." Arafat nodded agreement.

As I sat in the helicopter with Arafat, his team, and Bill Duncan, the air was so thick with tension it was hard to breathe. The PLO bodyguards were restless, eyes darting everywhere, feet tapping a nervous tattoo. They were fully armed and kept touching their weapons. They seemed so uptight I wondered whether this was their first time in a chopper. Arafat and I may have been the calmest people there. He trusted his men. I trusted our plan—and God.

This was the first time a helicopter ever landed on the UN grounds. Arafat spoke English, and I told him, "When we hit the ground, you must *run* to the armored car," which Ernie Graves was driving. It was about forty feet away. He said, "I understand." He ran. We drove the last hundred yards from where the helicopter landed to where he entered the UN.

There were no magnetometers to check for weapons.

Arafat went in and gave his speech, which ended with an ominous warning: "Today I have come bearing an olive branch and a freedom fighter's gun. Do not let the olive branch fall from my hand. I repeat: do not let the olive branch fall from my hand."

Arafat was tired and wanted to go to the Waldorf, his hotel. By the time he finished speaking, darkness had fallen. Now we could not avoid the streets, where furious New Yorkers lined the road to the hotel, screaming for blood.

It was time for "Plan Two": another motorcade.

Everyone at the United Nations watched us put the chairman in a black limousine. But about six cars back, there was another armored limo, "off the record." That is, it was armored but looked like a regular car. We exited the UN by tunnel, and right in the middle of the tunnel I stopped the motorcade. I explained to Arafat, "We're going to change cars." We had a heavy armored cape for him and he removed his burnoose. His bald head showed, and the awkward cape came up to his neck. But he was very dignified and quickly changed places with Jimmy Zedee, a New York policeman of Arab extraction, who took his place in the limousine. We drove out of the UN tunnel with the decoy in place.

Another first that day was the "muscle car" in the motorcade. It carried the "CAT" (counterassault team), with Kevin Hoolihan, Ken Lynch, Joe Carlon, and Art Rivers.

Along with maybe a thousand hostile demonstrators at the Waldorf, there must have been three hundred media types waiting in the "well," the entrance where VIPs emerged from their limos, protected from the weather. To get there, a car must pass another entrance on 50th Street. Well, the decoy ahead of us went up into the well, and while everyone was craning to see Arafat emerge from the limo, we stopped at the 50th Street entrance. Arafat without his burnoose, a couple of agents, and I just walked into the hotel, stepped into the service elevator, and rode up to his room—while the manager, all the press, and the hotel security officers were in the well. We didn't say a word to anybody. When we entered the suite, about forty agents were on duty with guns and shotguns—because we really were prepared for any trouble!

I heard that when Jimmy Zedee got out of that car, the people waiting in the well went nuts! They knew they'd been had. The manager—and even the hotel security officer—never could believe that we got Yasser Arafat into that hotel. But Don Edwards, Bill Duncan, and Chuck Zboril can attest to it. They were there.

As I left him at his room, Arafat said, "You can expect me to call you early in the morning."

I said, "We'll be ready." I liked working with him, because he knew how to be secure.

He said, "When I leave, I just want to go quietly. I want to go to the airport and get on an Algerian airliner to Havana."

"No problem. You tell us when you want to go."

At four o'clock in the morning we left in four cars, one of which was that unmarked armored car. We simply rode down in the service elevator. A New York police officer assigned to us appeared to be sleeping—on duty—at the elevator site. We walked right past him, got in the cars, and left. We crossed the Triboro Bridge, drove to the airport, put

Arafat on his airplane, and he left with Abu Hassan and his security team.

A postscript: I later learned that Abu Hassan's real name was Ali Hassan Salameh. He was chief of operations for Black September, the organization that had carried out the 1972 Munich Massacre. He lived an ostentatious playboy life and was rumored to be a conduit between the CIA and PLO, though the CIA denied this. Educated in Germany, he purportedly received military training in Cairo and Moscow and was fluent in at least four languages. In 1978 he married Georgina Rizk, a former Miss Lebanon who in 1971 had been named Miss Universe.

Under Golda Meir and continued by Menachem Begin, Israel pursued a secret plan to kill everyone connected to the Munich murders. And, systematically, they did it. Israeli Mossad operatives tracked Salameh to Beirut. He and four bodyguards with him—perhaps the very men I knew in New York—perished in a car bomb explosion on January 22, 1979.

And here's the most chilling thing I later learned: when we all climbed into the helicopter taking Yasser Arafat from JFK Airport to the United Nations on November 13, Abu Hassan and his companions were carrying live grenades, which they planned to detonate had the helicopter veered off the route to the UN. They didn't trust us.

I'll always wonder whether Arafat knew his "protectors" were prepared to kill everyone on the helicopter, including him, before allowing him to be taken prisoner.

CHAPTER 8

UP AND DOWN
THE LADDER

All who exalt themselves will be humbled,
and all who humble themselves will be exalted.

MATTHEW 23:12

1976-1981

I checked my watch again and steeled myself. In five minutes I was going to have a very tough conversation. One that would be painful for my colleague, the chief of the Executive Protective Service (EPS). And painful for me.

My mission: to persuade him to change his management style—or else. Considering what I'd heard in my new role as an inspector, it would not be easy.

For the first time in eleven years I was not assigned to protection. Since I had spent only two years in field offices (New York and Nashville), my career had become lopsided. I hadn't followed the usual track, to alternate between the field and protection. One reason was I was good at protection, and Headquarters believed they needed me there. But by reassigning me, they were not only developing my career but also doing me a personal favor. When Carolyn was accepted to Georgetown University law school, Secret Service director Stu Knight promised to keep me in DC for three more years to allow Carolyn to complete her degree without interruption. But I still needed to familiarize myself with other aspects of Secret Service work if I was going to move up. So instead of going to lead a field office, on December 7, 1975, I went from Foreign Dignitaries to the Office of Inspection. This change allowed me to leave protection and reacquaint myself with field operations while still based in Washington.

Inspectors were GS-15s, a high grade in government and a lateral move from my Deputy SAIC job. We traveled to field offices and other divisions to interview the Special Agents in Charge and other employees and to check out their systems, statistics, and paperwork. Our goal was to understand each office's particular challenges and to solve problems. We then wrote a report to the director.

We also investigated serious disciplinary matters: an employee's arrest, breaches of security, or complaints from the public or Congress. Sometimes our arrival was seen as good news; usually not so much.

A hernia operation almost caused me to miss the biggest assignment of my inspection career. Until the surgery I had never taken a single day of sick leave in thirteen years as an agent. If I'd known what I was stepping into, I might have taken another week off and let someone else handle the EPS assignment.

Jimmy Carter was now president. His first cousin, Hugh Carter, a White House aide, had gotten to know some of the EPS officers. They were the uniformed officers who protected the White House outer perimeter and foreign embassies in the United States. They had complained to him about their work situation. So the director called me in and said, "Take a team and go look at morale over there." I had no idea of the Pandora's box I was about to open.

Having learned from earlier crises about the value of listening, I took Tim McIntyre, George Hollendersky, and Dick Hankinson, good listeners all, and we simply showed up unannounced at EPS roll call in the White House basement early one morning. When I said, "We've come over to look at morale," the EPS officers laughed for five minutes! I noticed a framed picture of their boss—who never visited the basement—with a big technical security sticker pasted over his face. Other stuff was happening: an anonymous caller had sent a hearse to the chief's home.

His officers hated him.

It didn't take a genius to know the press would blow this problem out of proportion if it wasn't fixed. We were, after all, in the White House.

I told the officers, "We're going to interview every one of you who wants to talk. We'll keep what you say confidential. And we'll give you each as much time as you need." In field office inspections we normally interviewed employees, but this was a huge operation. I didn't really expect more than a dozen to want to talk.

I was wrong. They lined up, three deep! We had to bring in three more inspectors to handle the number. We interviewed more than six hundred people, one at a time. It took nearly four months.

The problem was the chief's autocratic, top-down management style. He hadn't come up through the ranks; he came from the DC Metropolitan Police into a culture that was working well and imposed his regime without any understanding (or consultation) about the effects of his changes.

A huge source of misery was mandatory rotations. People were now being forced to change shifts every two weeks. (This was also a problem for Secret Service agents, but with all our travel and advances, set shifts were often impossible. We had never known anything else.)

Under the prior chief a routine had developed that accommodated individual differences. Some officers liked midnights because they could study when things were quiet and go to college during the day. Or if they had working spouses, the couple could manage child care without the cost of a sitter. Some officers enjoyed meeting people and liked the posts at the gates. Others were more introverted and preferred posts away from the public. People could keep their assignments on a long-term basis.

Mandatory rotations turned people's lives upside down. The disruptions seemed unnecessarily arbitrary, even cruel.

One inspector fought back tears when he told me some of the stories he was hearing.

The more we learned, the bigger the investigation grew. I told the director, "We've got a time bomb here."

By the time I met with the EPS chief, I had the full picture. I wasn't sure what to expect from the meeting. Most of the inspectors had wanted to fire him on the spot, but I still hoped he would be willing to change. After what I'd heard, I realized the chances were slim. But in a confrontation I usually felt sorry for the loser, at least momentarily. Perhaps to spare myself, I stubbornly sought a happy ending. I laid everything out in plain English, but I tried to be tactful. "You have a lot of disappointed men and women, Chief. This morale problem is interfering with the mission."

He snapped, "Who's saying this? I want names!"

"I'm sorry, Chief," I said, "but we promised not to divulge that information. It's not just one or two people. The unhappiness is very widespread."

Red with rage, he sputtered, "I'll find out who the s.o.b.s are. They'll pay for this!"

That did it. The chief's style might work in the military or in other settings, but it wasn't working here.

Nevertheless, the chief deserved to be treated with dignity and respect. He was eligible to retire, and after a talk with Knight, he did. EPS was reorganized: it would be led by Assistant Director John Simpson, who would report directly to Director Knight. Simpson, a strong but compassionate leader, made immediate improvements. One was to open a path for EPS officers to become regular agents if they finished college.

Soon after, I received a personal letter from Director Knight:

June 6, 1977

Dear Jerry:
I want to commend you and your group for your enlightening and in-depth reports on the recently concluded study of the Executive Protective Service.
This most sensitive and challenging task was performed under difficult circumstances. The manner in which you and your associates conducted yourselves was most professional.
This was an important assignment and the results of your efforts are already evident. The improved morale and more effective operation of the Executive Protective Service will be a direct outgrowth of this team effort.
My sincere appreciation to you, Thomas Behl, Tim McIntyre, George Hollendersky, John Cook, Richard Hankinson, and Ned Hall.

Very truly yours,
H. S. Knight

* * *

I'd guarded a major contender in every presidential election: Humphrey for vice president in '64, Humphrey for president in '68, Agnew for vice president in '72, and in June 1976 I was temporarily pulled out of inspection to head another candidate detail. In my nonpartisan job, I was switching sides once again. This time the candidate would be a Democrat.

President Ford's opponent was Governor Jimmy Carter of Georgia, a newcomer on the national stage. Against the sordid backdrop of Watergate, Carter's outsider status gave him an advantage. A Naval Academy graduate who had served on America's first nuclear submarine, a Baptist, and a successful peanut farmer from tiny Plains, Georgia, Carter seemed a fresh and compassionate antidote to the cloak-and-dagger politics of the Nixon era. Voters liked his reputation for independent thinking, attacking government waste, and ending segregation in Georgia.

Carter chose Senator Walter "Fritz" Mondale from Minnesota as his running mate; I would lead Mondale's security.

Mondale was a liberal Democrat, a "boy wonder" sent to Washington in 1964 at the age of thirty-six to fill Hubert Humphrey's Senate seat when Humphrey became vice president. He'd won election in his own right in '66 and reelection in '72. More liberal than Carter, he brought both political and geographical balance to the ticket. I knew him as cochair of Humphrey's primary campaign for president in '68. After the Democratic Convention riots he'd said, "I didn't leave Chicago. I escaped it."

I could resonate with that.

I was with Mondale in New York on November 2, 1976,

when Carter defeated Gerald Ford. Next morning Mondale celebrated with Carter in Plains, a tiny Georgia town with a population of 653. There I met the president-elect for the first time. We didn't spend a lot of time together then, but perhaps because we shared Southern roots, I felt comfortable in his presence. After the election, I returned to inspection for another year and a half until I had the privilege of returning as special agent in charge (SAIC) of Mondale's detail in June 1978.

I was as happy as Brer Rabbit to be going back into the briar patch of protection.

But before I would officially change jobs, I needed to put a few pieces in place. Carolyn had graduated from Georgetown with honors in 1977, had passed the Maryland bar, and had begun to try tax cases for the IRS in the United States Tax Court. It was time for us to take a long-postponed family vacation with three weeks of my "use-or-lose" leave time. Since I was between divisions on May 16 when I made the request, I had to get permission from Bob Powis, the assistant director for Protective Operations. He and I hadn't always seen eye to eye, and I wasn't sure he'd grant it. In my memo I tried to cover all possible objections up front:

> I have planned to take 120 hours annual leave in August of this year with your approval.
>
> The other supervisors at VPPD know the dates involved, July 30 to August 20, 1978. We will work around these dates accordingly, and there will be no problems with adequate supervisory coverage.

I have rented a 25′ RV and plan to take the family west to California and return via the southern route. None of the family except myself has been west of the Mississippi River.

Since there is considerable expense involved in this trip, I am making the annual leave request at this time.

Since I'll be on the road most of the time, I plan to call in every other day to make contact with the Division.

Permission was granted. Carolyn's boss at the IRS also agreed, and the whole family started to study maps and campgrounds and the etiquette of camping in RVs.

Ours came equipped with a shortwave radio, the kind truckers use on the road, and Kimberly, now sixteen years old, read up on trucker jargon. "Smokey" was a code word for the highway patrol. While I had fleeting feelings of guilt at the notion of trying to avoid fellow cops, just maneuvering that twenty-five-foot vehicle was enough to occupy my mind. Kim got a kick out of her conversations with drivers of 18-wheelers.

Our first few days went well, but when the RV started to cough, we limped into the first gas station we could find. It was in a little town called Oakley, Kansas.

When we pulled in, the mechanic-owner diagnosed the problem and held out his keys. "I'm afraid you'll have to spend the night," he said. "You can take my car." I was astonished. *Is this what they mean by Midwest hospitality?* I wondered.

Oakley was less than two square miles in size. And flat. From where we stood in the garage, we could see the motel, a restaurant, and a movie theater. So we gratefully declined the car keys and decided to walk around town.

The town limits were obvious because that's where the houses stopped. Abruptly. At the edge of town, fields of wheat and other crops stretched as far as the eye could see. We drifted into a tiny museum of local history and were surprised by a photo exhibition of Oakley's founding fathers and mothers: among the earliest settlers was a family of black pioneers.

Coming out, we heard what sounded like carousel music. We came upon a county fair—out in somebody's field. Not only a carousel but a Ferris wheel, games, hot dogs, and lots of 4-H club exhibits. Eight-year-old Trish petted baby and grown farm animals and stared at the huge vegetables raised by children not much older than her. Teens the age of Kim and Jennifer proudly displayed clothes they'd designed and sewn themselves. Women stood behind their prizewinning pies and cakes. With a silent smile I imagined that, had we lived in Oakley, Jennifer would have captured a cooking prize: when she was only twelve, she'd made our entire Thanksgiving dinner from scratch, including a golden stuffed turkey and a cinnamony pumpkin pie! I identified with the farmers checking out the tractors. It felt like we'd stepped into a 1930s movie. Carolyn asked, "Where's Judy Garland?"

After lunch at the fair, the kids begged to go to the movie matinee in town. Like a good dad I shelled out cash for tickets and popcorn. But Carolyn and I decided to skip *The Incredible Melting Man*. We let them go alone. It was starting to feel safe here in Oakley.

Next day we picked up the RV, now in perfect shape. I asked hesitantly, "Will you take a check on an out-of-town bank?" The owner said, "Sure." I pulled out my driver's license, but he waved it off. "I'm sure it's good," he said.

This was not Oz—it was Kansas. And it was wonderful.

During this period of my career, in the stability of my now less-frantic schedule, our family found roots in a new faith community. Heritage Christian Church was a small and diverse congregation with a big heart. The first time Carolyn and I walked in, we saw a living sermon before Pastor Dick Miller even spoke a word. Two church elders greeted us at the door: Junior Crowell, a distinguished-looking white man I judged to be in his seventies, and Franklin Gee, a young African American real estate agent. Joanne and Floyd Jamsa came in with four children of different races: one was their biological child and three were adopted.

Judge Eugene Hamilton, an African American, and his wife, Ginny, pushed wheelchairs down the aisle on which sat identical twin children with cerebral palsy—white kids. I learned they had taken in dozens of hard-to-place kids of every race, some straight from the judge's DC Superior Court, where social workers brought them from abusive or negligent parents.

A couple across the aisle from us arrived with a child with Down syndrome who was happily embraced by the congregation and passed from lap to lap during the service. A woman presided over Communion; another chaired the congregation—our first church with women leaders. From the bulletin I also learned that Heritage members tutored neighborhood kids after school and ran a used clothes and grocery distribution center.

We had never belonged to a church like this, and we were thrilled. This community looked the way I imagine the heavenly banquet will, where everyone is welcome.

Another positive change in our home life came shortly after I took charge of Mondale's protection. Carolyn loved being a trial attorney, and the extra income allowed us to move from Silver Spring to North Potomac, Maryland. We bought a large, brand-new house on two acres with a swimming pool and a forest behind us full of deer and wildlife and a stream that ran into the Potomac River. I planted apple and peach trees and raised chickens and a turkey that followed me everywhere I went. With my little tractor, big garden, and poultry I fancied myself a farmer. I thought about my dad, who grew up on a farm in Ohio and always loved nature and living creatures. I missed him.

The space evoked my contemplative nature. I loved to sit outside amid the natural beauty and feel close to God. I read the Bible and also continued to be inspired by Thomas Merton. About that time Pastor Dick introduced me to another Catholic contemplative writer and activist, Henri

Nouwen, in person and through his writings. Nouwen would later become a personal friend.

Our new place was idyllic—except for the longer commute to work and my worry about our teenagers' daily drive back to their old high school (which we hesitantly allowed). And Heritage Christian Church was now more than twenty miles away.

✷ ✷ ✷

My promotion to SAIC of the VPPD for Mondale became official September 18, 1978.

Though my team members now addressed me as "Mr. Parr" or "sir," I was proud to be a simple agent. Even later on, when I became assistant director of the Secret Service, I always answered my phone "Agent Parr." It sometimes evoked surprised laughter on the other end—and sometimes distress by peers who considered it undignified. But I really thought of myself as an agent first. I didn't dwell on my job title, and I never demanded respect but always received it.

By this time I understood security at all levels, from standing post to leading complex advances to relating to world leaders at the highest levels. Administration, however, was never my strong suit. Fortunately, I was blessed with great deputies: Barney Boyett on VPPD, then Bob DeProspero on PPD and Ed Walsh in Protective Research.

Jimmy Taylor had left Mondale's detail in good shape. It had the strength of experience and the eagerness of youth.

I was glad because I wanted to avoid the "box phenomenon." That's the trap a detail can get caught in when there's an imbalance of youth and experience. Advances are critical and often complicated. But if the most-experienced agents are out on advance and the Man is surrounded with new agents, there's added danger in case of attack. On the other hand, if all the new agents are doing advances, then risk increases away from home. Agents can get trapped in one box or another. I tried to open the ends of the box, to maintain a flow of experience to enthusiastic young agents from veterans who could mentor them and to move agents back and forth between personal protective assignments and advances.

I expected to stay with Mondale quite a while.

I didn't hear Mondale talk much about God, but I knew that Walter Mondale's father was a Methodist minister with a strong social conscience, and the vice president grew up believing that Christians should help the poor. His wife, Joan, was also a preacher's kid. As a college student Mondale had helped Hubert Humphrey get elected mayor. After law school Mondale managed Orville Freeman's race for governor of Minnesota in 1958. The next year Governor Freeman appointed him state attorney general, at thirty-one, the youngest in America. Mondale prosecuted consumer fraud and protected civil rights. He won reelection twice by wider margins than any other state candidate. Like his mentor Humphrey, he was passionate about lifting the underdog.

In his interview with Carter, Mondale had made it clear he was not interested in a ceremonial vice presidency; he'd rather remain a senator in that case. That impressed Carter. He gave Mondale an office in the West Wing and ordered his staff to work closely with Mondale's people. Unlike his predecessors, Carter would rely strongly on Mondale's advice and would bring him into every important meeting and decision.

Middle East peace talks were no exception.

Perhaps because of his strong biblical roots, President Carter longed to see peace in the Middle East. He convened a meeting between Egypt's president, Anwar Sadat, and Israel's prime minister, Menachem Begin, which began at Camp David on September 5, 1978. The president took two old enemies and put them in a monastic environment—with a skeletal staff and no press—where they had to talk to each other. And they did. I saw Begin and Sadat walking side by side on a wooded path at Camp David, alone.

Carter's role began as mediator but progressed to active participant, including drafting the final agreement. The US team was Secretary of State Cyrus Vance, Secretary of Defense Harold Brown, and National Security Advisor Zbigniew Brzezinski. Since Carter remained on-site, Mondale stayed in Washington to handle whatever might come up.

But on the evening of September 14, 1978, President Carter urgently summoned the vice president to Camp David. After eight days of intense back and forth, negotiations were faltering. The parties seemed to have hit an impasse. Carter knew the Israelis trusted Mondale and thought his presence could be crucial in getting the talks unstuck.

At 10:55 on the night of September 14, we took a

helicopter, Marine 2, from DC to Camp David and landed in the middle of what looked like a failure. Mondale went directly to the cabin where Vance and Brzezinski were meeting. I was not privy to the talks and can't say what happened. But the stalemate was broken. Eleven days after the talks began—and three days after Mondale arrived—Begin and Sadat signed the Camp David Accords on September 17, 1978.

Looking back, it still seems to me that getting the agreement was a brilliant diplomatic coup. It would be the crowning achievement of Carter's presidency. It didn't buy him much traction from the US public, but it won him the Nobel Peace Prize.

I was with Mondale only a year—not long enough even to see his family move into the official vice president's mansion at the Naval Observatory, the first vice president to actually live there. While I was in charge of the VPPD, my old friend John Simpson headed the White House detail. In May 1979 an announcement from Headquarters came in over the wires: Simpson would be promoted to assistant director of Protective Operations.

I was honored—and humbled—to be chosen to lead the Presidential Protective Division.

* * *

Lost in the lush sound of Beethoven's Fifth Symphony, I was jarred back to reality by the insistent buzz of my pager.

Offering up a silent prayer of thanks for my aisle seat in the darkened Kennedy Center, I whispered to Carolyn, "Sit tight" as I left to take the call in the lobby.

Roger Counts was calling from Camp David. "The president ran out of gas."

"What was he driving?" I couldn't understand why that was an emergency.

"Not that kind of gas," Roger explained. "Oxygen. He was jogging up a hill here, trying to outrun some younger guys. They saw him turning gray and tried to get him to stop, but he kept going. Then his eyes rolled back and he collapsed. Jack Smith, Dale Wilson, and I threw him in the car and took him back to Aspen."

"Aspen" was the name of the central cabin at Camp David, where people ate communally and larger meetings took place.

I knew that hill. Carter had run up it twice before, to practice. On this day he was with runners in their twenties, and he wanted to race, to run and run and run. He couldn't keep up, but he wouldn't quit. His spirit was willing, but his flesh was weak. His body shut down.

Roger continued, "Dr. Voss got a line of glucose in him. He's okay now, but it's going to be in tomorrow's *Washington Post*, so I thought you should know."

I went back to the concert hall, but my ability to get lost in the music had vanished. I was concerned about this news but not surprised. I had already learned that Carter was a president who loved to take risks.

Going from vice presidential security to the White House was like moving from a suburban house to a palace. (In fact, before the Mondales occupied the new vice presidential mansion, that had been literally true.) The difference can be summed up in four letters: M-O-R-E. With a president there is more of everything. More threats. More agents. More press attention. More micromanagement from Headquarters. More perks.

And much, much more anxiety.

Since 1968—an aberrant year in every respect—only a few people have wanted to kill a vice president. But as the nation's ultimate authority figure, a president attracts crazies. A deranged person may see him as a neglectful or abusive father. To a religious fanatic, he may be the Antichrist. A revolutionary may hold the president responsible for the oppression of his or her people. A Nazi may believe the president wants to destroy the white race. Whatever the delusion, and whoever holds it, many people see the president of the United States as the ultimate enemy.

Mondale attracted very few threats. But like all other presidents, Carter drew hundreds a day. Credible threats: people who had the will to kill and the means to follow through.

About forty-five agents now guarded the vice president, but the White House detail had one hundred twenty. Administration and logistics were magnified: scheduling shifts, advances, days off, reviews, times for physicals and for shooting. Fortunately, I could rely on Bob DeProspero to cover that. But since I thought it important to know the agents on a personal level, I practiced "management by walking around." I often dropped in to W-16, the Secret Service work space directly beneath the Oval Office, just to take the pulse. It made me accessible and kept me in the loop about potential problems in a way I could not be if I stayed in my office all day.

There was another change I had to get used to: all day, every day, the national press scrutinize a president for the smallest misstatement or mistake. They watch us, as well. Regardless of political party, I learned that most presidential staffs—and most Secret Service leaders—regard the press with suspicion.

Tensions also arise between every White House staff and security. We have different jobs: they look after the president's political health, and we look after his safety. One requires high visibility; the other sometimes favors high fences.

I refused to buy into the notion that press and staff were the enemies of security. They had their jobs; we had ours. Sometimes we clashed. But whenever possible, by speaking respectfully and frankly about any problem that arose, I sought a collaborative win-win solution. I did understand the danger of being sucked into their differing agendas, and I hope I avoided that. But I treated White House press and staff as friends and colleagues. I got to know Helen Thomas, Sam Donaldson, Bill Plante, Judy Woodruff, Andrea Mitchell, and others. Chris Matthews, now host of MSNBC's *Hardball*, was a young speechwriter for Carter. As a former Capitol Hill police officer, Matthews shared an affinity of spirit with the agents. He still does.

I didn't realize it then, but the bread I was casting on the water would come back to me very soon.

Privileges came with the job as well as headaches. I could park on the White House grounds. I had a huge, beautiful office in the Old Executive Office Building. I rode on Air Force One. I could eat at the most exclusive dining room in Washington: the White House mess. The name is misleading—the dining room is more like that of an elegant private club, with a lovely formal setting. China and crystal, table linens, gourmet menu. Uniformed waiters. (I did get a monthly bill for my meals.)

Absolutely anyone—generals, senators, cabinet members, top media celebrities—would take my phone calls. It's a good thing I was nearly fifty years old and had a wife who kept me grounded. This was heady stuff.

But I never forgot for a single moment that my charge was to keep the leader of the free world alive. The thought of what could happen shadowed my days and troubled my dreams. A special telephone line direct to the White House was installed in my Potomac den. It seldom rang, but if it did, whoever was in the house sprang to answer it. Most often, in later years, it was Mrs. Reagan with a question or suggestion or concern—which I always took to heart. Once a king was on the other end of the line.

I began as "acting" SAIC on July 1; the promotion was official August 26, 1979. But my work with President Carter actually began before both dates.

From June 14 to June 18 I accompanied the president

to Vienna, where he participated in the Strategic Arms Limitations Talks (SALT II) negotiations with Leonid Brezhnev. They reached agreement and signed the treaty on June 18. Although it was never ratified by the US Senate—at least partly because in December the Soviets invaded Afghanistan—both sides honored the treaty until Reagan withdrew, accusing the Soviets of violations.

While I was still in acting SAIC status, President Carter decided to cruise down the upper Mississippi River on the *Delta Queen*, an American stern-wheel steamboat that is a national historic monument. Built in 1927, it is 285 feet long, 58 feet wide, and draws 11.5 feet. It can carry 176 passengers. Carter's route would take him from St. Paul, Minnesota, to St. Louis, Missouri, a distance of about fifteen hundred miles. He would stop along the route to meet and greet folks from Middle America.

The logistics required were enough to give me a second hernia. I thought perhaps the tour with Emperor Hirohito had been a practice run for this. Sometimes God's gifts are only recognized in looking back.

Since Carter was the first protectee in the twentieth century to take a riverboat cruise, the security planning was unprecedented. Between St. Paul and St. Louis lay the towns of Prairie du Chien, Wisconsin; Dubuque, Davenport, and Burlington, Iowa; Hannibal, Missouri (birthplace of Mark Twain); and numerous others. The Mississippi runs downhill. Beyond St. Louis the country is flat, but the president's chosen route took the *Delta Queen* through twenty-six locks and dams. In each we would be temporarily immobilized and helpless.

What we had was a nineteenth-century conveyance with a twentieth-century president aboard, moving seven miles an hour down a river with banks within shooting distance on both sides. This chicken gizzard was impossible to chew! We had to cover both sides of the river: three thousand miles of shoreline. We put human beings on every bridge. We advanced each stop and each lock. Two countersniper teams rode on board, continuously scanning the banks through binoculars for potential danger.

As commander in chief, the president required instant capacity to leave in case of an attack or nuclear war. This meant we had to be accompanied by a Coast Guard river ship big enough to carry a presidential helicopter.

During the daytime a second helicopter circled above us for surveillance ahead and behind. Following along the shoreline would be a skeletal motorcade: an armored car, a backup vehicle, and an SUV to carry agents and critical staff in case at any point we had to abort the cruise.

All the way, day and night, we needed fast watercraft escorts for two purposes: to prevent other boats from approaching and to outrun an aggressor in case of attack. A lot of Coast Guard auxiliary members volunteered. But after the first night—when they realized this was going to be a 24-7 operation—they peeled off and left it to the Coast Guard regulars.

Everyone—police, Coast Guard, Secret Service, helicopter

pilots—had to be connected by a radio matrix set up and monitored by the White House Communications Agency.

Steve Garmon and I shared supervision for the whole spectacle. From the time we started on August 17 until we disembarked on August 24, I never got more than four hours' sleep a night.

We constantly made creative adjustments. Often President Carter left the boat to run. We radioed ahead for the location of a high school track. He really could run: at Burlington, Iowa, he ran four miles flat in twenty-eight minutes—four seven-minute miles—at the age of nearly fifty-five! He liked to compete with the younger agents I assigned to run with him: Larry Cunningham, Jack Smith, and Doug Laird. He loved the challenge. Once he asked me, "Jerry, why don't you run with me?"

"Mr. President," I said, "I only have so many heartbeats, and I don't want to waste any." I wasn't about to let him prove he could outrun me!

One night on the river a huge thunderstorm engulfed us. Lightning struck all around, and the radar went white with hail and rain. Carter, a former naval officer, went up and stood in the pilot's cabin. Our pilot was the best riverboat man on the Mississippi, brought out of retirement for this assignment. He seemed a little worried. He said, "I don't want this wind to get behind us."

An eighty-mile-an-hour wind buffeted the ship; I thought the glass was going to break. I told the president, "We ought to get downstairs. This is really getting serious."

"I'll just stay for a few more minutes," he said. And he did. More accurately, *we* did.

The captain said, "If that wind gets off to the side, we'll be pushed around. I don't want it to push us back toward a lock." The smaller escort boats were already being blown all over the river, calling, "Mayday! Mayday! Mayday!" With a lot of effort they managed to get to shore and tie off.

We couldn't do that—the wind could have broken the ship, pounding us against whatever we were tied to. Instead, the captain drove that riverboat right into the bank, head-first! He kept the steam engine at full blast and the paddle wheel going the whole time, positioning the curved bow on the bank so that it could slide off if necessary. When the wind passed, he just reversed the paddle wheel and backed off into the river. It was brilliant.

Carter took a lot of chances. Once, impatient with the two minutes it took to lay down the gangplank, he climbed up on the ship's rail and leaped from the boat to the dock. Had he slipped, he'd have fallen maybe thirty feet into the space between. And had he survived the fall, he could have been crushed by the movement of the ship.

The trip was well publicized, and crowds gathered along the shore to watch the *Delta Queen* and its retinue pass by. One evening in the dark we could see that a large crowd had gathered. No event was planned there, but Carter ordered the boat to stop. Standing on the deck, he held a spotlight and shined it on himself while he spoke to the crowd. I died a thousand deaths. The crowd was in the dark with only a handful of security people; the president of the United States was a lit target. There was absolutely no way any agent could have spotted an assassin with a weapon. I just prayed the first shot would miss and I'd be able to push the president down fast enough. God was good.

* * *

When I first came to the PPD, the president; his wife, Rosalynn; and his young daughter, Amy, often went home to Plains. It was a hot and humid little farming town where he and Rosalynn grew up. The president loved to walk in the freshly plowed fields. I enjoyed walking with him. The musky scent of rich, damp soil awakened my sleeping farmer genes.

Carter would walk slowly, contemplatively, eyes downcast. One day I asked him why he always looked down. He said, "I'm looking for arrowheads. Our old plows dug twelve inches down and turned up many Cherokee relics. But the new plows have eighteen-inch blades. So older artifacts are showing up." From time to time he actually found some.

Carter took Jesus' saying "Blessed are the peacemakers" to heart. To that end, he had instituted a number of changes in US foreign policy, some before I came aboard and some after. He signed a controversial treaty returning the Panama Canal to Panama. He negotiated the arms limitation treaty with the Soviets. He established diplomatic ties with mainland China. And he organized and led the Camp David Accords.

The international community admired these initiatives, but they were not always welcomed by the American public, especially conservatives.

One day as Carter was delivering a White House briefing on SALT II, an invited guest stood up, approached the president, pulled out a glass container, and started dumping ashes on the carpet and all the furniture in arm's reach. I was standing in the back of the room; other agents were near the president, but they seemed paralyzed. As the protester headed toward the president, I rushed to the front, firmly grasped the gentleman's arm, and not so gently escorted him out. After the event was over, I gave the agents a little refresher course about why they were drawing a paycheck.

In June 1980 we went to Rome, Venice, Belgrade, and Lisbon and finished up in Madrid. The king of Spain shook hands with President Carter and then greeted me with a big smile. He said, "Jerry! How are you doing?" The president was puzzled: how would I know the king? The answer was I had protected him at foreign digs when he was Prince Juan Carlos, and he remembered me. In fact, one day the White House phone at my home rang, and he was on the other end. "Hi, Jerry. This is Juan Carlos. I'm in town and just called to say hello." If Juan Carlos had been a regular guy instead of a king, I think we'd have been good friends.

Despite the president's other foreign policy successes, on November 4, 1979, the framework for peace he was trying to build fell apart. Two weeks after the United States admitted the exiled and dying shah of Iran for cancer treatments in late October, militant Iranian students stormed our embassy in Tehran and took sixty-six United States citizens hostage.

This was a gross violation of international diplomatic protocol, which recognizes foreign embassies as the inviolable territory of another country. Henry Kissinger once said that diplomacy is the art of restraining power. A country can withdraw diplomatic relations, close its embassy, and leave, or it can declare an individual diplomat "persona non grata" (an unwelcome person) and send him or her home. But invading another country's embassy and capturing its citizens is almost tantamount to an act of war.

In spite of universal international condemnation, Iran's leader, Ayatollah Khomeini, praised the students' action. After a few days he did release thirteen hostages: five white women and eight African American men. One other hostage was released much later, suffering from MS. The remaining fifty-two prisoners were held 444 days.

The hostage takers demanded we return the shah for trial in Iran, plus give them billions of dollars they claimed he had stolen. The money was negotiable, but turning over a dying man who trusted us was not.

Historian Gaddis Smith said of the hostage taking that from its beginning "the crisis absorbed more concentrated effort by American officials and had more extensive coverage on television and in the press than any other event since World War II." It certainly absorbed President Carter. As a compassionate man and a peacemaker, he seemed torn about the right course of action.

Carter declared he would not go home to Plains until the hostages could come home. So he and Mrs. Carter and their daughter, Amy, celebrated Christmas at Camp David in 1979. The president invited three men to bring their families: his helicopter pilot, his personal physician, and me.

Carolyn, Kim, Jennifer, and Trish arrived by car on Christmas Eve. They were greeted with Christmas cookies, hot chocolate, and a warm fire in the Aspen lodge. Each family had a comfortably furnished, fully equipped log cabin to themselves. While I was on duty, Carolyn and the kids walked the forest paths in the crisp, cold air and drank in the star-filled night sky. We shared a traditional family-style Christmas dinner with the Carters in Aspen. Eleven-year-old Amy was so excited about her Christmas roller skates she wore them to the table. I appreciated the president's thoughtfulness in providing this opportunity to spend Christmas with my family in such a lovely setting.

Two days after Christmas the Soviets invaded Afghanistan. On January 20, 1980, Carter announced that the United States would boycott the summer Olympic Games in Moscow if the USSR did not withdraw. They didn't, and we did. We also stopped selling the Soviets our wheat, an act that hurt US farmers.

None of Carter's diplomatic attempts to get the hostages freed had any effect. Not unanimous international condemnation nor a freeze on Iranian assets nor expelling Iranian diplomats from the United States.

Not even secret, backdoor negotiations helped. For a

few days in February things looked hopeful when the newly elected president of Iran, Abolhassan Bani-Sadr, said he believed the hostage crisis could be solved quickly. He ordered the militants to turn over the hostages to the Revolutionary Council that he headed. They refused. He called them "dictators who have created a government within a government." But Khomeini supported the kidnappers, and the stalemate continued.

While President Carter sometimes took chances with his personal safety, he never wanted to risk harming others. But in desperation he approved a highly dangerous secret commando mission to free the hostages by force. In the predawn darkness of April 25, 1980, eight helicopters rendezvoused in the desert. A fierce sandstorm struck, forcing three choppers to return to their ship. Since at least six helicopters would be required to carry everyone out, and only five remained, the mission was aborted.

Then things got even worse. Preparing to leave the desert, but before taking off, eight men were killed and at least one survivor was horribly burned when a helicopter collided with a C-130 support aircraft in a refueling area at the site.

The United States was humiliated. With the element of surprise now blown, another rescue attempt would be impossible. The militants immediately dispersed the hostages to different parts of Tehran.

After that, Carter almost never smiled. I saw him losing weight. His grief for the hostages was now magnified by losing the rescuers. And, I imagined, he grieved for his own helplessness. A week after the failed rescue, he said, "Jerry, I want to fly to Texas. Keep this as quiet as you can. I don't want any publicity."

The president and I flew to Lackland Air Force Base in San Antonio, where I had done my basic training thirty years before. No press knew of the trip. Our destination was Brooke Army Medical Center, where a surviving pilot was being treated for severe burns.

As we walked into the hospital, I flashed back to Clark Air Force Base in Manila with Humphrey thirteen years before, where I'd witnessed firsthand the horrors of war. But this was my first time with burn victims; the Vietnam burns were sent to Japan.

At the burn center, a doctor led us to a huge window through which we could see a large room with several beds. Since this was peacetime, only one was filled. The lone patient was swathed from head to toe in bandages. Only his eyes, mouth, and nostrils were exposed. A nurse attended him. The only sound was the hiss of oxygen tanks and the musical *ping, ping* of machines connected to tubes that ran into different parts of the patient's body.

"He's conscious," the doctor said, "but we don't expect him to live."

President Carter said, "I'd like to go in and speak to him. May I?"

The doctor hesitated. He was, after all, in the US Army— and his commander in chief stood before him. But he wanted to protect his patient. After an awkward minute he explained his dilemma. "He's totally vulnerable to infection. We have to maintain a sterile field. If you go in, you'll have to dress in surgical greens and cover your nose and mouth."

Carter readily agreed. We both changed our clothes, covered our hair and shoes, and put on facial masks. But then Carter looked at me, and I thought, *He wants to go by himself. He wants private time with a man he sent into a situation that may have killed him or ruined his future.*

I recalled Jesus' words: "All who humble themselves will be exalted," and I thought, *This president is humbling himself. That takes a different kind of courage.*

The patient was physically vulnerable, but the president was making himself emotionally vulnerable. I said, "Mr. President, I don't have to go in. I'll just watch through the window."

Carter entered and stood beside the soldier's bed. Like the patient, only the president's eyes were visible. He said something, and the soldier turned his head very slowly toward the sound of the voice. Then this man, wrapped from head to toe in bandages and in unspeakable pain, raised one hand and saluted! Carter returned the salute.

Watching through the window, gratitude filled my heart and spilled down my cheeks. I knew I was witnessing a supreme act of compassion, a holy moment born of mutual pain and forgiveness.

When the president came out, neither of us said a word. There are times when silence is more profound than words could ever be.

The soldier lived.

The hostage crisis dominated the president's thoughts. It also dominated the consciousness of the press and public. But Americans were enduring serious economic and other domestic problems as well. During the Carter years, home mortgage rates climbed above 15 percent; the prime rate hit 21 percent. Consumer prices rose 18 percent in one year. Draft registration—which had ended after Vietnam—resumed. Gasoline prices skyrocketed in the face of an OPEC cartel, and long lines formed at the pumps. Four out of ten Americans stopped buying large American cars, and Japan led the auto industry.

The shah of Iran died in Egypt on July 27. But still the hostages did not come home.

Nineteen eighty found me once again in the midst of a presidential election. Ted Kennedy mounted a challenge, but President Carter (and Mondale) won easy renomination at the Democratic Convention in August. In a hard-fought contest, Ronald Reagan defeated Tennessee's Howard Baker, John Connally of Texas, Bob Dole, and George H. W. Bush for the GOP nomination. Reagan chose Bush as his running mate, and Baker later became his chief of staff.

After that, Carter's travel got a little crazy as he campaigned across the United States. We were in the air so much that I forgot my own birthday until the president's staff and flight crew emerged midflight from the galley with a birthday cake. On September 16, 1980, I celebrated my fiftieth birthday on Air Force One.

We hit about sixty towns in September and October,

ranging from huge cities like New York to small towns like Beaumont, Texas, and Bristol, Tennessee. In the first four days of November, we shot through eight more, including Springfield, Portland, and Seattle.

One night on the campaign trail in New Orleans, I got a report that a couple of guys were seen with guns. I told the president, "You can't work this rope line." He agreed, but as soon as we got to the speech site at the end of the rope line, he got out of the car, jumped up on the trunk, and then stood up on the roof of the car. I learned to pray with my eyes open.

Sometimes we had to improvise as we went along. One hot day in Kentucky, the president again was on top of a car. I sat up there with him, my left hand holding him by the back of his belt, my right hand free if I had to shoot. An agent inside the car opened a door to push back the crowd lining the street, and I steadied myself by jamming my foot into the crevice between the open door and the car frame. This technique was not in any training manual.

Dennis Finch drove slowly through the crowd, trying to see between the president's legs dangling down over the windshield. That wasn't in the manual either.

Since I couldn't complain about everything, I had to pick my battles. But if I did warn the president about something—with great seriousness—he listened and took my advice. Some things I just had to live with. We walked in a bubble of grace.

In any crowd agents look at hands and eyes. An agent

went along the rope line ahead of the president, saying to the crowd, "Please pull your hands out of your pockets. We need to see your hands."

At one stop Jimmy Ventola was working the rope line up ahead. I was on the president's left, and Tom Holman was behind him. Holman thought Ventola wasn't getting the hands out fast enough, and he shouted, "Talk to 'em, Jimmy! Talk to 'em!"

Carter turned around to Holman with a surprised look and said, "I *am* talking to 'em!"

Besides hands, we also look at eyes. Most people in a crowd are anticipatory, excited, happy to see the president. We look for eyes that glitter with hatred—or faces with no expression.

As I would learn a few months later, one young man with an expressionless face had been present at a rally in Dayton, Ohio, on October 2, 1980, and again in Nashville on October 9. He was stalking President Carter. He wanted to kill a president.

His name was John Hinckley Jr.

The last day of the campaign—November 3, 1980—was a heavy day. ASAIC Bob Horan and an eight-agent shift were with me. We started in the Midwest with two stops in Missouri and one in Michigan. We flew from there to Portland and Seattle. It was getting late. En route, the president got a report that the latest polls in key states indicated the election would not be close. He knew he had lost before he got to Portland. But there were big crowds waiting in

Portland and Seattle, and the president campaigned bravely to the end, knowing it was futile.

The air was thick with sadness late that night, flying back to Plains, where Carter would vote.

Reagan won 90.9 percent of the electoral votes. It was a crushing landslide. Like me, my youngest daughter, Trish, then ten years old, always hurts for the loser. When I got home, she asked me, "Daddy, how does the president feel?"

"Well, honey, he's grieving. And wounded."

"Will he ever feel better?"

I thought for a long minute before I answered. "Yes, I believe he will. God has called him to be a peacemaker. And God will make a way for him to answer that call."

* * *

Presidential transitions are always stressful. I decided to stay with Carter and send Bob DeProspero and a few key PPD agents to go with President-Elect Reagan. I made a revolving transition, sending people back and forth so Reagan and his staff would get to know us and how we worked, and vice versa.

There's a big difference between working a candidate, a president-elect, and a president. Reagan had been a candidate in '68, '72, and '76, so he already had three opportunities to work with the Secret Service. He knew John Simpson and a lot of agents. Somewhere in that interlude I met Reagan's chief of staff, Mike Deaver, and Mrs. Reagan. So when I rode to the inauguration with President Carter and President-Elect Reagan, in the backseat of the limousine together, my face was familiar to both of them. From my perspective it was an easy transition.

On Inauguration Day, the choreography at the White House is planned to the last second. The incoming president and spouse arrive, are greeted and enjoy a few minutes of friendly chatter with the current residents, get in a limo, and ride together to the Capitol, where the change in command will take place at high noon.

Then everything at the mansion goes into fast-forward. All photos of current occupants, as well as personal items, are wrapped, labeled, catalogued, boxed, and removed. Photos of the new president, selected ahead of time, are hung. This happens not only in the family living quarters, but also in all hallways, all offices of all prior staffers, the Oval Office— everywhere. All party symbols are changed. Closets are cleared out, and any unpacked clothing is boxed and shipped to the former first family's forwarding address. It's a massive undertaking. And it's always done unobtrusively and to perfection in about three hours' time.

Until the very last minute, President Carter had continued to seek release of the hostages. Then, on the morning of the inauguration, word came that the hostages were sitting in an airplane on the runway in Tehran, preparing to take off.

Before we got in the limousine, Carter said, "Jerry, I've given instructions for the military to radio you the minute the airplane takes off. If I'm still president, I don't care what's happening, you let me know. Will you?"

"Yes, sir. I will." I was touched by Carter's trust.

President Reagan knew about this and agreed.

All during the inauguration I listened for the word that never came. As he left the podium after the ceremony to board a helicopter, Carter caught my eye. He sounded weary. "They never called, did they?"

"No, Mr. President. No one called. I'm sorry." He just looked down at his feet, seemed to gather his thoughts, and walked away.

The ayatollah had his revenge. Thirty minutes after Ronald Reagan became president, the hostages were airborne for Germany.

CHAPTER 9

SHOTS FIRED! MEN DOWN!

We few, we happy few, we band of brothers;
For he today that sheds his blood with me
Shall be my brother.

WILLIAM SHAKESPEARE, *Henry V*

MARCH 30, 1981

President Reagan and I were six or seven feet from the open car door when I heard two staccato shots, followed by four more. Loud, shrill, piercing—stinging the ear. A sound I recognized from years of shooting practice. I'd been waiting for that sound for almost nineteen years and hoping it would never come.

But I didn't think about that. No time to think. Training and muscle memory took over.

At the sound of the first shot I was already moving. *Cover and evacuate.* I grabbed President Reagan by the back of his belt and pants, pushed his head down with my right hand, and hurled him into the car. At the same moment Ray Shaddick thrust us both forward. We flew into the limo behind Tim McCarthy—who faced the shooter and spread out his big Irish body to extend the protection of the armored door as we threw the president behind it.

Reagan extended his arms to block the fall, his chest smashing into the transmission riser with my full weight on top of him, his head hitting the seat. Then Shaddick shoved our feet and legs in and slammed the door behind us.

"Get out of here! Go! Go! Go!" I yelled. Three seconds from the time the first shot was fired, the limo took off.

Driver Drew Unrue hit the gas, and we burned out, heading for "Crown"—the White House, the safest place. As I helped the president to a sitting position, I noticed a mark on the right rear bulletproof window. That window had stopped a shot. Through the back window, I saw three men down on the sidewalk. I began to absorb it: *Someone really tried to kill the president.*

Unlike President Carter, Reagan paid attention to security. A three-time candidate, he'd always worked well with the Secret Service. He had formed a personal relationship with the temporary detail that protected him when he sought the Republican nomination in 1976. In fact, after losing to Ford, Reagan wrote detail leader Joe Parris:

October 7, 1976

Dear Joe:
This is to report serious deficiencies in the security at both the Palisades location and Rancho del Cielo. It has

been a matter of some several weeks now and we've been unable to detect any on-site personnel at either location. In fact, we seriously doubt that the agent caught in the chimney last Christmas eve is still on duty. In lighting a fire in the fireplace, we hear no coughing or choking sounds.

At the ranch, the lion has been sighted virtually in the front yard, Ft. Drone is showing signs of deterioration due to lack of occupancy, and Gwalianko and No Strings have been asking why the little chestnut filly doesn't come around anymore. Worst of all no one brings us the morning paper.

If my wearing a gun lately is the reason for your invisibility, come out, come out wherever you are, and I'll take it off.

Seriously, Nancy and I miss you all very much. Barney and Dennis walk by the windows now and then to cheer us up, but things just aren't the same. The other night we were going out to dinner and both of us got in the back seat and waited for you to get in and drive. Nancy Reynolds [a family friend] is learning Karate and Rocket has left home (to go to Yale).

Please know how grateful we all are for all that you did. We miss you and wish you all the very best.

Sincerely,
Ronald Reagan

The president took our suggestions, grumbling only occasionally about the discomfort of a bulletproof vest, even as he put it on. I grimaced to think he wasn't wearing one that day. The Hilton was an easy, familiar site to protect, one our charges used all the time—the last place I expected any trouble.

At the moment we careered out of the hotel driveway, Carolyn was tearing across the street, desperate to identify the three bodies she saw lying there. Agent Bob Wanko, holding an Uzi (a 9-millimeter submachine gun), screamed at her, "Get back!"

Dashing to another part of the sidewalk, she saw Press Secretary Jim Brady lift his grievously wounded bald head. She knew he wasn't me.

Then she heard a woman screaming. Realizing it was her own voice, she clapped a hand over her mouth to stifle it. In desperation she ran back to Wanko, who was watching her. "I'm Jerry Parr's wife! Where is he?"

He pointed. "In the car. With the Man."

In the car, I was half sitting, half kneeling on the floor before the president. Checking him for blood, I methodically worked my hands around his body from the belt line up, under each arm, along his back, neck, and head—looking for blood, feeling for a wound or a painful spot. With immeasurable relief, I assessed that he had escaped unharmed, at least for the moment. But there was no telling what dangers might still be lurking. We needed to secure the president.

I radioed Shaddick in the follow-up car. "Rawhide is okay.

We're going to Crown." I had a choice to make: head to the ultrasecure White House or divert to George Washington University Hospital. I chose the White House.

But about twenty seconds into the run, I noticed the seventy-year-old president was pale, and he grimaced every time he took a breath.

I asked, "Is it your heart?"

"I don't think so," he said in a soft, clear voice. Then, matter-of-factly, "I think you broke my rib."

I caught my breath. All I could think was, *God, I hope not!*

The president took a napkin from his pocket and touched it to his lips. It filled with blood. "I must have cut the inside of my mouth," he said. But I remembered my "Ten Minute Medicine" class: frothy, bright red blood was oxygenated—a sign of a lung injury. My own heart was pounding, though my head was clear. *Maybe I hurt him when he hit the riser! What if a rib punctured a lung? What if I killed the president trying to save him?*

His pallor was now gray and his lips were blue. His breathing was becoming more labored. As we passed through the tunnel under Dupont Circle, I made a decision. "Mr. President, we're going to GW Hospital."

I saw concern and strength in his eyes. He didn't argue.

We'd left the follow-up car and the entire presidential motorcade in the dust, but they managed to catch up. Unrue radioed Agent Mary Ann Gordon. "We want to go to the emergency room of George Washington." The lead police car overtook us and went in front as usual. What was not usual was that no agent was in it. That meant they didn't get the radio message of our revised destination and sped on to the White House. Mary Ann Gordon pulled ahead of us to replace the lead car and take the brunt of any traffic we might encounter. I grabbed Unrue's mike (mine had torn off my belt as I hit the limo floor) and ordered Shaddick, "Get an ambulance. I mean, get a stretcher out there. Let's hustle!" Our sirens were wailing as we tore toward the hospital on Washington Circle.

"Should I take a shortcut and go the wrong way around the circle?" Unrue asked. Seconds were precious, but I said no. The last thing we needed was a head-on collision.

We screeched to a halt at the GW entrance at 2:30 p.m., just under three minutes from the time we peeled out of the Hilton driveway. Shaddick leaped out of the follow-up car and opened our door. I climbed over the president and extended my hand, but he didn't take it. Though pale and gaunt, he was determined to walk in on his own steam. I was on his left, no more than two inches away. Shaddick was on his right. Dale McIntosh and Russ Miller caught up with us to create a circle of protection around him. As we walked about twenty feet, the president's eyes suddenly rolled back in his head and he dropped. Shaddick and I caught him as he collapsed. Nearly two hundred pounds of deadweight. The four of us and an ambulance attendant carried him to Trauma Room 5 in George Washington Hospital's emergency room.

President Reagan was pale. The doctors and nurses

immediately ripped off his clothes and took his vitals. I heard a nurse say his blood pressure was too low to get a systolic reading. His pulse was faint. At first the team suspected a heart attack.

Feeling helpless and sick to my stomach, I tried unsuccessfully to stifle the nagging memory of JFK and the fear of losing another president. I did the only thing I knew to do: I told Shaddick, "Set up a perimeter."

Later the Treasury lawyers preparing for a congressional inquiry had a hard time understanding what that meant. But every agent knows how to set up a perimeter: we start with the president's body and systematically cut off access to him. I stayed with the president, close enough to observe without hindering the trauma team.

When an emergency room nurse caught my eye, I asked her, "Do you know all the doctors who belong in here?" She nodded. I told her, "We don't have time to check people out. If you let them in, they'll come in. If you don't, McIntosh will keep them out."

She may have ticked people off, but that nurse did her job. Word traveled with lightning speed through the hospital, and many doctors started to show up just to watch a part of history: pediatricians, gynecologists, whoever. But the right people got in, and those who didn't belong were turned away. It may have looked like chaos to an outsider, but that perimeter held.

Joseph Giordano, the surgeon in charge, and his trauma team found the wound, a narrow slit. I thought for a moment that maybe the corner of the door had hit him. A surgical intern who had been in Vietnam recognized it as a bullet wound. It wasn't round; the president had been hit by a ricocheted bullet, flattened out like a dime. We later surmised it struck the car and bounced through the narrow space between the car frame and the door, which opened toward the back. It must have hit the president's left side as he threw his arms forward to catch himself. Because he held his arm close to his side in the car, his arm had closed the wound. That's why there had been no blood on the outside.

I could hardly believe it. A lone bullet from the would-be assassin, who I would later learn was John Hinckley Jr., had found its mark. And now the president was suffering massive internal bleeding.

Giordano got a chest tube in to suck out the blood, then gave the president a transfusion and glucose; his blood pressure started to rise almost immediately. He quickly regained consciousness and looked puzzled. He could speak, and his mind was clear. A doctor on the trauma team asked, "Mr. President, do you know what happened?"

"No, not really."

"Someone shot you. There's a wound on your left side. We're giving you blood. In a few minutes we'll take you to the operating room and remove the bullet."

I silently prayed, *Lord, let him live.*

Then another doctor said what the president and all of us wanted desperately to hear, but something of which he himself was unsure: "You're going to be fine."

Soon Mrs. Reagan arrived, along with her agents. She rushed to his side, frantic with worry. At the sight of her, his face lit up. With a twinkle in his eye, he said, "Honey, I forgot to duck."

Mike Deaver (deputy chief of staff) had come in the follow-up car from the Hilton; soon Jim Baker (chief of staff), and Ed Meese (counselor to the president for policy) hurried in. When the president saw his "Troika," he began to crack one-liners. "Who's minding the store?" he asked, with a wink to Baker.

With mock seriousness, he turned to me and said about the doctors, "I hope these guys are Republicans." I smiled. Later in the operating room, he would repeat that wish to the doctors there, and they burst out laughing. Dr. Giordano, a dyed-in-the-wool Democrat, assured him, "Mr. President, today we're all Republicans." It broke the terrible tension.

Always considerate of others, Reagan was playing the consummate host, putting his guests at ease even in the emergency room. It worked. I even began to relax a little. But the relief was premature. From the number of transfusions he was getting, I could see that the president was still losing blood at an alarming rate. (Half his body's blood, I later learned.) The low blood pressure was a sign of shock: first symptoms are weakness, loss of control. Then the body's organs begin to shut down. There is a point of no return from so much blood loss.

The ER was beginning to look like a battlefield. Soon Jim Brady arrived. He was still conscious, with gray matter oozing from his head. Tim McCarthy was also brought to the ER. None of them could see each other.

The other wounded man was a policeman, Thomas Delahanty, who was taken to the Washington Hospital Center because GW couldn't handle any more. All the men who took a bullet that day were Irish. By God's grace they all survived, though Jim Brady would never fully recover.

We had plenty of agents: the day shift who'd been at the hotel and Mrs. Reagan's agents, and soon the four-to-midnight shift, who heard about the shooting on TV like everyone else, drove right to the hospital. In addition we had support from the Washington field office.

Pat Miller did a wonderful survey, a protective plan, right on the spot. These guys knew what to do, and it relieved me of a lot of worry. The inner perimeter was holding, but we needed middle and outer perimeters. There were all kinds of problems. People were trying to get into the hospital just to be there. The press was trying to stake out territory; senators were arriving, expecting to be handled with deference.

At 2:57 p.m.—thirty minutes after he was shot—the president was on his way to the operating room.

I went into the operating room with the president. Though I'd dressed in scrubs with President Carter in the burn unit, I'd forgotten how they went on. To the nurses' amusement I put them on backward, but nobody mentioned it. I covered everything—clothes, face, hair, shoes—so as not to violate the sterile environment. I introduced myself to Ben Aaron, the senior thoracic surgeon, and Kathleen Cheyney, a thoracic surgical fellow. While junior to Aaron, she herself had eight years' experience with chest surgery. I took my place about four feet behind the president's head.

I watched the surgeons open his chest, then use a rib spreader that looked like a torture instrument from the Inquisition. Dr. Aaron started hunting for the bullet revealed by X-rays taken in the trauma room—a flattened-out bullet, like a curved dime. Aaron couldn't find it. He put his hand in the president's chest to feel for it. Still no luck. Finally, he turned to me in frustration and asked, "Do you really want it?"

As a criminal investigator I knew we needed it to establish the "chain of custody" evidence for trial. I'd heard we had the lone gunman, but we needed the bullet to be sure it came from his gun. Our plan was for the bullet to go from the president's body, to Dr. Ben Aaron, to me, in a cup. Then to Agent Joe Trainor, and from Trainor to an FBI agent. And then they would trace it back to John Hinckley.

On the other hand, I didn't want to increase the president's danger by keeping him open and sedated longer than necessary. I gulped and took a giant leap of faith. "Well, we'd really like to have it."

They re-X-rayed him in the operating room. I kept looking at the monitor up there, and his blood pressure stayed in a good range. Mine was probably higher at that point!

At the very same time, in the next operating room, Agent Tim McCarthy was undergoing surgery for a gunshot wound to the upper chest. The bullet had migrated to his abdomen, nicking several organs on the way. He was young and strong and got out of surgery first.

In another operating room, Dr. Art Kobrine was working on Jim Brady. That was a much longer, much more serious operation. Brady would survive with his mind intact, but he would be in a wheelchair the rest of his life and unable to work again.

Peering through the large observation window overlooking Reagan's operation, I saw a figure dressed in surgical green, mask and all. I recognized his eyes and motioned him to come in. It was John Simpson, then assistant director of Protective Operations (he later became director). He had guarded Reagan in earlier campaigns and had a deep respect and affection for him and Mrs. Reagan. I knew he wanted to be there, whether the president lived or died.

Dr. Aaron finally found the bullet and removed it from the president's lung. Then he still had to stop all the internal bleeding in Reagan's chest. He discovered the problem— a damaged artery—and stitched it shut. They had to clean the wound, sew up the tissue and muscles inside, then close the rib cage and sew up the skin. They left drainage tubes in that would be removed in a few days.

The surgery lasted about three hours. The doctors had done their best. I was praying it was good enough to save Ronald Reagan.

In the recovery room, about 7:15 that night, the president regained consciousness. He had tubes running in and out, draining out fluids that weren't supposed to be accumulating, like clots and secretions, and putting in fluids he needed, like saline. He was on a ventilator and couldn't speak. He tried to pull out his breathing tube. Agitated, gesturing for a pen and paper, he scribbled, "I can't breathe." Under it, he made ditto marks. The second line read " " " " at all." He handed me the paper, his eyes full of fear. He was the color of ash. Two nurses, Denise Sullivan and Cathy Edmondson, were monitoring his blood pressure, drainage tubes, and breathing, but they were not in the room. I longed to comfort him, to protect him, but I was helpless—and on the verge of panic myself.

Like Abraham in the Bible, I started to argue with God. *Surely you didn't bring him through all this to suffocate before my eyes!* I motioned desperately to nurse Cathy Edmondson, telling her, "He feels like he can't breathe!" I showed her Reagan's note. She touched his arm and said gently, "Mr. President, the ventilator is breathing for you. Try to trust us. You're getting all the oxygen you need." Once he relaxed and let it work, he (and I) felt better. That's when I finally started to believe the president would live.

The hospital staff was very kind, but I realized the president needed to know he had a protector, a familiar agent he could trust. I couldn't stay in the hospital all night.

I gave an order: "While he's in this hospital, I want a White House agent in the room at all times. I don't care what else is going on. I don't care if the FBI is getting a deposition. I don't care if they're giving him a bath and he's buck naked. I want an agent in here, all the time." My order was kept for the whole length of the president's hospital stay.

At that point I understood that I—we—could control only a little chunk of Ronald Reagan's life, but a very important chunk: at that moment we had to be with him until he either survived or passed.

In a very real sense, my own destiny hinged on the president's survival. The drive to protect him came from nearly nineteen years of training, yes. But I operated from an even deeper protective instinct, one I'd always known, a drive so essential to my being that it defined who I was. To fail at protecting the president would have called into question my life's purpose.

But Ronald Reagan proved to be very robust. Years at the ranch chopping wood, building his own fences, and riding the range had been good for him.

All the doctors agreed that we'd have surely lost him if I'd taken him back to the White House. Though I had hints of it, only later did I learn how very close he had come to dying. I learned that during those tense moments in Trauma Room 5, while they were reassuring him he'd be okay, most of the doctors and nurses feared he would die. He was seventy years old. His blood pressure had plunged dangerously low. His grievous loss of blood had put him in shock; not until the surgery was nearly complete were the doctors able to stem the flow. Surgery revealed that the bullet had torn up a lung and lodged only an inch from his heart. For foreign policy reasons as well as domestic stability, the president's real condition had been downplayed.

I thanked God for helping me make the right decision.

Shortly before the president regained consciousness, around six o'clock, I had finally been able to call Carolyn. That's when I learned she'd been an eyewitness. Her boss, Tom Morrison, and one of her colleagues, Larry Garr, had heard the sirens and looked out their office windows. They saw Carolyn staring into an Uzi, shaking and crying. Separately, each ran downstairs to try to help. Tom was stopped by an agent with dogs. Larry got to her and led her back up to her office. As they entered the lobby of the Universal North Building, they noticed a bullet hole in the ceiling—one of Hinckley's last bullets had apparently hit there, but it was never recovered.

Carolyn called W-16, White House Operations. They said they thought I was okay. She called the kids—Kimberly in college, Jennifer en route home from high school cheer-leading practice—but they'd already heard the incorrect report that three agents had been shot. Both girls sobbed with relief when Carolyn told them I was fine. Trish was still in elementary school. Her principal had not yet learned of the attempt. "Please," Carolyn begged, "find Trish. Tell her that Mom's on the way home and Dad's okay."

Larry Garr brought Carolyn home. The first thing they saw as they walked into the house through the laundry room was my bulletproof vest. Carolyn burst into tears all over again.

That night, after the president regained consciousness in the recovery room and the doctors thought he was going to make it, I still had an important job to do. Back at the

White House in W-16, I wrote a narrative affidavit of what had gone down as best I could recall. Then, suddenly realizing I had not eaten since breakfast, I went to the White House mess.

Ed Hickey, director of the White House Military Office, was there. Before I could get a bite, he asked, "Did you get the authentication card?" My heart sank. I had no idea what he was talking about.

The authentication card was carried by every president at all times. It contained the codes, in conjunction with the "football," to initiate nuclear war.

Frankly, I'd never heard of it. Through my time with President Carter and now with Reagan, nobody had ever told me there was such a thing. I had handed all the president's clothes, shoes, wallet, and cuff links to an FBI agent. I felt really dumb. "I guess the FBI has it," I said. (It took a lot of wrangling between agencies, but we eventually got it back.)

Ed said, "Well, why don't we have a drink?" So we did. Confession: I drank two glasses of vodka, and it had absolutely no effect on me! Then I drove home to Potomac in the midnight darkness and collapsed.

Unable to sleep much, I kept calling the hospital every hour to talk to the agents. That night the agents wouldn't leave when their shift was supposed to end. The same was true of the nurses. They didn't *want* to be relieved of duty. I learned that during the night the president started writing jokes to the nurses. "Does Nancy know about us?" he wrote

Denise Sullivan. To Marisa Mize, who replaced her, "Send me to LA where I can see the air I'm breathing."

Some of the notes were serious. He wrote Mize, "What does the future hold?" Then, "Will I be able to do ranch work, ride, etc.?" She assured him he'd be able to do all that in three months.

At three in the morning, to the president's immense relief, doctors removed the breathing tube. Reagan asked whether others were hurt and was told two were injured but recovering well. Nobody mentioned Jim Brady yet. Though hoarse, he was happy to be able to speak and entertained his audience, telling stories until four o'clock, when nurse Joanne Bell covered his eyes with a damp cloth, turned off the overhead lights, and ordered the president of the United States to go to sleep.

An hour and a half later, Reagan was moved from the recovery room to the ICU, where head nurse Lita Amigo and her boss Barbara Holfelner had been waiting since two thirty the prior afternoon. They would not go home for two days. The ICU had only fourteen beds and all but one were full. To make room for McCarthy and Brady, who preceded the president, the healthiest ICU patients were sent to the floor. Reagan had stayed in the recovery room while the nurses and Secret Service worked out traffic patterns and ID procedures and chose rooms in the ICU. The unit was crowded with security people and unbearably hot.

Dan Ruge, the president's White House physician, broke the news to Reagan about Brady's severe injury. The president wept.

ICU nurse Debbie Augsbach, who had waited sixteen hours, gave the president a newspaper around seven in the morning, the first he had seen. Although news of the attack covered the front page, she recalls, "He didn't discuss the shooting. Instead, he turned to me and asked, 'Do you know there was another child found in Atlanta?'" (A mass murderer was being sought in the deaths of several children in Atlanta.)

Later that day (Tuesday, March 31) Reagan met with the "Troika"—Meese, Baker, and Deaver—and proved he was still in charge by signing a dairy bill.

Reagan's recovery was phenomenal. As he prepared to leave the ICU that night, nurse Lita Amigo (who had been on duty two days) took his hand and said, "I'm praying for you, Mr. President."

He joked, "I'm not going to another world—just downstairs."

Two nights later I had two dreams. In one I went out to get in my car, and it ran away from me with nobody in it. The other involved a tractor that started without me, and I couldn't catch it. It didn't take a psych degree to interpret the symbolism.

I visited the president daily, often more than once at the beginning, and carefully quizzed the shift leaders and medical team about anything unusual. The nurses were touched by the president's consideration and humility. Barbara Benedict was on the floor with him after he left the ICU. She recounts the first time the president insisted he was well enough to wash himself in the bathroom without help.

He went in, closed the door, and stayed and stayed and stayed. She called, "Mr. Reagan, are you all right?"

"Yes, I'm fine," came the answer.

More minutes passed. No sounds came from behind the door. Now worried, but loath to violate his privacy, she tried again. "Mr. President, can I help you with anything?"

"No, I'm fine."

After more minutes passed, she announced, "Mr. Reagan, I'm coming in."

She discovered the president of the United States on the floor with a towel, wiping up a spill on his hands and knees. Embarrassed, he explained, "I made a mess and didn't want you to have to clean it up."

That consideration for others ran deep in Reagan's fiber and remained unaffected by his status. He wore contact lenses, and one day I had casually mentioned that my daughter Kimberly was having trouble removing hers. A few days later he called me into the Oval Office. He had a gift for me. It looked like a tiny suction cup. "I use one of these to take out my lenses," he said. "See if this would help Kimberly."

On April 11, the thirteenth day, the president went home. The nurses who had cared for him were there to see him off. Though they had worked twelve-hour shifts with no days off, many were weeping when he left. He had been an ideal patient––cheerful, undemanding, agreeable to any procedure no matter how uncomfortable. They had worked so hard and cared so much, and they knew as he left they would probably never have such an experience again.

Refusing a wheelchair, he said, "I walked in. I'm walking out."

A few days after the assassination attempt, I did something very unusual for the Service in those days: I got all the agents who had been on duty that day (except Tim McCarthy, who was still recovering) and let them talk.

I knew how much pain—and guilt—had been associated with the Kennedy assassination. In their book, *The Kennedy Detail*, Jerry Blaine and Clint Hill and others have spelled out how their lives were devastated. Jimmy Taylor, who was with Governor George Wallace when he was shot and paralyzed, never got over his guilt feelings. Dick Keiser, head of President Ford's detail, had hiccups for months after Squeaky Fromme and Sara Jane Moore each shot at Ford within a span of eighteen days. Larry Dominguez was in two assassination attempts, the attempts on Wallace and Reagan. The hypervigilance required to be responsible for someone's life, especially a president's, is exhausting. And when something goes wrong, the trauma runs deep.

So we got together in my office at PPD and talked about it for six or seven hours. Bill Green, the advance agent, especially wondered if he had done anything wrong. He later had to endure inspection, and then a Treasury Department investigation. I felt that because the Hilton was so familiar— we had brought presidents and vice presidents there more than a hundred times over the years—we may have become complacent. But given the protocols of the time—and the fact that the president lived—we escaped the type of criticism that might have otherwise followed.

Still, important lessons emerged. We had a problem with arrivals and departures. While we already knew that protecting the president in an open motorcade is impossible, that he must be in an armored, closed car, the attacks on Ford and Reagan showed us how very, very vulnerable we were on arrivals and departures.

We addressed the problem in two ways. First, we placed an armored cover where VIPs enter the Hilton Hotel. When a car drives in now, they shut the doors before the protectee emerges. Outsiders can't see the person.

Second, we acquired magnetometers, which we'd been trying to have at the White House for years. As soon as they were up and running, we discovered a lot of people going in there with guns—hundreds of them! Most meant no harm. Many were little old ladies, tourists afraid to walk on the streets of Washington, DC. (It's really quite safe in the tourist areas.)

Strangely, the president's would-be assassin and I had something in common: John Hinckley Jr., too, had been brought to that moment at the Hilton by a movie. He was obsessed with the film *Taxi Driver*, starring Jody Foster as Iris, a twelve-year-old prostitute. In the movie, Travis Bickle (Robert De Niro) plans to kill a presidential candidate to win the love of a woman and gain the redemption of Iris.

Hinckley set out to kill a president to win the love of Jody Foster.

Hinckley later told investigators that he had stalked Carter. He said of the day in Dayton, "I didn't make a move because I was 'looked off.'" I think he meant some agent—maybe me—locked eyes with him, and he lost his nerve.

About a week after following Carter from Dayton to Nashville, Hinckley was arrested at the Nashville airport when a security officer discovered three guns in his luggage: a .38 and two .22-caliber pistols, plus a pair of handcuffs and a box of hollow-nose bullets. Hinckley intended to board a flight to New York, which was the president's next destination. The police seized his guns and took him to jail. A judge let him go on $62.50 bail. They kept the guns, but no one in Tennessee connected him to the president's visit. Not until the assassination attempt did the FBI put the two events together.

We went back to look at the ABC camera crew's pooling pictures of that day in Dayton, and sure enough, there he is, about six or seven feet away from the president. Stopping the camera, one can see Bill Cotter, Mike Maddiloni, and me looking in his direction.

It made me believe that the Service, just by our presence, stopped that assassination attempt. Events such as these are unknown and uncelebrated victories.

On the night of the attempt on Reagan's life, Ed Hickey had said something to me as I sat in the White House mess eating a very late dinner. "I think you saved the president's life," he stated. It hadn't crossed my mind.

I did what every agent is trained to do. I was blessed with

quick reflexes, confidence, and good judgment. I knew my purpose. But I was in no way alone in saving the president's life. If it weren't for Tim McCarthy's courage in facing the assailant and spreading out his body, the bullet he took would have hit me or the president. The armor on the car and window stopped bullets. The hospital trauma and surgical teams had deep experience with serious gunshot wounds. The nurses were outstanding caregivers. The Secret Service training helped us all respond instantly and appropriately. The president's own robust constitution saved him. Saving the president was a team effort.

The press was very kind. They were calling me a hero on TV as soon as they identified me. Maybe the respect I'd always shown them came back to me. They could have called me something else. After all, a president was wounded and nearly died on my watch.

I wondered whether the Service would be criticized for putting a fifty-year-old in charge of the PPD. But a later commentator mentioned that my age may have been an advantage. A younger man might have hesitated to manhandle a president, he said, and the slightest hesitation would have been fatal. Because the White House was known to be secure, a less experienced person would almost surely have taken him there instead of to an unsecured hospital.

The Reagans never blamed me or the Service. From the very beginning, Mrs. Reagan repeatedly thanked me and still gives me a hug whenever our paths cross.

On April 28 Reagan addressed Congress, praising Tim

McCarthy and the other wounded men. Four of us—Tim, Dennis McCarthy (who disarmed Hinckley), Ray Shaddick, and I—received awards from the US Senate and the Treasury Department, as well as the Presidential Rank Award. We were named "Top Cops of the Year" and featured on the cover of *Parade* magazine. I made a TV documentary for a weekly show called *Top Cops*, in which President Reagan introduced me, praising my work.

I have been thanked many times over, but my greatest reward is that Ronald Reagan lived twenty-three more years. Shortly after his recovery, Mother Teresa paid a visit. According to Mike Deaver, who was present, she told the president, "God has a plan for you. You were spared for a purpose." She confirmed his own belief that he was spared to be a peacemaker. Among his achievements would be a lasting nuclear arms reduction treaty negotiated with Mikhail Gorbachev of the Soviet Union in 1987. The Berlin Wall fell ten months after Reagan left office, and the Cold War ended two years later with the peaceful collapse of the Soviet Union.

And surrounding it all, embracing it all—the training, technology, human courage, medical skills, the president's personal strength, and his later achievements—was the grace of God. The grace of God.

Later I asked the president, "Did you know you were an agent of your own destiny?" I told him about seeing *Code of the Secret Service* many times as a little boy and being inspired to become an agent like Brass Bancroft when I grew up. He smiled. "It was one of the cheapest films I ever made."

✷ ✷ ✷

On the first anniversary of the near-fatal attack, I dreamed of being alone in a small rowboat far out in the ocean. The boat was about ten feet long with no oars. The sea was calm when the dream began. There was no wind, but I could smell the salty air I remembered so well from my childhood visits to Miami Beach.

As I sat alone, I could see an empty horizon. There was no telltale glow of city lights in any direction.

Then there appeared to be a dark cloud bank on the horizon. I assumed this indicated a possible thunderstorm, and rain and lightning would be in the offing, maybe soon.

The bank loomed closer. I began to sense that it was coming toward me and my boat slowly but inexorably—and I had no oars. As I pondered what to do, I realized the dark mass moving toward me was not a cloud; it was water, a gigantic wave from one end of the horizon to the other. This was what we'd call today a "rogue" wave, somehow created by fresh winds or an undersea earthquake. I felt totally helpless to do anything. I was afraid but could do nothing. I just had to ride it out.

The wave towered over me. As it got closer and closer, I could feel its immense power begin to lift me higher and higher.

I rose up the wave's silent side. This mass of dark water carried me higher to its crest. Then, at the crest, the water was calm again. There was no trough. There was stillness now and only the sound of water lapping the sides of the boat.

I woke up.

I continued to process this dream for a long time. It represented an overwhelming experience . . . a rendezvous with death had been escaped.

Perhaps it merely meant I had ridden out this crisis: the president was saved, and life went on for me. This was certainly true. The president lived for many more years, passing away in 2004 at age ninety-three. But I think there was a higher understanding.

My own reflection seems to say, *You were lifted by the event so you could see your entire life more clearly. God was lifting you up.*

A few years later I had lunch with Dr. Shervert Frazier, director of the National Institute of Mental Health in Bethesda, Maryland. He said my dream put the whole event together for me. I have never dreamed about that day since. But I never forget the relief and peace I felt at the crest of that wave.

MY ENCOUNTER WITH GRACE

CHAPTER 10

FROM THE WHITE HOUSE TO THE POTTER'S HOUSE

These are the words which came to Jeremiah from the LORD:
Go down now to the potter's house, and there I shall
tell you what I have to say.

JEREMIAH 18:1-2, REB

1985–1989

As the strains of "Pomp and Circumstance" filled the air, I adjusted my mortarboard once more and looked for Carolyn sitting near the front. We connected; she was looking back at me. She smiled and gave me a thumbs-up.

I was easy to spot. At fifty-six, I was one of the oldest graduates lined up on a beautiful spring day, May 16, 1987, about to receive a master's degree in pastoral counseling from Loyola University of Baltimore. I stood out for another reason. My mortarboard was a little different from the other master's candidates: I'd received it in Illinois a week before from Eureka College, President Reagan's alma mater, when

I gave their commencement speech. Eureka had named me an honorary Doctor of Humane Letters.

I had stayed with President and Mrs. Reagan for a year after the shooting, at their request. They wanted the stability of being with people they knew and trusted. And I felt that the agents protecting Reagan needed time to process the events of March 30 and to institute new procedures to prevent a similar attack in the future.

Nobody wanted me to leave. But protection is a young person's job. I was fifty-one. Like an aging athlete, I wanted to leave protection while I was still at the top of my game.

In 1982 I had been elevated to assistant director (Protective Research) of the US Secret Service. I moved from the White House to the director's office at Headquarters on G Street, a few blocks from the White House.

My assistant director peers were Larry Schaefe (Investigations), Ed Pollard (Protective Operations), Steve Garmen (Administration), and Bob Snow (Public Affairs). Together with Deputy Director Bill Barton and Director John Simpson, we seven set policy and led the US Secret Service from 1982 until I retired in 1985. We met in the director's conference room once a week or more often in an emergency.

My responsibilities included the Inspection, Technical Security, Liaison, and Intelligence divisions—and managing a $40 million budget. Though I knew almost nothing of computers, I took on the mission of bringing the Service from the file card system used since the administration of

President Grant into the digital age. Fortunately, I knew how to recognize the people who had the skills I lacked. Chief engineer Pat Shambach and my deputy Ed Walsh deserve a lot of credit for making me look good.

Even though my work responsibilities were weighty, I traveled less, and for the first time in years I actually had some discretionary time. I read more, prayed more, and thought about my future. By 1985 I had twenty-seven years in government service, including four in the Air Force. I was over fifty and eligible to retire. Many agents left for big-paying jobs in corporate security: oil companies, financial institutions, even professional football.

But neither money nor job titles nor perks appealed to me. My pension would be ample, and Carolyn's career had taken off. She was now special counsel to the assistant attorney general (Tax Division) at the Justice Department. And I sensed that even bigger things were in store for her. Though we still had private school and college costs to come for Trish, we'd be okay financially.

I had been called into the Secret Service as a way to nurture and protect life. Now I sensed God had another mission for me. But I wasn't sure exactly how that would look. As on that day twenty-three years before in the Vanderbilt coffee shop, I was again standing on the threshold of a major life shift.

My last day in the Secret Service was February 16, 1985. I felt a mixture of sadness and relief. I had really loved being an agent. I also loved the men and women who worked with me. I had met world leaders and traveled to every continent but Antarctica. In some ways I had lived a storybook life. That little boy riding on his dad's shoulders in Miami could never have imagined such a life might lie ahead. At the same time, for decades I had performed in a public fishbowl under tremendous pressure. I needed a change. I was ready to pursue my new call to serve God and others.

I filled out the final paperwork, cleaned out my desk, and walked over to the White House to say good-bye to President and Mrs. Reagan. As she always had since March 30, 1981, Mrs. Reagan greeted me with a warm hug. As the president extended his hand, he asked, with a twinkle in his eye, "You're not going to throw me over the couch, are you?"

* * *

As soon as I heard about Loyola's master's program in pastoral counseling, I thought, *This is the Lord's leading.* The combination of "pastor" and "counseling" resonated with my spirit. Over the years I had grown more firmly rooted in God's love and care, and I wanted to share that love with others. I knew I had a gift for listening. I could sense when people were hurting and connect deeply with them. Because of my working-class background—and my career in the halls of power—I was comfortable with almost everyone. I had seen pain in my mom and dad, in my stepfather Jack Cox, in winners and losers— even in presidents—and knew it could show up anywhere. I had experienced my own dark night of the soul.

And Jim Connolly's death continued to haunt me.

So in September 1983, while I was still assistant director, I started to attend night classes at Loyola. Most of my classmates were priests, nuns, or Protestant clergy. Jack Callope (later a monsignor), Fay Buford, and Mary Grealy became my study partners and close friends. We prayed for each other, learned from each other, and practiced on each other.

I had to postpone one requirement for graduation until I retired because it couldn't all be done on weekends and evenings: one thousand hours of supervised clinical practice at Affiliated Community Counselors in Rockville, Maryland. My supervisor was Hilda Weisman, PhD, who had studied under Harry Stack Sullivan. She was a great teacher. With the clients' permission, I would tape-record my sessions, and Hilda would listen and make comments. She'd say, "Jerry, you're talking too much."

"But what am I supposed to do when they stop talking?"

"Then you listen to the silence. Don't be in a hurry. Wait. If they don't start talking again, say, 'Tell me more.' There's always more."

Hilda also said, "Don't be afraid to take on the client's pain." From what I was learning in class, this was heresy. I protested, "But what about countertransference?"

Hilda just looked at me and asked, "How do you think they get well?" Hilda, a Jew, helped me understand what the Bible means when it says, "Bear one another's burdens, and in this way you will fulfill the law of Christ." Or the ancient Christian prayer, "Lamb of God, you take away the sins of the world." Hilda was saying that to take on another's pain, to ache with him or her, is a form of divine healing.

As an intern counselor at Affiliated Community Counselors, I wasn't paid. Our clients were too poor to engage a private therapist, but even so they paid ten dollars for an hour session on the theory that they should be expected to contribute to their own healing. They suffered from many kinds of mental illness: depression, schizophrenia, borderline personality disorders. I prayed for them all. And I almost always found something to love in each one.

In my write-ups I had to choose a diagnosis from a book called *The Diagnostic and Statistical Manual* (DSM), but I hated labeling people. Everyone was unique, and nobody neatly fit a category. Whatever the label, I tried to meet people where they were and help them move to a better place. I believed healing was possible and tried to give them hope.

For my thesis I chose to write about Vicki (not her real name). She was fortyish, overweight, and full of self-loathing. She was very angry. She said she'd hated school ever since fourth grade. She felt stupid and kept failing. I initially diagnosed her "borderline personality disorder" because nothing really fit, but one day I had a flash of insight. Handing her a book, I said, "Vicki, could you read that to me?"

She blushed with shame, and her eyes brimmed. "I can't read!" she whispered.

My own Trish had been diagnosed with a form of dyslexia when she was five years old, and I remembered the tears she spilled on the page where a specialist had her write the alphabet. My heart went out to Vicki.

"I think you have a learning disorder," I said. "It's called dyslexia. Cher has it. Vice President Nelson Rockefeller had it—he couldn't read until he was twelve years old. Lots of successful people have it. *You are not stupid.* We'll find you a teacher who can help you learn to read."

Now Vicki was sobbing, but the tears were of relief and joy. "There's a name for what I have? You mean I'm not crazy?"

"No, Vicki. You're not crazy. You never were."

✳ ✳ ✳

Less than a month after I graduated, Carolyn and I moved from Potomac, Maryland, to the Tenleytown section of northwest Washington, DC. Our kids parasailed into new adventures: Kimberly to Syracuse University and a career in advertising; Jennifer to the University of Maryland and, in 1986, to marry and start a home of her own with Richard Turek, whom she met at Heritage Christian Church and had loved since she was fifteen years old; and Trish to Purnell, a girls' boarding school in New Jersey horse country. Maintaining our large house just for the two of us no longer seemed worth the effort, and the daily two-hour round-trip commute to downtown DC had lost any charm it ever had.

After I retired, President Reagan appointed Carolyn to a fifteen-year term on the United States Tax Court. She was sworn in November 25, 1985, the second woman tax judge appointed in twelve years. While my White House connections undoubtedly helped, Carolyn came highly recommended by people I had nothing to do with: two commissioners of Internal Revenue, judges from both parties, two senators, and the Tax Section of the American Bar Association. Her work on illegal tax shelters had drawn praise from US attorneys across the country as well as lawyers who represented taxpayers. They wanted to see the bogus shelters shut down. Carolyn was becoming as well known in her field as I was in mine, and I was certain she'd make a good judge.

During our first couple of years in Potomac we'd continued to go back and forth to Heritage Christian Church. But when our pastor, Dick Miller, left for California, we looked for a Christian community in Potomac. We went to church, but until we moved to DC, we had never found one that felt like home.

One snowy night in January 1988 Carolyn and I nervously scanned the faces of sixteen strangers gathered around a table on the third floor of Christ House, a hospital for homeless men. We had signed up for Gordon Cosby's class in Christian growth after hearing him preach the week before at our first visit to the Church of the Saviour in DC. We had no idea what we were in for.

"We'll introduce ourselves," Gordon began. "But don't tell us what you do or where you're from. We'll learn that soon enough. Just tell us your name and your deepest pain."

Gordon was not smiling. In fact, he looked grim. He was deadly serious.

One woman stood up and said, "I can't possibly tell you my deepest pain." She left.

Grateful to be halfway around the circle and not at the beginning, I wondered what people would say. The first woman said, "My husband left me with four kids to raise. He wanted a younger woman. I can't forgive him."

Neither Gordon nor anyone else said a word. We just absorbed it in silence.

The next person said, "I watched my beautiful twenty-seven-year-old sister die from cancer. I keep asking myself, *Where was God?*"

A young man said, "I'm in my third year of seminary and have lost my faith."

When my turn came, I said, "My mother is in a nursing home with Alzheimer's. We tried to keep her at home, but it was impossible. My daughter Trish is the only one who can bear to go with me to visit her. It's very hard."

I had no idea what Carolyn would say. Later she told me she'd planned to say something like "Well, thank God everything is okay with me. I have a good job, a loving husband, healthy kids. I'm grateful to be so blessed." She wasn't in touch with any pain.

But what came out of her mouth, unbidden, was "I have a broken relationship with my oldest child." She was shocked to hear herself. She had never voiced how much this hurt her, and how helpless she felt to fix it. But I knew it was true.

When we finished going around the circle, nobody gave advice. Nobody tried to fix anybody else. But Gordon's brilliant and daring question evoked a deep and instant sense of community. We had been vulnerable to one another. We had been heard without judgment, accepted right where we were. We left with a deeper understanding of our own brokenness than when we came in. And as Gordon dimissed us in prayer, I sensed we were bonded in a fellowship of pain.

Most important, we filed out of the room that night knowing we were forgiven and loved by God—just as we were.

The first homework assignment seemed equally as odd as the introductions: find a time during the week when you can be alone and completely silent for one hour. No music, no reading, just sitting with silence.

As a contemplative with a monastic streak, I relished this. But that kind of silence was a completely foreign experience to Carolyn. Nevertheless, because she has always been an A student and done the teacher's assignment, she set the timer and sat alone in the dining room. About ten minutes into the hour, she told me later, she began to weep. Then to sob.

Now, Carolyn is not a weeper; she just sucks it up and moves on. At first she wasn't sure what the sobbing was even about, but she knew she was releasing repressed grief. Then she realized it had something to do with Kim.

She told me she felt two things at once. One was a deep conviction that she had unfairly tried to force Kim into a mold that wasn't Kim. And at the very same moment of being confronted with the truth, Carolyn felt loved and forgiven and embraced by God.

So when the hour was up, she called Kimberly in Syracuse.

She began, "Kim, you have been the center of a deep spiritual experience I just had, and I want to tell you about it." They wept together. Something that had been broken for years began to be healed.

The story of Gordon Cosby and the Church of the Saviour, which he and his wife, Mary, founded in DC in 1946, has been beautifully told by Elizabeth O'Connor in *Call to Commitment*. At Heritage Christian Church, Carolyn and I had read it in a small group. When we moved into the city in June 1987, we wanted to visit the community but kept putting it off, I think because we were afraid of the commitment that would be required.

In fact, our first contact was not with the ecumenical service that met on Sunday mornings in a Dupont Circle brownstone. We began to touch the life of the community at one of their missions, Christ House, in the Adams Morgan neighborhood of DC. We'd sent them a donation at some point, and they invited us to attend a Thursday night dinner and worship time with residents called "Table Fellowship."

Here's what we knew going into the dinner: Christ House opened in December 1985 as the first twenty-four-hour residential medical facility in the United States for sick homeless men with nowhere else to go. Women were included more recently. (As far as I know, it is still the only one in DC. They have treated more than seven thousand people since the facility opened.) Patients came with frostbite, gangrene, stab and gunshot wounds, tuberculosis, AIDS, and the multiple afflictions common to life on the street. Most were alcohol and drug addicts, and many were mentally ill. Many were also convicted felons. They were sent from hospital emergency rooms, homeless shelters, and a roaming medical van that treated folks living on the grates. Christ House had thirty-four patient beds and apartments upstairs for permanent staff.

The founders, Janelle and Alan Goetcheus, were Methodist missionaries who visited the Church of the Saviour when they stopped over in DC waiting for papers to go to Pakistan. When they saw the need in Washington, they changed their mission field. Janelle was a physician and Alan an ordained minister. Every day Janelle stood in front of a condemned crack house across the street from the Potter's House (another Church of the Saviour mission) and prayed for that building to become a hospital for the desperate.

One day a very wealthy visitor to the Potter's House heard Janelle speak. The visitor donated nearly three million dollars to purchase the building, create a state-of-the-art facility, and cover all expenses for the first six months of operation. She made the gift anonymously and never even asked to be on the board.

The Servant Christ, a sculpture by JIMILU Mason, graces the front. It shows a kneeling Christ, basin in hand, looking up at the live Christ House patients peering down from the windows. Jesus wants to wash their feet.

The residents protect this sculpture. It has no trace of graffiti or sign of disrespect.

Along with Janelle and Alan, Drs. David Hilfiker and Don Martin, their wives, and two nuns completed the medical staff. Some moved in to live with the patients and provide round-the-clock care. The Martins, Hilfikers, and Goetcheuses were Church of the Saviour members, but volunteers came from other churches in Washington and elsewhere.

This has been the pattern of Church of the Saviour missions: two or more people sound a call and commit themselves to carry it; money shows up, often unexpectedly; a wider community of volunteers provides support. This is the loaves-and-fishes miracle of how a faith community that has never had more than 150 core members at one time has started more than 65 missions, some with budgets well into seven figures, almost all touching some aspect of the pain of people at the margins.

Mary Cosby says there are four marks of call:

- You can say it in one sentence.
- It's impossible.
- It won't leave you alone.
- It can cost you everything.

These folks were called.

So we showed up one night at Table Fellowship. It was November and getting dark as we parked on the street and walked to the entrance. Carolyn was scared but wanted to come. My "street sense," honed in the days in New York's Bedford-Stuyvesant neighborhood, came flooding back.

I was keenly aware of my surroundings. But once we rang the bell and were admitted, we felt very safe.

In the brightly decorated dining room, we sat at one of several tables with a staff member and some homeless men. They were showered, shaved, and sober. They wore clean street clothes, not hospital gowns. They were quiet, well behaved, dignified even. A young volunteer, Jennifer Erickson, played gospel piano and led the singing with a crystal-clear soprano voice. Alan Goetcheus said grace. Then we shared home-cooked soul food family style and tried to make conversation. Some men eagerly told their stories: how they got there, what they hoped for when they were well. Others were quiet, like James, on my right.

I was surprised that there seemed to be no difference between staffers and patients. There was a sense of connection, an equality, a feeling of family. At the end of the meal, bread and grape juice were passed as Communion, and as we took it, we each said to the person beside us, "James (or Jerry or Rufus), God wants you to have this bread." As Carolyn passed the bread to her neighbor, I noticed tears running down her cheeks. I knew in my gut that God really did want those men to have that bread. And I was convinced God wanted us to serve it to them.

The experience reminded me of a poem attributed to Catholic priest Daniel Berrigan:

Sometime in your life,
hope that you might see one starved man,

the look on his face when the bread
finally arrives. Hope that you
might have baked it or bought it
or even kneaded it yourself.
For that look on his face,
for your meeting his eyes
across a piece of bread,
you might be willing to lose a lot,
or suffer a lot,
or die a little even.

From this first encounter, Carolyn and I realized that the Church of the Saviour was where we wanted to put down roots. Even so, we didn't get around to attending the ecumenical worship service at 2025 Massachusetts Avenue until the last Sunday of the year, December 27, 1987.

We did not hear a Christmas "feel-good" sermon. Gordon Cosby's topic was the "Slaughter of the Innocents."

This was vintage Gordon: take a very tough Scripture and force people to think about its implications. His question: "What must Mary have felt, knowing the birth of her son would cause the death of so many children?" We didn't get a pat answer, either. I don't remember the rest of the sermon. That one question blew me away. I thought about how many innocent people had died through the ages, killing each other in the name of God. The thought strengthened my resolve to nurture life in Jesus' name, not take it.

Gordon never sugarcoated Christianity, and his personal

faith in Christ was deep. As a chaplain of the 82nd Airborne Division with the troops that landed in Europe on D-Day, he had seen plenty of death up close. His unit lost half its men in just a few days. He won a Silver Star for going behind German lines and bringing out eleven wounded Americans, carrying them on his shoulders one at a time across a river in the dark. He never talked about it; his wife, Mary, didn't even know about it until she found the medal one day, tucked in the bottom of a drawer.

During the war, Gordon and Mary dreamed of starting a church that would be racially integrated and that would ordain lay members and prepare them for serious service by a process of deepening their faith. Theirs would be a robust, sacrificial Christianity. Members were challenged to give money generously, not to Gordon or to the church itself but to missions that small groups of members themselves would start based on their own gifts and calling, missions to touch the pain of the world.

They would go where Jesus went: to be with the undesirables and rejects of the world. The church would be ecumenical, drawing from many strains of Christianity, inviting members to share their own spirituality with the whole. Instead of a creed, Church of the Saviour members—after an intense period of preparation and internship—would make a commitment: "I unreservedly and with abandon commit my life and destiny to Jesus Christ. . . ."

Members would undertake an inner journey and an outer journey: to make God's love real in the world, even if it took them out of their comfort zones. And, as they did that, their own faith would grow.

Gordon's faith was built not on doctrine (though he didn't minimize its value) but on the premise that God's universal and unshakable love undergirds it all. He sometimes prayed, "Lord, help us believe against the data." He respected an honest doubter more than a smug "believer" who had an answer for everything. So Gordon had no problem with the doubts expressed that first night in our class. He encouraged us to say what we really felt. It was okay to pray, "Lord, I believe. Help my unbelief."

My contemplative nature and Carolyn's evangelical roots were equally respected and fed. We were challenged to take risks for Christ, to listen deeply to people in pain, to build relationships across class and racial lines, to get more comfortable talking about things that matter most. This was the kind of faith community we'd been looking for all of our married life. And we joyfully plunged in.

Even while I was still in the Secret Service, I knew of the Potter's House on Columbia Road NW, in the Adams Morgan district of DC. Ed Pollard and I went for lunch several times to look through the bookstore and just breathe in the atmosphere. At lunch social workers, intellectuals, musicians, and artists like sculptor JIMILU Mason and painter Mary Lou Barker mingled with characters from the street. Ed and I thought it was unique, the food was good, and the price was right.

Now I was learning the whole story. If "2025" ("Headquarters") was an ecumenical feeding station for members, then the Potter's House was the birthplace of missions. Over coffee or dessert young Christians and seekers of all ages evoked one another's gifts and shared dreams of a better world. Christ House, Academy of Hope, Jubilee Housing, Jubilee Jobs, Family Place, Samaritan Inns, and many others were born around the Potter's House tables. Small churches centered on ministries met at the Potter's House on Sunday mornings and some weeknights. Each had its own distinct flavor, and each was organized and pastored by ordained laypeople.

Begun in 1960, it was probably the first Christian coffee-house in the United States. A storefront with books in the window; art on the rough-hewn paneled walls; and home-made soup, salads, and sandwiches in the kitchen, it was a safe place for young people to gather and share their dreams. On weekends folksingers performed and writers read poetry and shared works in progress. People talked philosophy, the-ology, and politics. Church volunteers waited tables, offered warm hospitality to everyone who entered, and engaged in conversation with whoever wanted to talk. When people asked, "What kind of place is this? Who are you?" members joyfully shared their message of God's love—but nobody pushed their faith on anyone else.

When we arrived in early 1988, the Potter's House retained much of its original character. It still does. We wanted to taste it all. On Sundays we attended the ecumenical service in Dupont Circle, where Gordon preached. Monday nights found us at Jubilee Church with people of many hues from

Jubilee Housing. They sang gospel songs, clapped their hands, and praised God with joyful abandon. Homeless people and recovering addicts gave tearful testimonies. Little kids danced and crawled around under the tables. Gordon gave a five-minute sermon, almost always about God's inescapable love. Afterward our class with Gordon met. Wednesday was the Potter's House Church, practicing silence, singing Taizé chants, reflecting on Scripture, and discussing a "table question." That service attracted contemplatives and intellectuals. Thursdays found us at Christ House's Table Fellowship. We couldn't get enough.

After eight weeks we finished our first class in the School of Christian Living and signed up for a second, "Call," with Mary Cosby. We needed to complete two classes to intern in a mission group and five to be ordained. The process usually took around two years, but we would do it in eighteen months.

About that time the Potter's House needed a new manager. Gordon asked me to take it on. I knew absolutely nothing about running a bookstore, a restaurant, a nonprofit, or any kind of small business. My pay, when they had it, would be $6,000 a year—which may have been more than I was worth. I laughed, thinking about the six-figure sums my retired former colleagues were drawing. But I loved the folks who worked there, and I agreed to give it a try.

The first thing I came to believe was that God didn't want the Potter's House *ever* to make money. We lived on the edge of economic collapse every week. It would have driven a Harvard-trained MBA nuts.

The paid kitchen staff was wonderful. Rosa Easley was the main cook, a chubby, cheerful spirit who could pray out loud as well as anyone I ever knew. She said "affirmations" to herself as she walked to work: "Today's going to be a blessed day. Thank you, Jesus!" Her assistant, Mary Easley, a close relative, had a brilliant smile and a secret knack for baking wonderful bread, which doubled as Communion bread. Delphine Sherrod, our dishwasher, had a beautiful singing voice, loved Jesus, and had borne thirteen children. I loved those women, and they loved me.

Sometimes they even forgot I was white. Once I went to Kyrgyzistan on a teaching assignment for the State Department. When I returned, I mentioned I was surprised that I never saw a black person the whole time. Delphine touched my arm in empathetic concern. She asked, wide eyed, "Weren't you scared?"

A woman I'll call "Bertha," our outstanding bookkeeper, refused to be paid. She said, "No, this church saved my life when I was a drunk. I want to do all I can for you all." Bertha was a white woman from the Appalachian hills, crippled from childhood polio, who had survived alcoholism, six husbands (some without benefit of divorce), time in jail for manslaughter, and life on the street. She and her adopted son, Bobby, who was black, lived in one of the Jubilee buildings.

When we met Bertha, she was celebrating ten years of sobriety and had sponsored many new AA members who were trying to stay on the wagon. On cold evenings she carried hot food on her wheelchair tray to guys still living in the street. She said, "You all feed the hungry because you pity them. I feed them because I know how it feels to be out there."

Bertha was spooked when she learned my wife was a judge—but she got over it when she heard Carolyn play guitar and sing a song she wrote about the Good Samaritan. It ended, "For the wounded one was Jesus. / Could the stranger who cared be me?"

The Potter's House was a good place to get over assumptions.

Bertha was a salty saint. She reminded me of Peter. Down to earth, volatile, and competent. She was worth her weight in gold but was not always easy to manage. One morning she and another volunteer got into a shouting match just before we opened. I managed to separate them, but afterward Bertha confessed to me, "I put my hand on my blade." I sucked in my breath. I didn't know she carried a blade!

Thelma Hemker, another faithful volunteer, reminded me of a tiny hummingbird. The biggest thing about her was her eyes, full of love and wonder. When she looked at people, they thought they were seeing Jesus. Or at least that *she* was seeing him. At nearly ninety years old, she was stronger than she looked and came to work every day except the one she missed to recover from a mugging about a block from our entrance.

Thelma knew all the homeless people who came into the Potter's House, and she greeted them by name. The guy that got Thelma's purse probably had to change neighborhoods, because a lot of her friends were looking for him.

Thelma laughed when I'd introduce her as the oldest cashier in the world. She lived to be 105. She had a story about finding the church.

When her husband died, she'd been living in Baltimore. One night Thelma dreamed about a place in Washington, DC. A voice said, "I want you to go there." She wasn't sure whether the speaker was God or her husband. All she knew was that the place was in DC, and she saw a sign that said "P Street." She also saw a big building across the street, and people were going in and out with suitcases. She had no idea what her dream meant.

The next day she was visiting friends in Washington, DC, and they invited her to church with them in the brownstone at 2025 Massachusetts Avenue. As she and her friends came out, she noticed a hotel across the street and people going in and out with luggage. She said, "That looks like my dream, but this building is not what I saw." Nevertheless, she was offered a job as church secretary, and she took it because she was at loose ends, she liked the people, and the job came with an apartment on the third floor of our lovely Victorian headquarters.

A few days later she went out back to take out some trash. She saw a sign that said "P Street." Then she looked back at the building, and she recognized the one in her dream. She had seen the *back* of 2025!

That's her story, and she told it to everyone. I believed her.

One of the most difficult street persons was simply known as "Mr. Green." Unless someone had prevailed on him to take a shower at Christ House, he reeked of sweat and urine and was usually drunk. He talked loudly to himself. Most of the coffee shop's customers understandably avoided him, though they sometimes quietly told Thelma they'd buy his lunch. But even if anyone did try to engage with Mr. Green, the only one he'd talk to was Thelma.

One day he went through the line, got a sandwich, and sat down by himself to eat it. He began to talk loudly to his invisible voices. Then he shouted with a string of curses that turned the air blue. Conversations stopped. Everyone in the coffeehouse stared, but no one moved—except Thelma. She came out from behind the cash register, walked over to him, touched him gently on the shoulder, and said lovingly, "Mr. Green, you don't seem to be yourself today."

Mr. Green looked up. For a minute he seemed to be thinking over what she'd said. Then Mr. Green said, "You're right. I'm not." He finished his sandwich without another word and quietly departed.

One day word came that someone from Mrs. Reagan's staff would be paying a call on the Potter's House. Elizabeth Dole, a member of Reagan's cabinet and wife of Republican Senate majority leader Robert Dole, had a friendship with our writer and member Elizabeth O'Connor. We supposed Mrs. Dole may have mentioned that the Potter's House operated without government funding. Since the Reagans wanted to encourage private charity, a White House staffer decided to scope us out for a possible visit by the First Lady. Such a visit might help with fund-raising, which we always needed. The Potter's House staff and volunteers were excited at the possibility.

The advance person was due to arrive around ten o'clock, when we opened. But nobody told me about this. I planned to come in closer to noon. Thus I was not an eyewitness to the following events, but I heard about them the minute I checked in. A mission group member volunteered to meet Mrs. Reagan's assistant and show her around. But the guest arrived early, so the volunteer said, "While we're waiting, would you like to see one of the Jubilee Housing buildings?"

Just as they rounded the corner behind the Potter's House, sirens wailed, tires screeched, police jumped out of cruisers and surrounded the "Ritz." A cop screamed, "Stay back!"

Not waiting to learn whether they'd interrupted a drug bust or something worse, our guide quickly led the visitor back to the Potter's House. There was Mr. Green, drunk, sprawled across the entrance with his pants down around his ankles.

They stepped over him, and everyone pretended not to notice.

The First Lady did not visit the Potter's House.

The Potter's House was sometimes chaotic. Sometimes the relationships were messy. But it was—and is—a place to encounter God's redeeming love in action. I would eventually move on to other missions, but during my two years there as manager, I was proud to claim it as my own.

CHAPTER 11

DESCENT INTO JOY

Inasmuch as ye have done it unto
one of the least of these my brethren,
ye have done it unto me.

MATTHEW 25:40, KJV

1988-1993

As Carolyn and I pulled into the long driveway leading up
to the Gift of Peace, we had no idea what to expect. Mother
Teresa and her Missionaries of Charity had taken over an
unused convent in northeast DC and turned it into a hospice
for homeless men and women dying of AIDS. The large two-
story white wooden building rested in the center of a broad
green expanse of lawn and trees at 2800 Otis Street.

We had come to offer our services to Sister Dolores, the
Indian nun in charge. The year was 1988, a time when 100
percent of people who contracted HIV died—in those days
mostly gay men or needle-sharing addicts. AIDS struck

terror in every heart. Researchers were working desperately, but no effective way to prolong life had yet been discovered.

Dentists refused to treat AIDS patients, and many doctors and nurses also avoided them. Children who contracted HIV through blood transfusions were banned from school. Employment was out of the question: no one would knowingly risk placing an infected person in the workplace. Even patients with money could not find medical care or shelter outside of their own families. There were two exceptions. One was the gay community, who did the best they could to care for their own.

And the other was Mother Teresa.

On a visit to the United States in 1985 she encountered people dying on the streets, a sight she knew well in India but never expected to see here. She'd been called by Jesus to the "poorest of the poor," in whom she saw "Christ in his distressing disguise." Who could be suffering more than a homeless person, abandoned by family and friends, dying of AIDS? On Christmas Eve 1985 the Missionaries of Charity opened the Gift of Love residence in New York, followed by the Gift of Peace a few months later in the nation's capital. If Mother Teresa and her sisters couldn't save these people's lives, they would at least ensure that these "least ones" died with dignity, surrounded by love.

We rang the bell and were welcomed by a quiet, brown-skinned young woman wearing a white gauze sari with blue trim, the Missionaries' trademark. She ushered us into a small office, where Sister Dolores rose and took our hands.

Our interview had been arranged by Don McClanen, a volunteer and Church of the Saviour member. He'd warned us, "Don't be offended if Sister Dolores turns you down. As far as I know, I'm the only non-Catholic working there. But I gave you a good word, so she wants to see for herself."

Sister Dolores appeared to be in her forties. She was an imposing figure, big boned and direct. I guessed she had little patience for dilettantes. "Why are you here?" she began.

"We have friends," I explained. "A couple whose world-class concert pianist son with AIDS had no place to go when they grew too old to care for him. Desperate to find a peaceful place where he would not be shamed, they asked us to take him in. After struggling with what this might mean, we felt we had to refuse."

Carolyn interrupted, "I was still working full-time, and we felt incompetent and afraid. At least I did. It seemed overwhelming."

I finished the story. "The family had to move to Arizona, where they found a gay couple who would take their son into their home, along with five others. He died there."

Our refusal had haunted us, we explained. In some way we hoped that working at the Gift of Peace would be redemptive.

Apparently satisfied, Sister Dolores had one more question. She focused on Carolyn. "Can you change a diarrhea diaper on a grown man?"

Carolyn caught her breath. She paused. She wanted to answer truthfully and searched her heart and emotions. She'd changed plenty of diapers on our three kids but never on an adult. Finally she stammered, "I'm not sure, but I'll try."

Sister Dolores had one final test. She lasered in on me. I must have looked grim, thinking about the harsh reality of what we were taking on. "Can you smile?"

She continued. "I tell my nuns, 'These men and women are grieving, and they have too much to feel sad about. They don't need to see your tears. You must bring them joy. If you can't smile when you see them, you can't work here.'"

We promised to smile. We passed Sister Dolores's scrutiny.

What I hadn't mentioned was that as a rescuer and risk taker this assignment fit me perfectly. Carolyn's attitude was slightly different. Back in the car she said, with a kind of gallows humor, "If I have to die for Jesus, I guess AIDS is better than being burned at the stake."

We drew the Sunday night shift, 6:00 p.m. to 6:00 a.m. once a week. Five women and two babies with AIDS shared the first floor with the office, kitchen, nuns' living quarters, and a chapel. Men and another chapel occupied the second floor, where Carolyn and I worked.

The first night Jack, a Third Order Franciscan, taught us how to use gloves. Scientists had identified HIV as the virus that caused AIDS. They knew it spread through exchanging body fluids, most commonly through sexual activity, blood transfusions, dirty needles, and mother's milk. They believed the virus was not concentrated enough in tears or sweat to be dangerous. The jury was still out on saliva. So we'd wear gloves when we changed diapers or fed patients, but not in normal contact like handshakes or hugs. We'd also carefully cover any cut places on our own hands.

Jack taught us how to change sheets with a patient in the bed, drawing up his legs and using leverage to roll him from side to side.

Showing us the medicine chest, Jack warned us to keep it locked at all times and to wear the key on a cord around our necks. The only meds in the place were given by mouth; no syringes (so no fear of needle sticks, a relief to us), no IVs, no machines. One of the nuns may have been a nurse, but as in all hospices, care was palliative, designed only to make patients comfortable in their waning hours.

Jack alerted us about "Rufus," one of the few residents who did not have AIDS. He was a homeless alcoholic on whom Sister Dolores had taken pity. Jack said, "Rufus will cough and pretend he needs cough syrup. Don't give him any. He just wants it for the alcohol content."

The Gift of Peace was low-tech in the extreme. Everything was clean and bright but simple, some would say primitive. I supposed this was partly to save money, partly to keep the nuns in touch with the physical labor of the poor, and partly perhaps to preserve the planet. Whether she knew the term or not, Mother Teresa believed in making a low carbon footprint.

Patients' dirty sheets, towels, and hospital gowns went into specially marked bags to be picked up daily by Georgetown University Hospital, which washed and sterilized them to meet the DC Department of Health requirements. The nuns did their own laundry by hand and hung it out to dry.

Floors were swept, not vacuumed. There was hot water only one hour a day, between six and seven in the morning, for showers. No dishwashers. Dishes were soaked, then washed in cold water, detergent, and Clorox—the only agent known at the time to kill HIV.

There were no intercoms. If a patient needed attention, he would shout, "Volunteer!" and we were to go to him quickly so as not to wake up others.

Except in rare circumstances (like the Super Bowl or a special program) the sole TV was locked up. Many people offered to buy TV sets for the patients, but Mother Teresa refused; she didn't want them distracted from their prime task, which she believed was to get right with God before they met face-to-face.

Aside from the laundry rules, city officials were pretty lax with the hospice because they had no viable choice. At first the Health Department tried to require Mother Teresa to install an elevator, ramps, and other handicap-friendly features. But there was no money. The convent was donated and had been built long before. Mother was a tough negotiator. She listened patiently, then said that if DC insisted, she would just have to look for another city that was more hospitable. Since the alternative was sick people dying in the streets, the city caved.

With no elevator, if bedridden patients had to be moved out from upstairs, two nuns would carry them down on chairs. We practiced: with a person strapped to a high-back wooden chair, I held the back and Carolyn grasped the chair legs. This provided a good grip and sufficient leverage for two people to carry a patient.

When we arrived on a Sunday night, the nun on duty would brief us on new developments: who had died, who had arrived, who could no longer walk, who might need extra attention. Then she disappeared and we were on our own.

We quickly saw firsthand the brutal reality of AIDS. AIDS is called "slim disease" in Africa because most patients lose weight from diarrhea and nausea. Large purple skin cancers called Kaposi's sarcoma may appear. Many patients have a white film on their mouths from thrush. Some go blind. Some become demented. They become too weak to walk. They lose bowel and bladder control. Not everything happens to everyone, but we observed all of this.

The greatest suffering was the loneliness of abandonment.

And yet, at the Gift of Peace, the spirits of many residents thrived even as their bodies were wasting away. It was the first time some had experienced love in many years, if ever. Observing changes in the patients from week to week was like watching the opening of a flower or the growth of a fetus in time-lapse photography.

When they first arrived, men would be either deeply depressed or terrified or angry—or all of the above. A week later they were more calm and beginning to trust caregivers. Even as they grew weaker, smiles emerged and peace set in. Soon they were reaching out to console newcomers. The Gift of Peace lived up to its name. It was amazing and almost miraculous to see.

Little changes on the outside sometimes signaled bigger ones on the inside. One man freely expressed hatred for women, so I served him, not Carolyn. But one day when I wasn't there, he allowed her to feed him. His hostile look was gone. He could have been fed by another patient instead, so this felt to her like a great victory.

Among our duties was making and serving food to the residents. What was in the refrigerator for dinner depended on what DC Central Kitchen delivered that day or what some church group had brought. On a good day there might be chicken or lasagna or some kind of casserole, maybe some expiring vegetables from which a salad could be gleaned. On a bad day we might have to make soup from a can or scramble eggs or make peanut butter sandwiches. But like manna in the wilderness, there was always something. As I recall, the convent did buy milk and eggs and a few basics. Fresh fruit was very rare. Donated brownies were abundant.

"Armando," a blind man, always asked hopefully, "*Tienes jugo de mango?*" There must have once been mango juice, but now there was only Kool-Aid. If not for the prohibition on gift giving, I'd have brought him some mango juice myself.

We set the kitchen table for the eight or nine guys who were still ambulatory, delivered food to the bedridden patients who could still feed themselves, and hand-fed the others. Often the healthier men would help us.

"Franklin," a tall, thin, very dark-skinned man with luminous, depthless eyes, was especially kind and helpful to others. Once Carolyn was trying to get a very sick patient to take a little soup, but "Tyrone" wordlessly clamped his lips together. She coaxed and coaxed, but he would not open his mouth, even to speak.

Seeing her frustration, Franklin offered, "Let me try." He said, "Come on, Tyrone, this is Franklin. Take a little soup for me." Tyrone opened his mouth and took a bite, then another and another. Franklin patted Tyrone's arm and said, "I love you, man."

And Tyrone, who had not spoken a word for days, said something he may have never said (or heard) before: "I love you too."

After everyone was fed, Carolyn and I would sit down with the men in the kitchen, drinking coffee together and swapping stories. The men spoke of lost opportunities and lost loves, of survival in the streets or prison, and sometimes of regret. The stories were often sad but others were hilarious. I told lineman stories and sometimes lineman jokes that the men loved, not least because they'd have made the nuns blush. Carolyn and I talked about growing up in the South or our kids or current events.

We became friends with the men in every sense of the word. On Sunday night we loved being greeted with big smiles. "Hi, Carolyn! Hi, Jerry! We missed you. How's it going?"

Most but not all of them were young. "Jeremy" was a tall, thin, gay white man who had lost most of his teeth. He was ingratiating and tried to con us into smuggling in a copy of *The Blade*, a gay-oriented newspaper that the nuns wouldn't let him have. (Patients were allowed to read, but nothing the nuns considered salacious.) Rufus would cough and ask for cough syrup, until he realized we were on to him. Then he laughed as he told us a story.

He said, "Sister Dolores is tough!" Like other patients who were well enough, Rufus could leave during the day, but there was a strict curfew of 6:00 p.m. And regardless of where they went, they were not to use drugs or alcohol. "Once," Rufus said, "I came back late—and drunk. It was winter and freezing outside. I knocked and knocked on the convent window, begging to be let in. Finally, Sister Dolores took pity on me: she threw me a blanket."

But we all had our secrets. They never talked about how they got the virus, and Carolyn and I never revealed our work lives. Every Monday morning at 6:00 a.m., Carolyn would shower at the hospice, throw her jeans in a backpack, change into a dark suit and pumps, and drive to the United States Tax Court, where she was a judge. Only Sister Dolores knew about her day job. And no one at her court had any inkling about the Gift of Peace.

There were good reasons to keep our double lives secret. Most of the residents had spent time on the dark side of social acceptability, if not the law. Carolyn and I feared that our current and former jobs would come between us and serious friendship with patients. We worried they would be afraid and suspicious of our motives. Here at the hospice we wanted to be known for ourselves, not our job titles. We wanted to be real.

It's hard to imagine now, but in those days when AIDS was always fatal, Carolyn also feared that her colleagues would be terrified and perhaps even scandalized. She imagined they'd be afraid to shake her hand or sit beside her at the communal table in the judges' dining room. They might even think she and I had lost our marbles. I sometimes wondered myself. Neither of us had ever before, to our knowledge, touched gay men, addicts, or criminals in such an intimate way. I had never knowingly exposed myself to a fatal disease.

The only explanation I could think of was that God had brought us here. We never doubted that he was in this place.

We distributed meds at 6:00 p.m. and again at 10:00 p.m. I said the rosary with a man who asked me to, then it was lights-out. We slept on cots in our jeans and sweatshirts, half awake like parents of a newborn, listening for anyone who needed help.

One night we heard "Volunteer!" and recognized Franklin's voice. He was now unable to walk, and the virus had hit his brain. He had begun to have delusions. Once he asked about the dog in his room. I said, "Franklin, I don't see a dog." He just said sweetly, "Oh. I must have imagined it." Another time he thought Carolyn was his sister. But he had lost none of his gentleness, and the other men adored him. Before lights-out someone was always in his room, joking with him, talking seriously, praying, or holding his hand. As he had done for others.

When we answered Franklin's call, we were distressed at what we saw. He had soiled himself and was obviously in pain. We put on gloves, and I began to clean him up while

Carolyn set about changing the sheets. When we rolled him over, we saw a huge open sore that took up almost his entire left buttock. As I washed him and covered the wound with salve, Franklin cried out, "Thank you, Jesus! Sweet Jesus!"

We got him all cleaned up, and it came to me to take Franklin's hand and say, with as much faith as I could muster under the circumstances, "God loves you, Franklin."

Franklin looked straight at both of us, with his depthless eyes, and said, "I love you too." Not "God loves you too," but "I love you too."

Others may think that was just a demented man making a socially acceptable response. But to us it was a life-changing affirmation whose source was beyond Franklin and beyond death.

We had been Christ to Franklin, and Franklin had been Christ to us. Like the pair on the road to Emmaus who did not at first recognize Jesus, after that encounter with Franklin we couldn't shake the feeling that we had been addressed by the risen Lord.

We spent our Sunday nights at Gift of Peace for most of a year. But when Carolyn's travel schedule picked up, she often had to get substitutes, and Sister Dolores wanted more stability than we could offer. We left with regret, but our journey there had changed us forever.

* * *

By 1989 we had completed our required Church of the Saviour courses in Old Testament, New Testament, Christian

Growth, Christian Doctrine, and Christian Ethics—as well as others on call and community. We were setting aside an hour a day for prayer and Scripture study. We were tithing 10 percent of our gross income. We had interned in different mission groups who sponsored us.

On Sunday afternoon, September 19, we read our spiritual autobiographies to the assembled Jubilee Church and were ordained by Gordon Cosby. When I said, "I unreservedly and with abandon commit my life and destiny to Jesus Christ," I meant it.

So did Carolyn. She said, "You know, this feels a lot like getting married." It did.

Almost immediately we plunged into three major Church of the Saviour undertakings that would open in 1989 and 1990: Joseph's House, the Servant Leadership School, and a new congregation, Festival Church. All were located in Adams Morgan, near the Potter's House and Christ House.

Joseph's House became the Church of the Saviour's communal residence for eleven formerly homeless men living with AIDS. The founder was Dr. David Hilfiker (who also worked at Christ House and at a clinic for the poor); he would live there with his family. Carolyn was the first board chair, and I would follow her as a board member.

The Servant Leadership School was a people's seminary, classes open to everyone and taught by Bible scholars and lay leaders from across the spectrum of Christianity. Visiting speakers and teachers included Henri Nouwen, Richard Rohr, Jim Wallis, John M. Perkins, Walter Brueggemann,

Tony Campolo, and more recently N. T. Wright. Carolyn and I were founding members, teachers, and fund-raisers.

Festival Church was called to be a diverse, multicultural, and bilingual faith community that would welcome neighborhood Central American refugees as well as recovering addicts and other Christians of any race or class. It would become our primary faith community and place of belonging. Carolyn, who speaks Spanish, would serve as beginning copastor with Glennys Williams; after three years Rosy Cauterucci took Carolyn's place, and I copastored for twelve years with Margie Ford. We all served without pay.

Festival Church was born on an icy winter night in early January 1990, when Jubilee Church had four visitors. Reverend Charles Demeré had brought with him a Salvadoran family—Edgar Palacios; his wife, Amparo; and their two daughters, Xochitl (thirteen) and Amparito (fifteen). Charles was an Episcopal priest who worshiped at Jubilee and had ties to human rights workers opposing the military dictatorship in El Salvador.

At the end of the service the visitors introduced themselves. In broken English, a small brown woman with irresistible eyes stood up to speak. "I am Amparo," she began. "My husband, he is Baptist pastor. We come from El Salvador, from the war. No one in our family speak English but me. Please, if you speak Spanish, come talk with us."

Carolyn introduced herself. We learned that Edgar led the National Debate for Peace in El Salvador, a country the size of Massachusetts, ravaged by a decade of civil war. The family had fled with two of their three children[5] under UN guard after the military dictatorship murdered six Jesuits as well as the Jesuits' housekeeper and her fifteen-year-old daughter. Though Edgar's name was on the death squad's list, he would go back to his flock almost immediately. We invited Amparo and the girls to live with us. The girls returned to their Jesuit school in a couple of months. Amparo would stay to do all she could here to stop the killing in El Salvador. During the four years she was here, she helped us found Festival Church.

Amparo attracted miracles. With no space or equipment or money or help, she soon opened a US office of the National Debate. The Methodists gave her a space in their national building right across from the Capitol. Two Spanish-speaking volunteers showed up to help. A computer was donated. She found a free phone. More important, this woman who barely spoke English taught herself to lobby Congress to stop giving aid to the Salvadoran military. It was a quixotic undertaking. She never doubted she would succeed.

With a road map, a hearty round of good-byes, a few prayers, and plenty of black coffee, six of us set out on a beautiful April day in 1992 on a dangerous mission. In the midst of a civil war we were going to deliver a loaded school bus and two donated Hondas to Edgar's church, Shalom Baptist, in San Salvador.

Shalom had rescued twelve children orphaned by the

still-raging civil war. Six months before, on a Festival Church mission of solidarity with Shalom, Carolyn and I (and six others) had met and fallen in love with the kids. They ranged in age from one year to twelve. Some were siblings. In their sun-filled house they had proudly led us from room to room to show us their drawings and where they slept and brushed their teeth. They sat by us and wanted to be held. They sang for us. When we asked Edgar what they most needed, he said, "Transportation and a washing machine." We promised to do our best.

Right away we found the perfect vehicle: a like-new green-and-white Italian bus (an Iveco) that seated fifteen and ran on diesel. It had only fifteen thousand miles on it and cost five thousand dollars. The bus—packed with two washing machines, clothes, and toys—was to be transportation for the kids. We had assembled a small caravan: a used Honda for Edgar and another for his church. Though Festival had only twelve members, the money poured in.

We were a motley crew: two Methodist ministers, Andres Thomas and Doug Horner; Sally Hanlon, a former nun; Fanny Pantelis and Amparo, two bilingual pastors' wives; and me. Maybe because I missed my former adventurous life as a Secret Service agent, I had rashly volunteered to drive the bus. Andres, Amparo, and Doug would rotate driving the Hondas and sometimes relieve me on the bus. Sally and Amparo would focus on interpreting. Carolyn had to stay in Washington for court trials, so she was our home contact and liaison.

We knew it could be dangerous. On our first visit in 1991, soldiers had boarded a public bus our group was on and marched us off at gunpoint, hands on our heads. Open trucks carried military men who pointed guns at other drivers just because they could. We'd prayed in the rose garden at the University of Central America (UCA), where the six Jesuits and two women were murdered. We'd crossed over a bridge that was firebombed a few hours later. In 1991 El Salvador was a place of terror and suffering. Now, in 1992, a cease-fire existed and peace talks were being finalized—but the killing continued. El Salvador was still a dangerous place. Even so, I felt called to help.

In the six days it took us to drive from DC to El Salvador, we racked up over three thousand miles. Travel in the States was uneventful, but once we crossed the Mexican border, it seemed like a bizarre, never-ending chapter of *Alice in Wonderland*. We had driven in shifts twenty-four hours straight to the Mexican border at Brownsville, Texas, only to be held there for twenty-four hours with no adequate explanation. The farther south we drove, the more unreliable the maps became, not to mention the roads. We flounced from one pothole to another, and with each bone-jarring jolt, the washing machines strained against their makeshift moorings. I dodged all manner of varmints crossing the streets. Cows. Chickens. Coyotes. Stray dogs. Armadillos. I swerved to avoid hitting cars parked at night on the roads. Not on the roadside, *on the roads*.

More than once we found ourselves behind wagons piled

high with sugarcane, plodding along at three miles per hour. If I decided to pass, I was taking all our lives in my hands.

We stopped for gas at dilapidated stations with rusted pumps and no safety levers on the nozzles, which meant that gas from the nozzle backed up and spilled onto the ground. Which meant I stood in a half inch puddle of gas while I pumped. One spark, and the whole enterprise would have gone up in smoke. More accurately, a *huge* explosion, and then *I'd* have gone up in smoke.

There were no stripes on the road and no streetlights. By sundown my eyes were bleary from trying to stay on the road, which had been asphalted so many times the shoulders dropped off almost a foot in places. My sixty-something body ached. My neck ached. My back ached. My arms ached. My hands, even my fingers, ached. All I wanted to do was to stretch out and sleep. And take a bath. But it was hard to find a safe place. Robbers were everywhere, and Americans were easy targets—especially Americans in a bus full of supplies.

We finally stopped—before dark, as instructed—at a motel with ghetto lights and armed guards in the parking lot surrounded by barbed wire. This did not make me feel safe, but I was desperate for a bath and a bed. We were all tired and cranky. Sally criticized Doug for driving too fast, and he made a crude retort. She stormed into the parking lot to pout. But when a guard pointed a gun at her, she returned in a hurry, figuring she was safer with Doug than with the guards.

The next morning we threaded our way through the

mountain passes with their precarious roads. Then police stopped us, pointing a gun at Doug, who was then driving the bus. They threatened to arrest him for being shirtless. Amparo said, "They just want a *mordita*" ("a little bite," a handout). She and Fanny got out of the car and engaged in what seemed to be a very serious conversation with the officers. We waited nervously. Finally the women returned. The police walked away empty handed.

"What did you tell them?" I asked.

"I told them," Amparo said, "'We have a little money, but if you take it, you're going to be robbing orphans. These are babies whose parents were killed in the war. You seem to be nice men. I'm sure you wouldn't want to do that.'"

She was a small woman with a soft voice, but underneath that deceptive cover she had the spine of a junkyard dog. We kept our money.

At long last, after six days on the road, we arrived at the border between Guatemala and El Salvador. It was guarded by armed soldiers. I saw suspicion in their eyes and movements, and I knew anyone taking supplies into the country during the war was suspected of aiding the rebels. This moment could make or break our mission.

"*Descarguen el bus!*" the boss shouted, motioning for us to unload the bus.

The leader came up to me, studying my face. We had driven a long way to have it all end here. Our US citizenship gave us some protection, but the price they could get for a bus, two cars, and a couple of washing machines might be irresistible. I stared at him, showing no emotion. But I was thinking this *mordita* was going to be a big one.

The guard moved away and motioned for Amparo to come to him. He asked a question, looking down on her small frame, his hands still on his gun. Amparo, sweetly smiling as if he were her brother, answered. He looked back at me, then to her. Then an unexpected thing happened. The creases on his weathered face softened. They talked some more, and he smiled. He called to his partner. His partner looked at me and nodded approvingly. They laughed and seemed to congratulate each other. They came over and shook my hand. Baffled, I went with it, reaching out my hand as cordially as I could under the circumstances. Then they waved us on.

Amparo climbed in. "We don't have to unload anything. Just drive on."

I couldn't believe it. "What happened?" I searched Amparo's face to see mischief and amusement. But she didn't tell me until we were underway again, successfully inside El Salvador.

"The *comandante* asked me, 'Who's that guy? He looks familiar,'" she began. "Then I told him, 'That's Jerry Parr. He is American hero. He save Ronald Reagan's life.' 'Oh, yeah,' he said. 'I thought I recognized him! He was on TV last night!'"

Amparo's triumphant smile filled her whole face. "See," she said, "I tell you Jesus always goes before me!"

When Reagan's life hung in the balance, I had prayed.

And now I sensed that someone was praying for me, for all of us. Carolyn and all the people at Festival Church in DC were praying for our safety. So were the people at Shalom Baptist Church in El Salvador.

None of us quite understood what had happened at the border. But the mystery was solved when we got to the Palacios family's house that night. Xochitl grinned and produced a tape of me *speaking Spanish*. It was a *Top Cops* documentary of the attack on President Reagan—a program I'd filmed eighteen months before. Edgar said, "The Salvadoran channel advertised it all week. Many people were watching." The *comandante* must have been one of them.

It wasn't luck. That border crossing was one more in a string of dangerous near misses from which God continued to deliver me.

We had arrived during Easter week. I went with Edgar to help bury a young man who had lain dead in the street for four days. He was shot for breaking the curfew, trying to get water for his pregnant wife. Relatives were afraid to claim the body for fear of reprisals, and the police had left him there because they don't work during Holy Week. Unarmed, he wore only a pair of shorts. He lay in a makeshift morgue: in the back room of a little store, on a door spread across two sawhorses. A naked bulb suspended from a cord shone down on the corpse. The cruelty—the meaninglessness—of the violence came over me.

How did I wind up here? I asked myself for the umpteenth time. For the last thirty years or more God had taken me so many places I'd never expected to go. I had been to six of the seven continents. I had walked with paupers and kings. I had been wined and dined and had paint thrown at me. Some places, like the hospital in the Philippines, the burn unit at Lackland Air Force Base, and Trauma Room 5 at George Washington Hospital, were hard. Some, like Vietnam and El Salvador, were frightening. By now I was learning to trust God and learn what I could from the ride.

As we sat in the Palacios family's living room watching the tape again, my mind wandered to Shalom's orphans. I remembered their joyful hugs and kisses when we'd delivered the bus earlier in the day. The love between them and their houseparents was palpable. In just six months since the last time we'd met, they had grown in size and self-confidence. Proud to be attending school, they showed us their blue-and-white uniforms and their backpacks full of books, pencils, and pads. They read for us and showed us their homework. The oldest, a girl, was now thirteen. She struck me as a young Amparo, keeping a responsible eye on the younger ones, including her two brothers.

As my thoughts returned to the tape, I wondered whether a child somewhere in El Salvador—maybe even that young girl—might also be watching and thinking, as I did when I saw *Code of the Secret Service* as a nine-year-old in Miami, *When I grow up I want to be a lifesaver too.*

That thought made me smile.

EPILOGUE

The Lord has led me on many adventures in the years since that crazy mission to El Salvador. My body is slowing down, but my life in the Spirit is filled to the brim. I spend a lot of time visiting people in intensive care units and hospice, and a lot of time listening, holding hands, praying with people. I spend two or three hours a day on the phone simply being present to friends in distress. I accompany the dying, not only people in my church but also longtime Secret Service friends and their families. I sometimes bear loving witness to that most intimate moment when life leaves, moments when I know with certainty that I'm standing on holy ground.

It's a strange twist that having spent my so-called prime years protecting political figures from death, I now spend a lot of time helping people to surrender to it.

But the impulse to protect and the impulse to bear witness come from the same place. I know those impulses come from God and that God is love. The love that created me is the love that used the hard events in my life for good, even when I was unaware. In spite of all the risks I took and all the near misses, I have lived a long life. God's love has sustained me and sustains me still. It will carry me through my inevitable rendezvous with death.

Deep in my soul I'm certain of this: it's all about love. God's love holds the whole ordered universe together. As Thornton Wilder said, that love is the bridge between life and death. And that love is enough.

April 3, 1981

SAIC Parr — PPD   116-205.0

The Events of March 30, 1981

All Personnel - PPD

The events of March 30, 1981, which we will never forget, are now a part of American History.

The pride and admiration I feel for each of you moves me deeply. All of our actions together in that incredible moment, were professional and instinctive. Training can only do so much. It takes a more profound motive to respond the way Tim McCarthy did. It was a response, self-sacrificial in nature, which all Americans in general, current and future agents in particular, will write about and think about for as long as this Agency exists.

Drew Unrue's instant response and skill in that drive to George Washington Hospital were instrumental in saving the President's life. Ray's quick move in helping me with the President, Dale's fast response to the follow-up car, Jim Varey's good judgment and assistance to Jim Brady, Eric's move toward the assailant, Bob's coverage of the departure, Kent's move toward the gun, Bill's excellent security arrangements, Dennis' skill at the wheel of the follow-up car, Russ Miller's quick decision to fill McCarthy's position, Mary Ann's good judgment in the motorcade, Bob Weakley's driving, and Joe Trainor in W-16 who handled all of our emergency communications, were all performed in the very highest traditions of this Division.

Upon reflection, I believe the events of March 30 represent all that is worst in man and at the same time all that is best. Life is lived forward, but understood backward, and in the many paths to maturity the loss of illusions is part of that most human process.

As each of us move apart physically in time from that terrible moment, we are forever bound together by the sound of gunfire and the sure and certain knowledge that, in the words of William Faulkner, we not only endured, but we prevailed.

Jerry S. Parr
Special Agent in Charge

JSP:amr

cc: AD Simpson, Protective Operations
    SA Russ Miller, Counterfeit Div.

ACKNOWLEDGMENTS

I first met Del Wilber as he was writing *Rawhide Down* (Henry Holt & Co., 2011). When I shared with him the spiritual autobiographies Carolyn and I had written for our ordination in 1989, Del put them down and said, "You and Carolyn have to write your own book. Together." He helped us find a literary agent and has been unfailingly generous with time and advice. We owe him.

Our agent Greg Johnson was a perfect fit. To represent first-time writers our age was a huge risk, but he believed in our story and our ability to get it right. We thank Tyndale's Jon Farrar, Jonathan Schindler, and Kara Leonino, who always listened to our suggestions, even when they sometimes respectfully disagreed.

Ken Gire helped with the proposal and outline and got us off to a good start. Our talented writer friend Lauren Goodyear was our first line editor. She took our work into her heart, edited our drafts, changed the structure of certain chapters, suggested scenes, and taught us how to make the book come alive. Margot Starbuck, another talented writer and editor, suggested other changes that we adopted and appreciated.

Some treasures I had buried in the garage years ago served as an accuracy check despite the passage of time. I had saved all of my daily reports since my first day as an agent. I also found the transcript of three days of interviews with former Secret Service speech writer Darlene Simpson, conducted after I left the Service. Darlene later lost her battle to ALS, but her skill as an interviewer kept alive some of the best stories in the book. And Carolyn found the transcript of her own interviews in 1981 with nurses and female doctors who treated President Reagan at George Washington Hospital.

Mike Sampson of the Secret Service Office of Government and Public Affairs provided us with statistics and other hard-to-find information.

When they get together, Secret Service agents always tell stories, and they love a good laugh. Calls to old friends to confirm my recollections inevitably ended in hilarity. Tom Wells, Clint Hill, Ed Pollard, Hal Thomas, Don Bendickson, and Walt Coughlin shared their time and plumbed their memories; some of their favorite stories are included. Roger Warner, Mike Weinstein, Roger Manthe, Sam Sulliman, and Bill Barton contributed as well. Joe ("Jeff") Parris generously allowed us to use his letter from President Reagan, reprinted in chapter 9.

By photos and word Carol Holt, Glennys Williams, Doug Horner, and Amparo Palacios Lopez ("Amparito," our goddaughter) confirmed events of our trips to El Salvador described in chapter 11.

Finally, we are inexpressably grateful to Gordon Cosby and the salty saints in the Church of the Saviour who deepened and broadened our understanding of what it really means to follow Jesus.

TIMELINE
1930–1992

1930–1940	The Great Depression
1930 Sep 16	Jerry S. Parr is born in Birmingham, Alabama.
1930 Nov	Parr family moves back to Miami, where Jerry grows up.
1932 Nov	Franklin D. Roosevelt is elected president.
1937 Apr 17	Carolyn Miller is born in Palatka, Florida.
1939	Jerry sees *Code of the Secret Service* starring Ronald Reagan.
	Jerry's parents separate and divorce. (Jerry's mother marries twice more in three years.)
1941 Dec 7	Japan attacks Pearl Harbor.
1941 Dec 8	The United States declares war on Japan, entering World War II.
1945 May 7	Germany surrenders to the Western Allies.
1945 Aug 14	V-J Day: Japan surrenders, ending World War II.

1949 Jan	Jerry graduates from Miami Senior High School.
1949	Jerry is hired as a groundman, on track to become a lineman at Florida Power & Light Company in Miami, Florida.
1949	Jerry enlists in the Florida National Guard—211th Infantry Regiment.
1950 Jun 25	The Korean War begins.
1950 Jul	Jerry joins the Air Force, military police.
1950	Jerry is stationed in Finland, Minnesota, guarding an early warning radar site.
1952 Jul 9	Jerry marries Mary Henry.
1952	Jerry is stationed in Anchorage, Alaska, at Elmendorf Air Force Base. Jerry takes religious instruction and is baptized Catholic. He also takes some courses for college credit.
1953 Jul 27	The Korean War ends.
1954 Jul	Jerry leaves the Air Force in Alaska but initially stays in Alaska to work as a lineman. When Florida Power & Light notifies him that unless he returns to Miami, he'll lose his ten years seniority, he leaves Alaska.
1954	Jerry begins work as a lineman at Florida Power & Light and attends University of Miami at night on the GI Bill.
1955	Jerry and Mary Henry divorce in Miami.
1958 Aug	Jerry and Carolyn Miller meet in Miami.

1959 Jan 1	Fidel Castro takes control of Cuba.
1959 May	Carolyn graduates from Stetson University magna cum laude and receives fellowship offers from six universities, including Yale. She accepts a three-year National Defense Fellowship at Vanderbilt leading to a PhD in comparative literature.
1959 Oct 12	Jerry and Carolyn marry in Nashville.
1960 Jan	Jerry starts a joint program, Peabody College (education) and Vanderbilt University (philosophy and English).
1960 Aug	Carolyn receives her MA in English from Vanderbilt University and discontinues PhD program.
1960 Sep	Carolyn teaches English and Spanish at Hillsboro High School in Nashville.
1960 Nov 8	John F. Kennedy defeats Richard Nixon in the presidential race. Lyndon B. Johnson is vice president.
1961 Apr 17	The United States' attempted invasion of Cuba at Bay of Pigs fails.
1961 Aug 13	Barbed wire goes up around East Berlin.
1962 Winter	Jerry interviews with and receives job offers from the CIA and Secret Service. He accepts the Secret Service offer.
1962 Mar 25	Jerry and Carolyn's first child, Kimberly Susan, is born in Nashville.
1962 May	Jerry graduates from Peabody College with a BA in English and philosophy.

1962 Summer	Jerry works for Middle Tennessee Electric as a lineman and has a near-death experience.
1962 Sep	Family moves to New York and lives in Glen Oaks garden apartment in Queens.
1962 Oct 1	Jerry begins at the US Secret Service, New York field office.
1962 Oct 22	JFK orders a naval blockade of Cuba and announces the missile crisis to the public.
1962 Oct 28	Soviet ships carrying missiles turn back. The United States agrees not to invade Cuba; the USSR agrees to dismantle and remove missile sites.
1962 Nov 7	Eleanor Roosevelt dies. When both JFK and LBJ attend the funeral, Jerry gets his first presidential-protection assignment.
1963 Jun 11	JFK federalizes the Alabama National Guard to enforce federal court order to integrate the University of Alabama. After a speech, Governor George Wallace yields and permits two African American students, James Hood and Vivian Malone, to enter.
1963 Sep 17	Jerry and Carolyn's second child, Jennifer Lynn, is born in New York.
1963 Nov 12	Jerry is transferred to Nashville field office.
1963 Nov 22	JFK is assassinated. Lyndon Johnson is sworn in as president.
1963 Nov 25	Jerry is sent to Dallas, Texas, to protect Marguerite and Marina Oswald.

1964	Jerry is assigned to Nashville but is frequently called away to various temporary protective assignments.
1964 Jan 28	Jerry is stationed at LBJ Ranch, Texas.
1964 Feb 9–19	From the ranch to the White House (PPD), Jerry has his first encounter with LBJ and protects the British prime minister.
1964 Feb 26–28	Jerry works the presidential visit in Miami.
1964 May 8–Jun 19	Jerry attends Secret Service school in DC.
1964 Aug 7	Congress passes the Tonkin Gulf Resolution, enabling the president to employ military force against the Vietnamese Communists.
1964 Nov 3	LBJ and Hubert Humphrey defeat Barry Goldwater and William Miller.
1964 Dec 2	Jerry and his family move to Arlington, Viriginia, a suburb of Washington, DC.
1964 Dec 6	Jerry is transferred to VP-elect detail (Humphrey).
1965 Apr 7	LBJ's speech at Johns Hopkins announces that the United States will take a stand in Vietnam.
1965 Aug 11	Watts riots in Los Angeles damage white/black civil rights alliance.
1965 Dec 24–Jan 1, 1966	Jerry does first foreign advance in Manila, Philippines.
1965 Dec 31	Carolyn moves the family to Wheaton, Maryland, by herself.

1966 Jan 11–13	VP detail makes unplanned visit to New Delhi to attend funeral of Prime Minister Shastri of India.
1966 Feb 9–23	Jerry accompanies VP Humphrey on southeast Asia trip. Humphrey sees wounded at Clark AFB Hospital in Manila and also visits Seoul, Korea.
1967 Feb 10	The Twenty-Fifth Amendment to the US Constitution is ratified.
1967 Oct 28–29	VP Humphrey visits Saigon, Vietnam.
1967 Oct 30–Nov 6	VP Humphrey visits Jakarta, Indonesia, and Semarang, Central Java.
1968 Jan 31	Vietcong launches TET Offensive; the United States loses hundreds of men.
1968 Mar 4	In New Hampshire, peace candidate Eugene McCarthy comes within 230 votes of defeating LBJ in the Democratic primary.
1968 Mar 16	Robert Kennedy announces he'll run for president.
1968 Mar 31	LBJ announces he will not seek reelection.
1968 Apr 4	Martin Luther King Jr. is assassinated; riots break out in one hundred cities.
1968 Apr 23–29	Students shut down Columbia University.
1968 Apr 27	VP Humphrey announces he will run for president.
1968 Jun 5	Robert Kennedy is shot immediately after winning the presidential primary in California and dies the next day.

| 1968 Jun 6 | President Johnson orders US Secret Service protection for all presidential candidates. |

1968 Jun 6 President Johnson orders US Secret Service protection for all presidential candidates.

1968 Aug 26–29 The Democratic National Convention in Chicago nominates Hubert H. Humphrey as Democratic candidate for president amid riots.

1968 Nov 5 Richard Nixon defeats Humphrey in presidential race.

1968 Nov 17 Jerry transfers to VP-elect Spiro T. Agnew.

1969 Jul 13 Jerry is promoted to Shift Leader (ATSAIC) of Agnew detail.

1970 Apr 30 Nixon extends Vietnam War to Cambodia. Demonstrations flare up again and increase in intensity.

1970 Oct 3 Jerry and Carolyn's third child, Patricia Audrey, is born.

1970 Nov 30 Jerry is temporarily assigned to the Foreign Dignitary Protective Division (FDPD) to protect Jordan's King Hussein.

1970 Dec 13 Jerry is transferred to the FDPD.

1971 Feb 12 Jerry is promoted to ASAIC of Foreign Digs.

1971 First five female Secret Service Agents are appointed.

1972 Aug 1 Jerry returns to Agnew detail as a temp, alternating with FDPD as needed.

1972 Nov 7 Nixon and Agnew crush George McGovern and Sargent Shriver with 96.7 percent of the electoral vote.

1972 Dec 10	Jerry's transfer becomes official. Jerry is now ASAIC of VPPD.
1973 Jan 23	Cease-fire in Vietnam begins between North Vietnam and United States.
1973 May 17–Aug 7	Watergate hearings are televised.
1973 Jul 22	Jerry is promoted to Deputy Special Agent in Charge (DSAIC) of the VPPD.
1973 Oct 10	VP Agnew pleads *nolo contendere* to tax evasion charges and resigns.
1973 Oct 12	Nixon nominates Gerald Ford for vice president.
1973 Oct 13	Jerry is assigned to Ford as DSAIC of VPPD.
1973 Dec 6	Gerald Ford is confirmed by Congress and becomes vice president.
1974 Mar 17	Jerry is transferred back to Foreign Dignitary Protective Division as DSAIC (second tour).
1974 Jul 27	The House Judiciary Committee recommends President Nixon be impeached on grounds of abuse of power, obstruction of justice, and contempt of Congress.
1974 Aug 8	Nixon resigns; VP Ford becomes president.
1974 Sep	Carolyn enters Georgetown University Law School.
1974 Sep 8	President Ford pardons former president Richard M. Nixon.

1974 Nov 13	Yasser Arafat addresses the United Nations on behalf of the Palestine Liberation Organization. Jerry in charge of his security in NYC, where Arafat is hated by pro-Israel citizens.
1974 Dec 19	Nelson Rockefeller is confirmed and sworn in as vice president.
1975 Apr 17	North Vietnam defeats South Vietnam.
1975 Apr 30	Vietnam conflict officially ends.
1975 Dec 7	Jerry becomes an inspector. (He is in Inspection through Jun 17, 1978.)
1976 Nov 2	Jimmy Carter and Walter Mondale defeat Gerald Ford and Robert Dole in presidential election.
1977 May	Carolyn graduates from Georgetown University Law School.
1977 Sep 7	Carter signs treaty giving Panama Canal back to Panama, effective December 31, 1999.
1977 Sep	Carolyn begins her legal career with the IRS as a trial attorney.
1978 Sep 6	Carter meets with Egyptian president Anwar Sadat and Israeli prime minister Menachem Begin at Camp David.
1978 Sep 17	Camp David Accords reached, ending thirty years of conflict between Egypt and Israel.
1978 Sep 18	Jerry promoted to SAIC of VPPD for VP Mondale.

1979 Jan 1	The United States establishes diplomatic ties with mainland China, the first since 1949.
1979 Jun 18	President Carter and USSR's Leonid Brezhnev sign SALT II.
1979 Aug 26	Jerry is named SAIC of the PPD for President Carter.
1979 Oct 1	Iranian students storm US embassy in Tehran and take employees hostage.
1979 Dec 25	Parr family spends Christmas at Camp David with President Carter, Mrs. Carter, and daughter Amy.
1979 Dec 27	Soviets invade Afghanistan.
1980 Jan	President Carter announces US athletes will not attend summer Olympics in Moscow unless the Soviet Union withdraws from Afghanistan.
1980 Apr 25	The US mission to rescue hostages in Iran is aborted after a helicopter and cargo plane collide.
1980 Apr 30	Carter secretly visits the hospital in San Antonio where a burned helicopter pilot is being treated.
1980 Jul 14–17	Republican Convention is held in Detroit, Michigan. Ronald Reagan of California is nominated for president and George H. W. Bush of Texas as vice president.
1980 Sep 16	Jerry celebrates his fiftieth birthday with a surprise cake on Air Force One.

1980 Nov 4	Ronald Reagan defeats Carter for president.
1981 Jan 20	Jerry attends the inauguration with President Carter and returns to the White House with President Reagan. US hostages in Iran are released when Carter is no longer president. Reagan sends Carter to greet them in Germany, where they are flown.
1981 March 30	Ronald Reagan is shot in the chest by John Hinckley Jr.
1982 Feb 13	Jerry works his last day with Ronald Reagan.
1982 Feb 14	Jerry is promoted to Assistant Director for the Office of Protective Research.
1982 Oct	Carolyn is appointed Special Counsel to the Assistant Attorney General, Tax Division, at the Department of Justice.
1983 Sep	Jerry begins a master's program in pastoral counseling at Loyola College in Baltimore, Maryland.
1985 Feb 16	Jerry retires from the Secret Service.
1985 Nov 25	Carolyn is sworn in as a judge for the United States Tax Court.
1987 May 9	Jerry is awarded an honorary degree (Doctor of Humane Letters) from Eureka College in Eureka, Illinois.
1987 May 16	Jerry earns MS in pastoral counseling from Loyola College.
1987 Jun 3	The Parrs move from Potomac, Maryland, to Washington, DC.

1987 Dec 27	The Parrs first visit Church of the Saviour and hear Gordon Cosby.
1989 Sep 19	Jerry and Carolyn are ordained by the Church of the Saviour.
1989	Jerry becomes the manager of Potter's House, a Christian coffeehouse, performance venue, art gallery, and bookstore in the Adams Morgan area of DC.
	Jerry and Carolyn secretly volunteer at Gift of Peace, a hospice for homeless men with AIDS.
1989 Nov 16	Six Jesuits, their housekeeper, and her fifteen-year-old daughter are murdered by the military in El Salvador.
1990	Carolyn helps found Joseph's House for homeless men with AIDS and serves as their first board chair.
	The Parrs help found the Servant Leadership School, a people's seminary focused on inner-city ministry.
	The Parrs help found Festival Church, an ecumenical, multicultural, bilingual Christian faith community in Adams Morgan. At different times each will serve as pastor.
	The Parrs form a friendship with Edgar Palacios, pastor of Shalom Baptist and executive director of the National Debate for Peace in El Salvador. They invite his wife, Amparo, to live with them while she represents the National Debate in the United States.

1991 Nov	The Parrs and five others from Festival Church make a dangerous trip to El Salvador to offer solidarity and support for Shalom Baptist. They meet twelve children whose parents perished in the civil war.
1992 Jan 16	Salvadoran peace accords, partly drafted by Edgar Palacios, are signed, ending a twelve-year war. But tensions continue to run high.
1992 Apr	Leading a group of six, Jerry drives a bus to El Salvador from DC to donate to Shalom Baptist Church for the orphans. A miracle occurs at the border between Guatemala and El Salvador.

NOTES

PROLOGUE

1 *There is always one moment . . .* Graham Greene, *The Power and the Glory* (New York: Penguin, 1990), 12.

2 *CODE OF THE SECRET SERVICE Code of the Secret Service* was a 1939 film that Reagan later claimed was the worst movie he'd ever made. The budget was so low he had to do his own stunts.

CHAPTER 1: JUST ANOTHER DAY AT THE OFFICE

8 *. . . enchanted by this poem.* This story is told by James Douglass in *JFK and the Unspeakable: Why He Died and Why It Matters* (Maryknoll, NY: Touchstone, 2008), 225–26.

CHAPTER 2: INAUSPICIOUS BEGINNINGS

19 *". . . whither he went."* Hebrews 11:8, KJV.

23 *"Knights of the Spur."* Edwin B. Kurtz and Thomas Shoemaker, *The Lineman's Handbook* (New York: McGraw-Hill, 1928, 1942, 1955). The dedication, "Knights of the Spur" by Edwin B. Kurtz, reads, "To all linemen everywhere, those twentieth-century knights of the spur who serve for only one cause, 'just service to man. . . .'" I believed then and believe now that being a power lineman is a noble calling.

28 *"Love covers . . ."* 1 Peter 4:8.

CHAPTER 3: FROM NEW YORK TO DALLAS: "THE PRESIDENT IS DEAD"

47 *We arrived in New York City . . .* The dates and events in this and subsequent chapters have been confirmed by my daily and weekly reports, which I

saved since my first day in the Service; interviews with other agents; and contemporary news reports. Agent Hal Thomas, who followed me, was especially helpful in confirming many details of life in the New York field office.

55 *This revelation . . . became public on October 22.* See "Fourteen Days in October: The Cuban Missile Crisis," by Kurt Wiersma and Ben Larson, http://library.advanced.org/11046/. See also "Cuban Missile Crisis," John F. Kennedy Presidential Library and Museum, http://www.jfklibrary.org /JFK/JFK-in-History/Cuban-Missile-Crisis.aspx.

61 *Of those who disliked Kennedy . . .* A poster of Kennedy, front and side view with caption, read "Wanted for TREASON." See "11/22/63, the Warren Commission, and the 'torrid atmosphere of political rage in Dallas,' 1963," *Historiann* (blog), November 21, 2011, http://www.historiann. com/2011/11/21/112263-the-warren-commission-and-the-torrid-atmosphere-of-political-rage-in-dallas-1963/. "Reader letters to the *Dallas Morning News,* 1963," collected by *New York* magazine's 48th anniversary of JFK's death, November 20, 2011, http://nymag.com/news/frank-rich /dallas-morning-news-2011-11/.

62 *. . . Kennedy made a speech announcing ongoing talks with the USSR . . .* "Nuclear Test Ban Treaty," John F. Kennedy Presidential Library and Museum, http://www.jfklibrary.org/JFK/JFK-in-History/Nuclear-Test -Ban-Treaty.aspx.

65 *Suddenly Walter Cronkite was on the screen.* "Walter Cronkite announces death of JFK," YouTube video, 5:44, original CBS news broadcast on November 22, 1963, posted by "maxpowers518," March 27, 2009, accessed May 12, 2012, http://www.youtube.com/watch?v=2K8Q 3cqGs7I.

70 *Ich bin ein Berliner.* "1963: Kennedy: 'Ich bin ein Berliner,'" BBC News, On This Day, June 26, 1963, http://news.bbc.co.uk/onthisday/hi/dates/stories /june/26/newsid_3379000/3379061.stm; "Kennedy—I am a Berliner— Ich Bin Ein Berliner," YouTube video, 4:42, posted by "forquignon," November 5, 2006, http://www.youtube.com/watch?v=hH6nQhss4Yc.

71 *. . . "a moral issue."* "Radio and TV Address on Civil Rights, 11 June 1963: Executive," John F. Kennedy Presidential Library and Museum, http:// www.jfklibrary.org/Asset-Viewer/Archives/JFKWHCSF-0926-041.aspx; "John F. Kennedy Civil Rights Address 11 June 1963 Part2," YouTube video, 7:01, posted by "zzahier," March 23, 2008, www.youtube.com /watch?v=tkOlCU5aMcM.

72 *. . . last night's frightening attack on Adlai Stevenson.* "Disgraced Dallas Delivers Apologies for Mistreatment of Adlai Stevenson," originally

printed in the *Schenectady Gazette*, October 22, 1963, http://news.google
.com/newspapers?nid=1917&dat=19631022&id=MnUhAAAAIBAJ&
sjid=_4gFAAAAIBAJ&pg=5988,4423922. According to Warren Leslie,
in the 1960 campaign, racists in Dallas opposed to Johnson's support
for civil rights cursed and spat on LBJ, and Mrs. Johnson as well. Leslie,
former reporter for the *Dallas Morning News*, wrote *Dallas Public and
Private: Aspects of an American City,* published four months after Kennedy's
assassination. At the time he wrote the book, he was a vice president and
chief spokesperson for Neiman Marcus.

74 *According to Roger Warner . . .* Roger Warner, Secret Service agent, personal
interview by the author, May 27, 2012. Warner was an agent in the Dallas
field office when John F. Kennedy was shot.

75 *"Marina's going to get rich . . ."* "The Day the President Was Shot," http://
www.allangrant.com/oswaldstory.htm. Accessed on April 10, 2013. For
a sample of Marguerite Oswald, see "1964 Interview with Marguerite
Oswald," YouTube video, 4:29, posted by David VonPein, May 28, 2011,
www.youtube.com/watch?v=HxVozhyf6SI.

76 *Dental records conclusively proved . . .* W. Tracy Parnell, "The Exhumation
of Lee Harvey Oswald and the Norton Report," parts 1 and 2, 2003,
http://mcadams.posc.mu.edu/parnell/lhox1.htm and http://mcadams.posc
.mu.edu/parnell/lhox2.htm.

77 *. . . Abraham Zapruder.* The Zapruder film can be seen on YouTube. "The
Undamaged Zapruder Film," 1:25, posted by Robert Harris, April 15, 2008,
http://www.youtube.com/watch?v=kq1PbgeBoQ4.

CHAPTER 4: VIETNAM: GOING FROM BAD TO WORSE

79 *Vietnam: Going from Bad to Worse.* In addition to my own memory
and contemporaneous notes, I mined the memories of Agents Walter
Coughlin, Tom Wells, Hal Thomas, Mike Weinstein, Roger Manthe,
and others.

85 *George Reedy, President Johnson's press secretary . . .* George Reedy, *The
Twilight of the Presidency.*

86 *. . . official vice-presidential residence.* The Naval Observatory is America's
official timekeeper. It houses an atomic clock and monitors complete
sun and moon data for the US Navy. The nineteenth-century mansion
previously housed the US chief of naval operations. See "The Vice
President's Residence & Office," the website of the White House, www
.whitehouse.gov/about/vp-residence.

91 *. . . Gulf of Tonkin.* The resolution authorized the president to "take all
necessary measures to repel any armed attack against the forces of the

United States and to prevent further aggression." It passed both houses of Congress in August 1964 with no dissents in the House and only two in the Senate. There was never a declaration of war in Vietnam, but President Johnson used this resolution in its place.

92 *And only in such a world will our own freedom be finally secure.* Lyndon B. Johnson, "President Lyndon B. Johnson's Address at Johns Hopkins University: 'Peace Without Conquest,'" April 7, 1965, LBJ Presidential Library, http://www.lbjlibrary.net/collections/selected-speeches/1965/04-07-1965.html.

92 *The East Room of the White House* . . . "The East Room," The White House Historical Association, accessed May 15, 2012, http://www.whitehouse history.org/whha_history/whitehouse_tour-east-room.html.

102 *Humphrey apologized to Weaver.* I was on the trip but elsewhere in Vietnam when this occurred. Walt Coughlin, Secret Service agent (Deputy SAIC at the time of the incident), personal interview by the author, May 27, 2012.

104 . . . *can't bear to talk about it yet.* Walt Coughlin was with me and overheard this exchange. Coughlin interview.

104 *Tom Wells tells this story.* Tom Wells, Secret Service agent, personal interview by the author, May 26, 2012.

105 *In the Watts section* . . . *National Guard troops to quell the riot.* "Watts Riots," Civil Rights Digital Library, http://crdl.usg.edu/events/watts_riots /?Welcome&Welcome.

106 . . . *immediate aftermath of fires and riots* . . . Wells interview.

107 . . . *Gianni Buzzan. Pittsburgh Post-Gazette*, Friday, March 31, 1967, extracted from the Internet via www.newspaperarchive.com.

108 *Hal Thomas saw a guy* . . . Hal Thomas, Secret Service agent, personal interview by the author.

CHAPTER 5: 1968: THE YEAR FROM HELL

113 *No one in human history* . . . Lawrence Kushner, *Eyes Remade for Wonder* (Woodstock, VT: Jewish Lights Publishing, 1998), 62.

116 . . . *Benjamin Spock and celebrities such as Joan Baez and Jane Fonda were actively encouraging draft-age youth to resist.* "Dr. Benjamin M. Spock," the website of Oregon Public Broadcasting, http://www.pbs.org/opb/the sixties/topics/war/newsmakers_3.html; "Jane Fonda & The Vietnam War," the website of Wellesley College, http://www.wellesley.edu/Polisci/wj /Vietimages/fonda.htm; "1967: Joan Baez arrested in Vietnam protest," BBC News, On This Day, October 16, 1967, http://news.bbc.co.uk/on thisday/hi/dates/stories/october/16/newsid_2535000/2535301.stm.

116 *"Love your enemies."* Matthew 5:44.

117 *Hal Thomas had a formal-looking folder* . . . Hal Thomas, Secret Service agent, personal interview by the author.

120 *In Kinshasa, Congo* . . . Walt Coughlin, Secret Service agent, personal interview by the author, May 27, 2012.

121 *Walter Cronkite* . . . *"did the best they could."* "Walter Cronkite's 'We Are Mired In Stalemate' Broadcast, February 27, 1968," University of Richmond, https://facultystaff.richmond.edu/~ebolt/history398/cronkite_1968.html.

122 *President Johnson announced* . . . *"another term as your president."* "President Lyndon B. Johnson's Address to the Nation Announcing Steps to Limit the War in Vietnam and Reporting His Decision Not to Seek Reelection, March 31, 1968," LBJ Presidential Library, http://www.lbjlib.utexas.edu/johnson/archives.hom/speeches.hom/680331.asp.

122 *Rev. Martin Luther King Jr. had been shot and killed.* Coughlin interview.

123 . . . *the anger that followed closed the university* . . . "History," Columbia University 1968 Conference website, http://www.columbia1968.com/history.

123 . . . *Agent Don Bendickson actually got it.* Don Bendickson, Secret Service agent, personal interview by author, June 16, 2012; Thomas interview.

127 *A story Walt Coughlin tells* . . . Coughlin interview.

130 *Approximately 668 protesters were arrested.* "1968 Democratic National Convention (August 26–29, 1968)," South Loop Historical Society, http://www.southloophistory.org/events/1968convention.htm. For more information about the Chicago Convention and riots, see "Brief History of Chicago's 1968 Democratic Convention," CNN All Politics, http://www.cnn.com/ALLPOLITICS/1996/conventions/chicago/facts/chicago68/index.shtml. See photos: http://chictrib.image2.trb.com/chinews/media/photo/2007-12/34472391.jpg; http://chictrib.image2.trb.com/chinews/media/photo/2007-12/34472412.jpg; Haynes Johnson, "1968 Democratic Convention: The Bosses Strike Back," *Smithsonian* magazine, August 2008, http://www.smithsonianmag.com/history-archaeology/1968-democratic-convention.html.

CHAPTER 6: TWO DEATHS

133 *Two Deaths* Thanks to agents Sam Sulliman, Clint Hill, and Ed Pollard for augmenting my own recollections.

133 . . . *where Agnew would make history* . . . For a contemporaneous account of Agnew's court appearance and resignation see the *New York Times* account by James M. Naughton, "Agnew Quits Vice Presidency and Admits Tax Evasion in '67; Nixon Consults on Successor," October 10, 1973, *New*

York Times Learning Network, http://www.nytimes.com/learning/general
/onthisday/big/1010.html. Also, much material is available through the
Maryland State Archives, www.msa.md.gov. See also Britannica Encyclopedia
online, http://www.britannica.com/EBchecked/topic/9318/Spiro-T-Agnew
?overlay=true&assemblyId=61044, showing a photo of the vice president
leaving the courthouse with me on one side and Agent Jimmy Taylor on
the other.

133 *Only a handful of people . . . knew . . .* Ed Pollard, an agent in the follow-up
car (who later became assistant director for Protective Operations), recalls,
"We were told the VP was going to Baltimore that day, but were not told
we'd be going to the courthouse. . . . We were all stunned that that's where
we were. Agnew pled. We were shocked, did not want to believe it." Agent
Ed Pollard, personal interview with the author, July 18, 2012.

137 *Conservatives including Senator Goldwater rushed to Agnew's defense . . .* Even
after Agnew resigned and pled *nolo contendere*, conservative columnist
William S. White quoted Goldwater approvingly as saying that Agnew was
"hounded from office" and excoriated the Justice Department for publicly
"crowing over the broken body" of the vice president. William S. White,
United Feature Syndicate column, October 17, 1973.

140 *. . . letters of resignation to be hand delivered . . .* Agnew's resignation letter
to Secretary of State Henry Kissinger and President Nixon and Nixon's
response, all on October 10, 1973, are a part of the national archives. A link
to them can be found at the website of the Maryland State Archives, http://
www.msa.md.gov/megafile/msa/speccol/sc3500/sc3520/001400/001486
/images/nixonletter.jpg.

141 *Hands trembling, Agnew then read . . .* Agnew's statement to the court is
available at the website of the Maryland State Archives, http://www.msa.md
.gov/megafile/msa/speccol/sc3500/sc3520/001400/001486/images/agnew
statement.jpg, reprinted in *U.S. News & World Report,* October 22, 1973.

142 *". . . part of a long-established pattern of political fund-raising in the state."*
For a discussion of this, see "Kickbacks, Agnew Payoffs Part of Maryland's
Political Back-Scratching," by David Goeller, Associated Press, October 11,
1973. Published in the *Daily Mail,* Hagerstown, MD.

143 *In an interview with Ben Bradlee . . .* "Spiro Agnew and the Golden Age
of Corruption in Maryland Politics: An Interview with Ben Bradlee
and Richard Cohen of *The Washington Post,*" Center for the Study of
Democracy, vol. 2, no. 1 (Fall 2006), http://www.smcm.edu/democracy
/_assets/_documents/agnewpaper.pdf.

143 *All the world's a stage . . .* William Shakespeare, *As You Like It,* Act 2, Scene 7.

144 *Judge not, that ye be not judged.* Matthew 7:1, KJV.

CHAPTER 7: SINNERS AND STATESMEN:
WATERGATE AND THE WORLD

152 *The Watergate saga began . . .* Watergate has been written about extensively. A good summary can be found at "Watergate Scandal," History Channel website, www.history.com/topics/watergate.

154 *Solicitor General Robert Bork . . . did the deed.* Carroll Kilpatrick, "Nixon Forces Firing of Cox; Richardson, Ruckelshaus Quit," *Washington Post,* October 21, 1973, www.washingtonpost.com/wp-srv/national/longterm /watergate/articles/102173-2.htm.

156 *FDPD was born in 1970 . . .* "Report That Pompidou May Cut Short His Visit; 10,000 Demonstrate in Chicago," *Jewish Telegraphic Agency,* March 2, 1970, http://archive.jta.org/article/1970/03/02/2952573/report-that -pompidou-may-cut-short-his-visit-10000-demonstrate-in-chicago.

160 *"No people can get along without others."* Albin Krebs, "Léopold Senghor Dies at 95; Senegal's Poet of Négritude," *New York Times,* December 21, 2001, http://www.nytimes.com/2001/12/21/world/leopold-senghor-dies -at-95-senegal-s-poet-of-negritude.html. See also Mark Doyle, "Senegal's 'poet president' dies," BBC news, December 20, 2001, http://news.bbc .co.uk/2/hi/africa/1722156.stm.

163 *Several of those women hired . . .* D. Darlene Simpson, "Women in Secret Service," Women in Federal Law Enforcement website, http://www.wifle .org/conference1991/pdf/46-52.pdf.

166 *. . . six months before the emperor's planned visit.* Hirohito's visit was widely covered in the US press. See, e.g., "The Nation: Hirohito Winds Up His Grand U.S. Tour," *Time,* October 20, 1975, www.time.com/time/magazine /article/0,9171,946563,00.html and "Once a God, and a Bitter Wartime Foe, Emperor Hirohito Is Now America's Guest," *People,* October 6, 1975, www.people.com/people/archive/article/0,,20065719,00.html.

172 *The leader was Abu Hassan.* A Google search of Abu Hassan, aka Ali Hassan Salameh, reveals material of a spy thriller. In fact, according to one source, he has been the model for characters in several novels and films, including Steven Spielberg's *Munich.*

174 *. . . do not let the olive branch fall from my hand.* Arafat's entire speech can be found online: "Speech of Yasser Arafat Before the UN General Assembly," MidEastWeb: Middle East, November 13, 1974, www.mid eastweb.org/arafat_at_un.htm.

CHAPTER 8: UP AND DOWN THE LADDER

178 *When Carolyn was accepted to Georgetown University law school . . .* Her acceptance letter arrived in April 1974.

183 *Voters liked his reputation* . . . "American President: A Reference Resource," Miller Center, University of Virginia, http://millercenter.org/president /carter/essays/biography.

183 *Carter chose Senator Walter "Fritz" Mondale* . . . See essay by Mark O. Hatfield, with the Senate Historical Office, *Vice Presidents of the United States, 1789–1993* (Washington: US Government Printing Office, 1997), 517–25, http://www.senate.gov/artandhistory/history/resources/pdf /walter_mondale.pdf.

191 *I saw Begin and Sadat walking side by side* . . . For a chronology of the Camp David Accords, see "Camp David Day By Day," Camp David Accords— Framework for Peace, Copyright American-Israeli Cooperative Enterprise, reprinted with permission, http://www.jewishvirtuallibrary.org/jsource/Peace /cddays.html. For the treaty language, see "The Camp David Accords: The Framework for Peace in the Middle East," ibiblio online database, http:// www.ibiblio.org/sullivan/docs/CampDavidAccords.html. For an overview, see also "Peace Talks at Camp David, September 1978," PBS online, http://www.pbs.org/wgbh/americanexperience/features/general-article /carter-peace/.

193 . . . *Carter was a president who loved to take risks.* I mean no disrespect here. I admire him very much. As I write this, President Carter is still taking risks to help desperately poor people around the world. For biographical information see Steven H. Hochman, "Jimmy Carter," ibiblio online database, http://www.ibiblio.org/lia/president/Carter Library/GeneralMaterials/Biographies/JimmyCarter-bio.html; "Jimmy Carter-Biography," Nobelprize.org, May 7, 2013, http://www.nobelprize .org/nobel_prizes/peace/laureates/2002/carter-bio.html.

197 . . . *negotiations with Leonid Brezhnev.* For an extensive discussion of the treaty talks, see Matthew M. Oyos, "Jimmy Carter and SALT II: The Path to Frustration," American Diplomacy, University of North Carolina at Chapel Hill, December 1996, http://www.unc.edu/depts/diplomat/AD _Issues/Amdipl_2/Oyos_1.html.

197 . . . *President Carter decided to cruise down the upper Mississippi River on the Delta Queen* . . . For more information on the *Delta Queen*, see "Delta Queen Steamboat," National Trust for Historic Preservation, http://www .preservationnation.org/travel-and-sites/sites/eastern-region/delta-queen -steamboat.html#.UX57UaKKKDk.

201 . . . *the president* . . . *often went home to Plains.* For more details on President Carter and Plains, Georgia, see "Welcome to Plains, Georgia: Home of the 39th President of the United States and Nobel Peace Prize

Winner," Plainsgeorgia.com, http://www.plainsgeorgia.com/plains_to
_the_white_house.html.

201 *Blessed are the peacemakers.* Matthew 5:9.

203 *. . . militant Iranian students stormed our embassy in Tehran . . .* For a good
overview of the Iran hostage crisis, see "The Iranian Hostage Crisis," PBS
online, http://www.pbs.org/wgbh/americanexperience/features/general
-article/carter-hostage-crisis/; "Iran Hostage Crisis," History Channel
website, http://www.history.com/topics/iran-hostage-crisis.

203 *Historian Gaddis Smith said of the hostage taking . . .* "The Iranian Hostage
Crisis," PBS online, http://www.pbs.org/wgbh/americanexperience/features
/general-article/carter-hostage-crisis/.

205 *Preparing to leave the desert . . . eight men were killed.* According to one report,
in addition to the eight men who died, five were injured. I was unable to
learn what happened to the other four. "Hostage rescue mission ends in
disaster," History Channel website, http://www.history .com/this-day-in
-history/hostage-rescue-mission-ends-in-disaster.

206 *Our destination was Brooke Army Medical Center . . .* For a brief description
of what this survivor would have been dealing with, see article by Melissa
Block, "Army Burn Center Sees Some of Worst War Wounds," NPR online,
http://www.npr.org/templates/story/story.php?storyId=5570807.

210 *He was stalking President Carter.* Hinckley admitted this a few months later.

211 *Reagan won 90.9 percent of the electoral votes.* "1980 Presidential General
Election Results," Dave Leip's Atlas of U.S. Presidential Elections, http://
www.uselectionatlas.org/RESULTS/national.php?year=1980.

213 *. . . the hostages were airborne for Germany.* When newly sworn in President
Reagan learned that the hostages had taken off, he made a magnanimous
gesture: he sent former-president Carter to Germany to greet the returning
Americans.

CHAPTER 9: SHOTS FIRED! MEN DOWN!

217 *Sincerely, Ronald Reagan* Thanks to Agent Joe Parris for sharing his letter
from President Reagan, dated October 7, 1976.

220 *We screeched to a halt at the GW entrance at 2:30 p.m.* Some technical details
and hospital events are taken from *Rawhide Down* by Del Quentin Wilber
(New York: Henry Holt and Co., 2011), a riveting and well-researched
book about the events of March 30, 1981.

227 *Like Abraham in the Bible . . .* This story is found in Genesis 18:24-33.

231 *. . . head nurse Lita Amigo and her boss Barbara Holfelner had been waiting
. . .* In July 1981 Carolyn and my daughter Kimberly interviewed female
nurses and doctors at George Washington Hospital about their roles

in saving the president for an article by Kimberly that appeared in *Us* magazine in August 1981. The tape and transcription of those original interviews provide the basis for my description of several events that occurred at the hospital when I was not present.

236 *About a week after following Carter from Dayton to Nashville* . . . Deputy Darrell Long, who arrested Hinckley at the Nashville airport, interview by Dan Whittle, "Hinckley stalked Carter in Tennessee," *Murfreesboro Post*, January 1, 2012, http://www.murfreesboropost.com/hinckley -stalked-carter-in-tennessee-cms-29647.

CHAPTER 10: FROM THE WHITE HOUSE TO THE POTTER'S HOUSE

247 *Bear one another's burdens* . . . Galatians 6:2.

253 *The story of Gordon Cosby* . . . See "The Potter's House Story," The Potter's House website, http://www.pottershousedc.org/about. The history of this little community of believers has been lovingly chronicled by Elizabeth O'Connor, one of its members, and published by Harper & Row. See *Call to Commitment,* 1963; *Journey Inward, Journey Outward,* 1975; *Our Many Selves,* (HarperCollins, 1971); *The New Community,* 1976; *Letters to Scattered Pilgrims,*1979; *Eighth Day of Creation,* 1975; *Cry Pain, Cry Hope* (Potter's House, rev. ed., 1993); *Servant Leaders, Servant Structures* (Potter's House, 1991); and *Our Rag-Bone Hearts* (Potter's House, 1993). Most of Elizabeth's books are now out of print, but may be available from the Potter's House bookstore, http://www.pottershousedc.org/bookstore.

256 *Sometime in your life* . . . "Communion" appeared on inward/outward.org of the Church of the Saviour on September 7, 2012, with notation "source unknown," http://inwardoutward.org/2006/11/23/communion.

259 *Help my unbelief.* See Mark 9:24.

259 . . . *I knew of the Potter's House* . . . See www.pottershousedc.org.

264 . . . *"Mr. Green."* Like "Bertha," this is not his real name.

CHAPTER 11: DESCENT INTO JOY

269 *Children who contracted HIV* . . . Ryan White, a student in Kokomo, Indiana, was the best-known child banned from school. His struggle received national attention. He died at age eighteen. See his obituary dated April 9, 1990, in the *New York Times*: http://www.nytimes.com /1990/04/09/obituaries/ryan-white-dies-of-aids-at-18-his-struggle -helped-pierce-myths.html. As I write there is still no cure for AIDS, but drug advances have now converted it from a disease that is always fatal to a chronic one that can often be controlled with drugs.

269 *Our interview had been arranged by Don McClanen* . . . Don was the founder of the Fellowship of Christian Athletes. His story is told in his biography, *Caution to the Wind,* by Joe Murchison (Grand Island, NE: Cross Training Publishing, 2008). Don was a member of the Church of the Saviour.

271 *Jack alerted us about "Rufus"* . . . Names in quotation marks are fictitious to protect privacy. The stories are real.

278 *Like the pair on the road to Emmaus* . . . See Luke 24:13-32.

280 *The family had fled with two of their three children* . . . An older son, Edgar Jr., had been sent to school in Mexico for his own protection.

281 *. . . the military dictatorship murdered six Jesuits* . . . On November 16, 1989, the victims were pulled from their beds, lined up, and shot in the rose garden next to the chapel of UCA, the University of Central America, where they taught. We visited their graves in 1991. A good source of material on their murders and the Salvadoran conflict is found at "As it happened, November 16, 1989," Creighton University Online Ministries, http://onlineministries .creighton.edu/CollaborativeMinistry/WPnov16.html.

EPILOGUE

292 *Love is the bridge between life and death.* Thornton Wilder, *The Bridge of San Luis Rey,* 1927.

INDEX

A

Aaron, Dr. Ben *224, 225, 226*
Agnew, Spiro T. *86, 101, 126, 131, 133, 134, 135–45, 147, 151–54, 183, 301, 302, 313, 314*
Air Force *20, 40, 42, 44, 59, 89, 245, 296*
Albert, Carl *144, 145*
Amigo, Lita *231, 232, 317*
Arafat, Yasser *165, 170, 171–74, 175, 176, 303, 315*
Augsbach, Debbie *232*

B

Baker, Howard *208*
Baker, Jim *223, 232*
Balge, Ken *156, 159*
Bani-Sadr, Abolhasan *205*
Barbuto, Rick *102, 106*
Barker, Mary Lou *259*
Barton, Bill *165, 244, 294*
Begin, Menachem *176, 191, 192, 303, 316*
Behl, Tom *109, 182*
Bell, Joanne *231*
Bendickson, Don *126, 149, 294, 313*

Benedict, Barbara *232*
Bernstein, Carl *136, 152, 153*
Bork, Robert *154, 155, 315*
Boyett, Barney *189*
Bradlee, Ben *143, 314*
Brady, Jim *218, 223, 224, 226, 231*
Brandt, Willy *68, 159*
Brown, Ham *172*
Brown, Harold *191*
Brzezinski, Zbigniew *191, 192*
Buford, Fay *247*
Burke, Bob *94*
Bush, George H. W. *208, 304*
Butterfield, Alexander *154*

C

Campbell, Shawn *164*
Camp, Bob *74*
Camp David *191, 192, 193, 201, 204, 303, 304, 316*
Carlon, Joe *174*
Carlyle Hotel *60*
Carter, Jimmy *131, 144, 179, 183, 184, 190–94, 196, 197, 199–208, 210–213, 224, 236, 303–5, 316, 317, 318*
Cheyney, Dr. Kathleen *224*

Christ House 250, 253, 254, 260, 261, 265, 279

Church of the Saviour 250, 253, 254, 255, 257, 258, 269, 278, 279, 294, 306, 318, 319

Clark Air Force Base 103, 104, 206

Clarke, Kathy 164

Code of the Secret Service 2, 24, 238, 288, 295, 309

Connally, John 65, 66, 67, 71, 77, 208

Cosby, Gordon 250, 251, 252, 253, 257, 258, 259, 260, 261, 279, 294, 306, 318

Cosby, Mary 255, 258, 261

Coughlin, Walt 86, 94, 96, 120, 122, 124, 127, 128, 129, 294, 311, 312, 313

Counts, Roger 49, 94, 193

Cox, Archibald 154, 315

Cronkite, Walter 65, 66, 121, 310, 313

Cuban Missile Crisis 55, 61, 310

D

Daley, Mayor Richard Daley 127, 169

Dean, John 153, 154

Deaver, Mike 13, 211, 223, 232, 238

"Deep Throat" 153

Delahanty, Thomas 224

Delta Queen 197, 200, 316

DeProspero, Bob 148, 189, 194, 211

Dole, Elizabeth 265

Dole, Robert 208, 265, 303

Dominguez, Larry 234

Donaldson, Sam 195

Duncan, Bill 171, 172, 173, 175

E

Easley, Mary 262

Easley, Rosa 262

Edwards, Don 172, 175

Ehrlichman, John 153

Executive Protective Service (EPS) 89, 163, 177, 179, 181, 182

F

Florida Power & Light 27, 33, 40, 44, 296

Ford, Gerald 14, 145, 151, 152, 155, 156, 169, 171, 183, 184, 216, 234, 235, 302, 303

Foreign Dignitary Protective Division (FDPD) 135, 156, 157, 159, 162, 164, 301, 302, 315

Foster, Jody 235

G

Garmon, Steve 199

Garr, Larry 229

Gasquez, Joe 62, 63

Gaugh, Bob 64, 67, 68

Gibbs, Harry 56, 57, 63

Giordano, Joseph 221, 222, 223

Gittens, Charles 50

Giuffre, Jack 94, 106

Goldwater, Barry 84, 91, 137, 299, 314

Gorbachev, Mikhail 238

Gordon, Mary Ann 13, 164, 219, 220

Graham, Billy 144

Gulf of Tonkin Resolution 91, 114, 311

Guy, Johnny 12

H

Haldeman, H. R. *153*
Hanlon, Sally *282*
Hassan, Abu (Ali Hassan
    Salameh) *172, 173, 176, 315*
Hemker, Thelma *263*
Heritage Christian Church *187,
    188, 189, 249, 250, 253*
Hickey, Ed *230, 236*
Hill, Clint *61, 78, 135, 158, 159,
    234, 294, 313*
Hilton Hotel
    (Washington, DC) *12–15, 17,
    122, 235*
Hinckley, John, Jr. *210, 222, 225,
    229, 235, 236, 238*
Hirohito (Japanese emporer) *165,
    167, 168, 169, 170, 197, 315*
Hoffman, Walter E. *140, 143*
Humphrey, Hubert *84, 86, 90,
    92–95, 99–103, 104, 105–110,
    111, 113, 114, 116–20,
    122–31, 182, 183, 190, 206,
    299–301, 312*
Hussein (King of Jordan) *157, 159,
    165, 301*

J

Jaworski, Leon *155*
Johns Hopkins speech
    (President Johnson) *91, 93, 114,
    299, 312*
Johnson, Lady Bird *68*
Johnson, Lyndon *58, 68–70, 80,
    81, 82, 84, 91, 93–95, 100, 104,
    105, 114, 116, 121, 122, 127, 130,
    297, 298, 301, 311–13*
Jukes, George *50, 55*

K

Kaddoumi, Farouk *171, 172, 173*
Keiser, Dick *234*
Kellerman, Roy *59, 77*
Kennedy, Jacqueline *60, 61, 68, 69,
    78, 81*
Kennedy, John F. *8, 14, 47, 50,
    55, 58–66, 68, 70, 71, 77,
    78, 81, 91, 93, 125, 150,
    297, 310, 311*
Kennedy, Robert *14, 68, 121, 124,
    125, 131, 300*
Kennedy, Ted *68, 164, 208*
Khomeini (Ayatollah) *203, 205, 213*
King, Martin Luther, Jr. *14, 106,
    115, 122, 124, 300, 313*
Kippenberger, Jack *139*
Kissinger, Henry *140, 203, 314*
Kleindienst, Richard *153*
Knight, Stu *178, 181, 182*
Kobrine, Art *226*

L

Lackland Air Force Base *206, 288*
Lawson, Win *95*
Liddy, G. Gordon *153*
Lineman *20, 21, 22, 23, 41, 42,
    44, 275, 296, 298, 309*

M

Malcolm X *71*
Mason, JIMILU *254, 259*
Matthews, Chris *195*
McCarthy, Dennis *238*
McCarthy, Eugene *121, 125, 127,
    130, 300*
McCarthy, Tim *17, 18, 216, 224,
    225, 231, 234, 237, 238*
McClanen, Don *269, 319*

McCord, James W. *153*
McGovern, George *135, 301*
McIntosh, Dale *17, 220, 221*
McNamara, Robert *93, 105*
Meese, Ed *223, 232*
Meir, Golda *151, 160, 163, 176*
Merton, Thomas *43, 188*
Missionaries of Charity *267, 268*
Mitchell, Andrea *195*
Mitchell, John *136, 152*
Mize, Marisa *231*
Mondale, Walter *86, 183, 184, 190, 191, 192, 194, 208, 303, 316*
Morrison, Tom *229*
Mother Teresa *238, 267, 268, 271, 272*

N

National Debate for Peace *280, 281, 306*
Naval Observatory *86, 192, 311*
Nixon, Richard *125, 126, 130, 133–36, 140, 141, 145, 151–57, 164, 297, 301, 302, 313–15*
Nouwen, Henri *189, 279*

O

O'Connor, Elizabeth *253, 265, 318*
Oswald, Lee Harvey *68, 70, 72, 73, 74, 75, 76, 77, 311*
Oswald, Marguerite *73, 74, 75, 76, 298, 311*

P

Palacios, Amparo *280, 281, 282, 285, 286, 294, 306*
Palacios, Edgar *280, 281, 282, 287, 306, 307*

Palestine Liberation Organization (PLO) *165, 170, 172, 173, 176, 303*
Parr, Carolyn *12, 17, 18, 19, 22, 23, 26, 27, 40, 41, 42, 43, 44, 45, 47, 48, 53, 54, 55, 57, 58, 64, 65, 66, 83, 85, 88, 91, 97, 98, 129, 138, 147, 164, 170, 178, 184, 185, 186, 187, 188, 193, 204, 218, 229, 243, 245, 249, 250, 251, 252, 253, 255, 256, 257, 259, 263, 267, 269, 270, 272, 274, 275, 276, 277, 278, 279, 280, 282, 287, 293, 294, 295, 296, 297, 298, 299, 301–3, 305, 306, 315, 317*
Parris, Joe *216, 294, 317*
Parr, Jennifer *63, 139, 186, 204, 229, 249, 256, 298*
Parr, Kimberly *45, 54, 57, 58, 61, 185, 229, 233, 249, 252, 297, 317, 318*
Parr, Patricia (Trish) *135, 138, 164, 186, 204, 211, 229, 245, 248, 249, 251, 301*
Peabody College *19, 23, 297*
Pforr, John *170*
Plains, Georgia *183, 184, 201, 204, 211, 316*
Plante, Bill *195*
Pollard, Ed *244, 259, 294, 313, 314*
Pontius, Ron *82, 83*

Q

Quinn, Tom *150*

R

Reagan, Ronald *2, 3, 15–18, 125, 131, 197, 208, 211,*

212, 213, 215, 216, 217,
218–25, 226, 227, 228,
229–33, 237, 238, 244,
249, 286, 287, 294, 295,
304, 305, 309, 317
Richardson, Elliot 140, 141, 143,
154, 315
Rockefeller, Nelson 86, 125, 169,
249, 303
Rome Opera House 107
Rowley, James J. 110
Ruby, Jack 70, 72, 73
Ruckelshaus, William 154, 315
Rundle, Paul 144, 145
Rusk, Dean 93

S

Sadat, Anwar 167, 191, 192, 303,
316
SALT II 197, 202, 304, 316
Saturday Night Massacre 152, 155
Semarang, Indonesia 109, 110
Senghor, Léopold Sédar 159, 160,
161, 165, 315
Shaddick, Ray 17, 215, 216, 218,
220, 221, 238
Shalom Baptist Church
(San Salvador) 281, 282, 287,
306, 307
Sherrod, Delphine 262
Simpson, John 49, 135, 162, 181,
192, 211, 226, 244
Sinatra, Frank 144
Stevenson, Adlai 71, 72, 310
Sulliman, Sam 80, 81, 133, 134,
135, 138, 145, 161, 163,
294, 313
Sullivan, Denise 227, 231

T

Tachibana, Maseo 165, 166, 167
Taxi Driver 235
Taylor, Jimmy 94, 189, 234, 314
Taylor, Robert 26
Thomas, Hal 108, 109, 117, 119,
124, 126, 131, 172, 294, 310,
311, 312, 313
Thomas, Helen 195
"Troika" 223, 232

U

Unrue, Drew 216, 219, 220

V

Vance, Cyrus 191, 192
Vaughn, Albert 24, 25, 58
Vietnam 67, 79, 91, 92, 93, 101,
102, 103, 104, 105, 108, 110,
111, 114, 115, 121, 122, 128,
130, 134, 136, 152, 206, 208,
222, 288, 299, 300–303,
311, 312, 313

W

W-16 11, 195, 229, 230
Walker, Edwin 72, 77
Wallace, George 14, 125, 130,
234, 298
Wanko, Bob 17, 218
Warner, Roger 72, 74, 75, 94,
109, 294, 311
Washington Post 136, 143, 152,
153, 154, 193, 314, 315
Watergate 135, 136, 137, 151,
152, 153, 154, 155, 156,
183, 302, 315
Waverly, Minnesota 88, 89, 130, 131

Weaver, Glenn *86, 94, 102, 110, 128, 312*

Wells, Tom *104, 106, 117, 146, 294, 311, 312*

Whitaker, Alfred E. *50, 52, 53, 54, 57, 63*

Wong, Al *50*

Woodward, Bob *136, 152, 153*

Z

Zapruder, Abraham *77, 78, 311*

Zboril, Chuck *49, 172, 175*